THE
AMERICAN
PUBLIC
SCHOOL
TEACHER

THE
AMERICAN
PUBLIC
SCHOOL
TEACHER

———∞∞∞———

Past, Present, & Future

Darrel Drury *and* Justin Baer

HARVARD EDUCATION PRESS
Cambridge, Massachusetts

Library of Congress Control Number 2010942142
Hardcover ISBN 978-1-934742-91-4

Published by Harvard Education Press, an imprint of the
Harvard Education Publishing Group

Harvard Education Press
8 Story Street
Cambridge, MA 02138

Cover Design: Sarah Henderson

The typefaces used in this book are Adobe Garamond and Hoefler Text.

For America's 3.2 million public school teachers—
the dream keepers of our nation's youth.

Contents

Reflections and Conclusions

Foreword

A little more than a decade into the twenty-first century, America's teacher workforce is much in the public eye and figures prominently in policy discourse. In recent months, a major city newspaper provoked a firestorm of controversy by publishing the names and student test-score results of more than six thousand elementary teachers. At least five states have taken steps to eliminate or modify tenure laws, with more likely to follow suit. A national news magazine has launched a project to grade more than a thousand of the country's university- and college-based teacher-education programs. And private foundations have invested large sums to promote alternative pathways into teaching. Tumultuous times.

Meanwhile, a sense of urgency pervades our collective efforts, both nationally and locally, to propel the American education system into this new century while also erasing stark and long-standing disparities in educational outcomes. This sense of urgency manifests itself in the hopes and expectations we express for what teachers can and must accomplish. It would seem a timely moment to take stock of what it means to be a teacher in America.

In this book, a fifty-year profile of public school teachers provides a common point of departure for quite diverse and provocative commentaries from teachers, union officials and other education leaders, education researchers, government leaders, and corporate executives. Derived from surveys of teachers conducted in five-year intervals from 1955 to 2005 by the National Education Association, the data reveal points of continuity and change in the composition of the teacher workforce, teachers' perspectives on their careers, and the environments in which teachers work. Yet data do not speak for themselves—indeed, they may support quite different judgments about what proves worthy of attention, what interpretations and explanations seem plausible, and what guidance one might glean for practice and policy. The book's task might thus be defined as finding the story (or stories) in the numbers.

The book's central device—a set of invited commentaries—affords substantial latitude to the contributors, who attend selectively to what they consider salient aspects of the fifty-year profile and who also draw on numerous other sources of information and insight. The result is a wide-ranging conversation that spans most of the key issues now compelling public, professional, and policy attention. While some of the recurring themes evoke commonly shared views, others mark disputed and complicated terrain. For example, contributors concur about the need to support teachers in making productive use of new technologies or in teaching an increasingly diverse student population. They are more likely to disagree on issues surrounding teacher preparation and licensure, compensation, and evaluation. In these contested domains, the commentaries help to expose the dimensions of complex issues and the contours of key debates. The very design of the book invites readers to join the fray, beginning with the profile constructed over the span of half a century and imagining the commentary one would contribute if invited.

The book's scope is ambitious, embracing past, present, and future. Perhaps not surprisingly, the present looms particularly large here. Nonetheless, readers will also find reminders that familiarity with the past will likely aid us both in grappling with present concerns and in envisioning future scenarios. An introductory chapter offers a broad overview of teaching from the founding of public education to recent decades in which accountability movements have held sway and market-based reform initiatives have multiplied. Selected commentaries point to the ways in which the NEA survey itself is a product of its historical moment, requiring other sources to amplify what is inevitably an incomplete picture. We learn, for example, that the NEA began collecting data on teachers' race only in 1970, even though the 1954 *Brown* decision and subsequent years of desegregation profoundly affected African Americans' presence and participation in teaching. And in the future? What might surveys of this sort help us track and understand about the composition of the teacher workforce? Latino/a teachers, Asian-American teachers, immigrant teachers, and those trained outside the United States are not yet visible in this portrait.

Just as the commentaries dwell most firmly in the present, so do they concentrate on the institutional and policy face of teachers' work. Yet each of the issues highlighted by the individual contributors—from technology use to performance-based pay—plays out in the lives and day-to-day work of teachers in schools and districts. Teacher-authored vignettes embedded throughout the text provide a helpful counterweight and tap aspects of professional experience for which surveys are but blunt instruments. Echoing historical portraits of teaching that stretch back decades, these contemporary accounts illuminate the intimate, challenging, energizing, and enervating world of classroom teaching. It is a world that is constant across time and place in its intensity and immediacy, but also a world changing in multiple and consequential ways. Most of the vignettes zoom in close to the classroom and to connections with children, with "making a difference" the recurrent refrain. A smaller number move beyond the classroom to demonstrate how the workplace matters: brief glimpses of mentors who build a novice's confidence; a principal who reignites enthusiasm in a teacher on the brink of burnout; a professional development experience that transforms a teacher's understanding of the wealth of resources to be found in poor communities.

Together, the commentaries and vignettes offer certain surprises. Among them, one would have to rank emerging evidence of a generational divide among teachers, with new recruits to teaching (including career changers) often differing from their veteran colleagues on some of the most controversial issues of the day, including the future of the single-salary schedule, performance-based pay, peer evaluation, and the appropriate role of unions. In other respects, the surprises reside in which contemporary developments go relatively unnoticed. For example, several commentaries and vignettes center on the instructional and communication possibilities associated with the use of digital technology, but none highlights another outgrowth of technology—the introduction of administrative data systems that enable states to link teacher and student data, track teacher mobility, and supply "value-added" assessments to schools, districts, and teacher education programs.

The book's final chapter brings the contributors into direct conversation with one another, focusing on the four strands of workforce demographics, workplace conditions, teacher capacity (preparation, licensure, evaluation), and the professionalization of the teaching occupation. Here, one can easily imagine a round table at which the individual contributors discover their points of agreement and disagreement and press one another on both the scope of their attention and the merits of their arguments. For example, in the section on teachers' working conditions, the authors point to signs that schools' traditional "egg crate structure" (with individual teachers exercising autonomy behind the proverbial closed classroom door) may be beginning to give way to an organization built on "professional learning communities," while cautioning that existing barriers continue to impede a more complete transformation. Members of the round table might agree that evidence warrants the vigorous pursuit of more collective responsibility and mutual support within schools, but might also maintain that the rhetoric of "professional learning community" has far outpaced the reality of teachers' daily experience. Similarly, the book's authors argue that the lack of an accepted core knowledge base in teaching has undermined the movement to professionalize teaching. The argument is a familiar one, and thus a reasonable charge to the round table—and to readers—would be to grapple with how well we are now positioned to define essential knowledge and skills for teaching (this is not a blank slate by any means), what remains to be known, and by what means we gain agreements as a field. These two aspects of teaching—a knowledge base on which teachers may rely and an organization that enables them to be effective—are both crucially important and complex, as are other issues broached throughout the book. It is in this concluding chapter that one especially gains an appreciation for the complicated task of juxtaposing past, present, and future.

The impetus for this book lies in the fifty-year history of NEA-sponsored surveys of American public school teachers. The authors rightly claim that, with these surveys, the NEA launched an unprecedented effort to trace the evolving shape and experience of public school teaching. Of course, no survey can encompass all aspects of teachers' work and careers, and the conversation that unfolds in these pages ventures into far wider territory, invoking a wide array of policy initiatives, practical experience, and accumulated research. What might then be accomplished in the next generation of teacher surveys? Some information sought by the NEA surveys, especially that concerning who teaches and where, is increasingly available by other means. Yet the impulse to capture teachers' experiences and perspectives—and to do so on a large scale—remains crucially important in an era when our educational needs are truly urgent and when our hopes for meeting them rest so squarely on those who teach.

—Judith Warren Little
  Dean of the Graduate School of Education
  University of California, Berkeley

Acknowledgments

A project of this scope and magnitude could not have come to fruition without the encouragement, dedication, and support of many. We especially wish to thank our friends and colleagues at the National Education Association (NEA). Dennis Van Roekel quickly grasped the potential of this book to inspire an important national dialogue on the past, present, and future of teaching and gave it his immediate and enthusiastic endorsement. John Wilson displayed equal passion for the project and, over the course of its development, contributed directly to its success in more ways than we can possibly recount here. John Stocks shared our vision for a work that would transcend institutional thought boundaries to tell the story of the American public school teacher in a fair and balanced way, and his support in realizing that vision was indispensible. Ron Henderson, more than any other individual, must be credited with making this book possible. Not only did he oversee the administration of the NEA surveys at the heart of the book for many of the past twenty-five years, but he also provided continuous inspiration, insight, and collegial support at every phase of the project.

Other current and former colleagues at the NEA and its affiliates to whom we owe a debt of gratitude include Mary Ann Blankenship, Kay Brilliant, Drew Cullen, Peg Dunlap, and Segun Eubanks for their advice and feedback during the initial conceptualization of the book; Leah Gandy, Kathy Tuck, and Brooke Whiting for their meticulous work on the NEA surveys; Cynthia Chmielewski for her oversight of all legal matters related to the project; Russell Forman for his research assistance; and Kirsten Nelson for her administrative support.

We also wish to thank several of our colleagues in the education research community who helped us lay the groundwork for this work as well as those who facilitated its publication. In its early developmental phase, the project benefited immeasurably from the guidance and support of Pam Grossman, Richard Ingersoll, Susan Moore Johnson, Mark Smylie, Gary Sykes, Wayne Urban, and Ana Maria Villegas. Douglas Clayton, director of the Harvard Education Publishing Group, believed in the idea of this book from its inception and, at every juncture, made us feel that its publication was his first priority. As developmental editor, Monica Jainschigg helped us cast our ideas in language accessible to a broad range of potential readers while simultaneously juggling impossible deadlines. Marcy Barnes conscientiously shepherded the book through production, and Joanna Craig copyedited the entire manuscript with a scrupulous eye for detail.

Finally, we shall remain forever indebted to our wives, Joan and Sandra, for the enabling environment that they created through their unwavering love and support, and to our children, Dylan and Julia, who provided both inspiration and purpose as we applied ourselves to this work.

Setting the Context

I

Introduction

O UR NATION HAS SUCCEEDED in building the most extensive school system in the world, providing an educated citizenry that is the lifeblood of our democracy and fueling an economy that has provided unprecedented strength and prosperity. But in recent decades there have been increasing signs that America's gains in education have stalled. At the same time, other nations have aggressively advanced their own educational systems, gaining ground in the new global economy and challenging the United States' long-standing preeminence in world affairs. Symptoms of America's arrested development include high school graduation rates stuck at around 75 percent; limited progress in closing historic gaps in achievement across students from different racial, ethnic, and socio-economic backgrounds; and disappointing performances by our students in international assessments of reading, mathematics, and science. In short, the educational system that once nourished the aspirations of the nation is increasingly perceived as falling behind and ill-prepared for the challenges of the twenty-first century. Little wonder that a recent Gallup poll reports that nearly four out of five Americans would give the nation's public schools a grade of C or lower.[1]

Against this backdrop, many have come to see teachers and the human capital they represent as essential to any long-term strategy to improve public education in the United States. For some, this will seem self-evident, given teachers' frontline position in classrooms across the country. But until recently, the pivotal role that educators play in determining the success of the nation's schools was neither fully appreciated nor acknowledged. For much of our history—from the colonial era of the one-room schoolhouse through the mid-twentieth century—more emphasis was placed on expanding *access* to public education than on improving its *quality*, and even less emphasis was placed on the quality and effectiveness of teachers themselves. Only in the past fifty years or so have we as a nation begun to turn our attention to improving the productivity of our schools, and only in the past two or three decades have research and public opinion converged in identifying teachers as key to that enterprise.

Education for All: The Emergence of the American Public School

During America's colonial and revolutionary periods, most schooling was provided through an unregulated patchwork of institutions typically functioning under the auspices of religious groups and generally dependent on parents to pay all, or at least part, of the cost. Educational goals were modest, emphasizing basic training in literacy and numeracy along with instruction in religious and cultural values. Though laws and customs generally limited or even forbade the teaching of slaves and free African Americans, primary schooling was available to most other children, often in so-called Dame Schools run by women with limited education but impeccable moral character. The sons of the elite could extend their education by enrolling in Latin grammar schools, where they received a classical education in preparation for attendance at one of the colonies' newly established colleges, such as Harvard and Yale. Teachers in these schools were usually young, single men who taught for a brief interlude before moving on to more stable careers. There were no formal academic requirements for becoming a teacher; most were selected for the job based on their moral fiber and adherence to local religious values rather than for their instructional skills.[2]

Beginning in the early nineteenth century, the *common school* movement expanded the depth and breadth of American public education in response to the fledgling republic's growing need for an educated citizenry. Whereas enrollment in the colonial- and revolutionary-era Latin grammar schools had been largely reserved for the sons of the privileged classes, the new common schools provided free education for most children, although they still excluded African Americans.[3] The student population surged over the course of the century, and by 1870 the nation's common schools enrolled more than 6.8 million students.[4] Private academies, the forerunner of today's high schools, also emerged during this period, replacing the Latin grammar schools as the dominant form of secondary education. By the mid-nineteenth century, these privately run academies enrolled more than a quarter of a million students, providing single-sex and coeducational schooling in both a traditional college preparatory curriculum and a general curriculum for those who had no educational aspirations beyond secondary school.[5]

As the nineteenth century drew to a close, the combined influence of industrialization, urbanization, and immigration gave rise to the need for a labor force with more specialized skills than those taught in the common schools. The private academies offered such education for a limited number of relatively privileged students, and, beginning in the early 1880s, a few public high schools opened their doors as well, providing similar instruction to a broader spectrum of society.[6] However, the widespread growth of public high schools did not occur until a series of court decisions in the 1870s gave local school districts the authority to levy taxes in support of free secondary education.[7] By 1890 these schools enrolled more than twice as many students as the private academies.[8] As of 1900 enrollments reached 630,000.[9] New laws requiring school attendance were enacted during the first part of the twentieth century, and as World War I drew to an end, all states had compulsory attendance statutes on the books, thirty requiring full-time attendance until age sixteen.[10] As a result, by 1940 more than 80 percent of school-age children were enrolled in the nation's public schools, with nearly eight million at the high school level.[11]

A Shift in Focus: From Access to Quality

The World War II era witnessed one of the most severe crises in the supply of teachers the nation has ever experienced. The war effort produced an abundance of jobs paying more than the relatively low wages earned by teachers, and the result was predictable: many educators left the classroom to pursue these opportunities, resulting in large-scale teacher shortages.[12] The number of emergency teaching certificates issued by states rose quickly, from 2,305 in 1940–1941 to 108,932 by the war's end.[13] During the postwar period, teacher shortages continued as schools struggled to accommodate an influx of baby boomers. Several states raised formal training requirements for elementary and secondary teachers, but with emergency certificates being issued by the tens of thousands, maintaining standards was an uphill battle for a workforce that was grossly overworked, demoralized, and underpaid.[14] In 1950 Ralph McDonald, the first executive secretary of the National Commission on Teacher Education and Professional Standards, expressed anguish over the "deterioration of teaching," citing the "low standards of preparation and of admission to teaching" as the underlying cause.[15]

By the early 1950s, states began to undertake comprehensive reviews of their teacher certification programs, motivated in part by increasing concerns about the decline of teacher education. The publication of two influential books—historian Arthur Bestor's *Educational Wastelands: The Retreat from Learning in Our Public Schools* and Rudolf Flesch's best-selling attack on progressive education, *Why Johnny Can't Read*—raised doubts among the public as well.[16] Collectively, these events laid the groundwork for the next half century, when the focus on improving access to schooling gave way to a new preoccupation with improving its quality.

The Soviet Union's successful launch of *Sputnik,* the world's first Earth-orbiting satellite, in the fall of 1957 brought a new sense of urgency to the nation's growing concern about the quality of its schools. The satellite's incessant beep from outer space sent shock waves across America, delivering a devastating blow to our national pride and focusing unprecedented attention on the need to improve our educational system. The following year Congress passed the National Defense Education Act, allocating nearly $1 billion for the improvement of math, science, and foreign language instruction in the nation's schools and colleges. The objective was clear: to train an elite corps of scientists and engineers to ensure America's competiveness in what was broadly perceived as an existential struggle for cold war survival and dominance.

Money poured in to support the development of new curricula in math, physics, chemistry, biology, and the social sciences, establishing the federal government as a key player alongside state and local governments in shaping education policy.[17]

In the 1960s public policy took another dramatic turn as America declared "war on poverty" under President Lyndon Johnson. Although the Supreme Court had made legalized school segregation unconstitutional a decade earlier, it was not until this period that equity in educational opportunity emerged as a major legislative priority. In 1965 Congress enacted the Elementary and Secondary Education Act (ESEA), directing billions of dollars to school districts with large concentrations of low-income students. One year later, the new emphasis on equity was bolstered by the publication of a congressionally mandated study by James Coleman and his associates that documented large racial disparities in student achievement.[18] Coleman showed that, on average, African American sixth graders lagged almost two years behind their white counterparts, and by twelfth grade the gap had widened to nearly four years. More fundamentally, this seminal study changed the way public education was perceived. First, it moved educational policy away from its traditional focus on *inputs*—such as the number of books in a school's library—and replaced that with an emphasis on student *outcomes*. And, second, it showed that the caliber of teachers, as measured by their verbal ability, was more strongly associated with student achievement than nearly every other school-related factor. For the first time, research provided empirical evidence consistent with commonly held intuitions concerning the importance of teachers.

In 1983 mounting concern with the standard of American public education peaked with the publication of *A Nation at Risk*, a report by the Reagan administration's National Commission on Excellence in Education. With great urgency, the commission warned of a "rising tide of mediocrity" in the nation's schools and concluded that the United States had squandered gains "made in the wake of the *Sputnik* challenge."[19] That report was soon followed by several others—including *Tomorrow's Teachers*, published by the Holmes Group in 1985, and *A Nation Prepared: Teachers for the 21st Century*, issued by the Carnegie

Forum on Education and the Economy in 1986—that set an ambitious agenda for the reform of teacher education and the professionalization of teaching.[20] A number of proposals contained in those reports, such as the development of the National Board for Professional Teaching Standards, were successfully implemented, although many others were not. Collectively, however, these reports sparked a national debate about the quality of teachers and teaching that continues to the present day and have inspired countless initiatives aimed at improving the nation's public schools. The standards and accountability movement, discussed at length below, also traces its roots to this period. As we will show, however, this reform, which has dominated education policy for the past two decades, has become as much a part of the problem as the solution to the challenges facing America's schools.

Since it first took up the challenge symbolized by a persistent beep emanating from outer space some fifty years ago, the United States has doggedly pursued excellence in public education. Yet progress has been slow and, in a number of respects, seems to have stalled of late. The obstacles to improvement have been many, but none more critical than the increasing complexity that teachers have encountered in the classroom during this period. In considering those obstacles, we establish the context for a detailed examination of teachers and teaching over the past half century.

The Growing Complexity of Teaching

Teaching, long considered a complicated and challenging occupation, has become ever more so since the mid-1950s, when education quality first emerged as a national priority in response to the Soviet challenge. Although a reduction in average class size, fewer out-of-field teaching assignments, and other positive developments have mitigated this trend somewhat, a confluence of major demographic, policy, economic, and social changes have raised the overall complexity of teaching to a level unimaginable a half century ago. An erosion of student discipline and dramatic incidents of school violence; classrooms in which one in five students suffer emotional, attention, or behavioral difficulties; and a recent upsurge in poverty that has left nearly six million school-age children surviving on less than seven or eight dollars a day all contribute to the new reality that teachers currently face.[21] Not surprisingly, a recent analysis of comparative occupational data from the U.S. Department of Labor found teaching to be most similar in skill set to the work of psychologists and social workers.[22] But of all the changes that have served to increase the complexity of teaching during this period, two stand out from the others: the phenomenal increase in the diversity and inclusiveness of U.S. public schools and the growing emphasis on standards and accountability that has dominated education policy for the past two decades.

The Diversity and Inclusiveness of America's Public Schools

Over the past fifty years, seismic shifts in the racial and ethnic composition of America's school-age population, combined with policies designed to promote within-school heterogeneity and inclusion, have resulted in a greater mix of students in the nation's classrooms than ever before. At the beginning of this period, *Brown v. Board of Education* overturned school segregation laws that had been in effect since the late nineteenth century, setting the stage for a new era of diversity in public education. But while *Brown* effectively removed legal barriers to school desegregation, entrenched patterns of *residential* segregation resulted in de facto racial isolation in America's schools that persisted until the early 1970s, when the Supreme Court upheld the constitutionality of busing as a means of achieving racial balance.[23] Over the next two decades, many urban districts, acting under federal court supervision, implemented mandatory busing plans. Some white families resisted by relocating from urban centers to the suburbs, while others enrolled their children in private or parochial schools. With time, however, various strategies designed to promote racial balance— including the redefinition of school boundaries, new school construction, and magnet schools—took effect, and by the early 1990s most districts had been released from court supervision, ending the tumultuous era of mandatory busing. Since then racial isolation in the nation's schools has increased once more, eroding many of the gains made in the decades immediately following *Brown*. Nonetheless, the impact of the desegregation movement on the job of the American public school teacher and its implications for her practice have been profound. In particular, many observers have expressed concern about the resulting demographic "mismatch" between teachers and their students, raising questions about the ability of a disproportionately white, middle-class teaching force to hold minority students to high expectations and provide effective role models.

A major wave of immigration, rivaling the influx from Europe at the turn of the twentieth century, has been another important source of growing diversity in our nation's public schools. Responding to a change in immigration law in 1965 that made family reunification a principal criterion for admittance, these latest arrivals come largely from the developing world.[24] By far, the greatest numbers originate in Latin America. In 1980 just 9 percent of children in the United States under the age of eighteen were of Hispanic origin, whereas today that figure has risen to 23 percent and, according to the U.S. Bureau of the Census, will advance to 39 percent in 2050, when children of Hispanic origin are projected to surpass all other racial/ethnic groups in size.[25] But the precipitous increase in the diversity of America's schoolchildren has not been limited to any one ethnic group or nationality. This was perhaps most vividly illustrated when an elementary school in one of Philadelphia's wealthiest districts recently decided to display a flag for each nationality represented in its student body. All told, at least forty flags were exhibited, from countries in the Far East, Africa, Latin America, Eastern Europe, and the Asian subcontinent.[26] While such multiculturalism undoubtedly adds greatly to students' educational experience, it also presents a challenge to teachers who must navigate across their students' various backgrounds and contend with new barriers to communication. According to government data, just 8 percent of school-age children spoke a language other than English at home in 1979, compared with approximately 21 percent today, and many of these students struggle to communicate effectively in English.[27]

The inclusion of students with disabilities in public education has further contributed to the diversity that has come to characterize America's public schools. Historically, these students either were excluded from school entirely, educated in separate classrooms, or placed in regular classrooms without meaningful support. Parents of such children, inspired by *Brown v. Board of Education* and the broader civil rights movement, sought redress in the courts, invoking the equal protection clause of the Fourteenth Amendment to the Constitution. In the early 1970s a series of court decisions and the enactment of laws in several states guaranteeing publicly funded schooling for challenged students created financial strains for state governments and local school districts.[28] In response, Congress passed the Education for All Handicapped Children Act (later renamed the Individuals with Disabilities Education Act [IDEA]), a federal grant program that mandated that students with disabilities residing in participating states were entitled to receive "free and appropriate public education" in the "least restrictive environment."[29] Though states can opt out, thus forgoing federal funds, none do. As a result, disabled children are currently educated in regular classrooms, sometimes with the use of supplementary aids and services. Where such supports are not sufficient, separate schooling is provided. IDEA represents a great victory for disabled students and their parents and an even greater victory for America's democratic ideals. But it also creates additional challenges for teachers, who must address the individual needs of students with a wide range of social and emotional difficulties and maintain discipline in these inclusive classrooms.

Still another form of diversity that teachers face today—the varying achievement levels of the students they teach—can be traced to a gradual metamorphosis in the organization of schools. Fifty years ago, junior high and high school students typically were assigned to one of three rigidly determined programs of instruction—academic, general, or vocational—based on their IQ or other standardized test scores. Many teachers found that sorting students by academic proficiency facilitated instruction and simplified their jobs by enabling them to pitch their lessons to the average ability level of the entire class. Consequently, traditional tracking programs earned the nearly unanimous endorsement of educators, as reflected in a 1962 poll in which more than nine in ten secondary school teachers favored the use of test scores to group students into classes.[30] By the mid-1970s, however, a growing number of critics began to point out that minority and economically disadvantaged students were disproportionately assigned to lower tracks, arguing forcefully that this practice reinforced existing social inequalities. Largely in response to such concerns, some school systems abandoned ability grouping altogether. But in most districts, tracking gradually evolved from its traditional deterministic origins to the more flexible model that predominates today, wherein students and parents have a greater voice in track placement and students are grouped subject by subject rather than by academic program. The effect of ability grouping on student achievement remains the focus of ongoing and sometimes contentious debate among researchers and policy makers alike, but for teachers the impact of the countermovement to *detrack* schools has been more certain. As the range of academic abilities represented in classrooms has increased, so too has the need for greater diversification of instruction, posing an additional challenge for today's teachers.

The Standards and Accountability Movement

Over the past two decades, standards-based education reform has emerged as the single most dominant feature on the American education policy landscape, adding yet another layer of complexity to teachers' work. Ironically, this powerful education movement, for which so many had such high hopes, has increasingly come to be viewed as more of a hindrance than a help to effective teaching. In response to growing concerns about the quality of our nation's schools, early advocates of standards-based reform espoused an ambitious vision for systemic changes to public education designed to promote higher levels of learning. Proponents foresaw clear standards that would identify what students should know and be able to do, reinforced by carefully aligned teacher education programs, curricula, instructional materials, and assessments.[31] Unfortunately, what they got was something less than that.

Building on several state-led initiatives in the late 1980s, the 1994 reauthorization of the federal ESEA established the legal framework for standards-based reform. This legislation, known as the Improving America's Schools Act (IASA), required states to develop challenging content standards for all students along with assessments aligned with those standards to measure student progress. But in contrast to the blueprint put forth by early advocates—which included a substantial focus on capacity building—the law that was ultimately enacted provided few meaningful supports for teachers, administrators, and other actors charged with improving student achievement. With little guidance for making the needed changes, few schools were able to successfully transform themselves.[32]

Over the course of the 1990s, all but one state established detailed content standards in core subject areas. They developed these benchmarks through a political process driven by state-level curriculum advisory committees composed largely of subject-matter specialists. As committee members each promoted their own areas of expertise, the number of curricular aims grew exponentially, and the path of least resistance was to include essentially "everything" about each particular subject.[33] Meanwhile, states rushed to buy off-the-shelf assessments or worked with testing companies to develop customized instruments, many of which were based on popular commercial designs. While such tests satisfied the needs of those who were primarily concerned with holding educators accountable, they were often poorly aligned with state standards and generally failed to assess the critical thinking skills that were the original focus of the standards movement.[34]

In 2001, with the passage of the No Child Left Behind Act (NCLB), the federal government took another giant legislative step, one that has determined the direction of the standards movement ever since. NCLB included three major changes to the previous law that are particularly noteworthy in the present context. The first and most positive was the law's emphasis on the disaggregation of assessment data to ensure that the performance of major subgroups—for example, racial or ethnic groups or those with limited English proficiency—could be tracked. The new law also ratcheted up the federal government's commitment to holding schools accountable for student outcomes, requiring a series of federally prescribed penalties for schools that failed to make *adequate yearly progress* on state tests (based on state-determined proficiency cut points). And, finally, in reaction to the public's perceived demand for greater progress in raising achievement, NCLB set an ambitious—some would say impossible—target of 2014 for achieving proficiency goals for all students.[35]

As this brief historical account suggests, standards-based education reform has evolved not as a single cohesive movement but, rather, as twin movements bearing the same name. On the one hand, there is the standards movement envisioned by early reformers: focused on higher-level learning, systemic in nature, with broad implications for change at every level of the educational system. On the other hand, there is a parallel reform that has focused almost entirely on the implementation of a regime of standardized testing aimed at holding schools and educators accountable. Unfortunately, this latter embodiment of the movement—which some critics refer to as its "evil twin"—has ascended to a position of dominance and has the full force of federal law. It is also the source of many frustrations for teachers.[36]

W. James Popham, a renowned expert in educational assessment, offers a vivid analogy for the situation teachers currently face under the accountability version of standards-based reform:

> Suppose you're standing in the middle of a circular shooting gallery. On the walls surrounding you there are one hundred bull's-eye targets, each about twelve inches in diameter. You've been given a loaded handgun and told to hit all one hundred targets dead center. However—and here's where this situation gets bizarre—you are only going to be allowed twenty seconds to do all of your shooting. You'll clearly not have time to make dead-center hits on all the targets. If you took really careful aim you might hit a few, but surely far fewer than required. If you aimed less carefully, you might hit more targets but almost certainly with less accuracy. And as if this scenario weren't bad enough, suppose you're told that only half of the targets will

actually count—but you won't be told which ones until after you've finished your twenty seconds of shooting.[37]

Like the hypothetical shooter, today's teachers are caught in a seemingly no-win situation. With a multitude of curricular demands and limited instructional time, some may attempt to shoot at every target, covering every element in the prescribed curriculum superficially. Others may try to target only those topics that have appeared on past exams. This latter strategy of "teaching to the test" might be a valuable tool for student learning if state tests accurately assessed the higher-level thinking abilities that state standards were envisioned to promote. But that's not the case. In a recent study of the alignment between test items and content standards in several states, researchers found that, on average, test items in five subject areas matched state standards in terms of content and "cognitive demand" just 18 to 30 percent of the time.[38]

Because high-stakes state tests tend to measure students' knowledge of discrete, disconnected facts—often at the expense of higher-level thinking skills—the vast majority of educators express concern that teaching has become too focused on assessment and report that they are "concentrating on tested information to the detriment of other important areas of learning."[39] This is particularly distressing given that the focus on test-preparation activities is especially strong in low-income, low-performing schools, where the need for more meaningful instruction is the greatest.

While standards-based reform as currently implemented represents a great source of frustration for teachers and an obstacle to their effectiveness in the classroom, this movement nevertheless continues to hold great promise. A commitment by states to prioritize content standards to produce more manageable sets of curricular objectives, combined with success in ongoing efforts to develop tests that authentically assess a broader range of skills, would go a long way toward restoring the original vision shared by so many early advocates of this important reform. Until then, the narrow focus of the present movement on testing for accountability will continue to distort that vision, diverting attention from higher-level learning and unnecessarily complicating teachers' work.

Purpose and Overview

The phenomenal growth in the diversity and inclusiveness of America's public schools over the past half century is wholly in keeping with this nation's pluralistic values and democratic ideals, and there is no doubt that public education has benefited greatly from the vitality and energy that have accompanied these changes. But it also must be said that changes of this magnitude, occurring over a relatively brief period of time, would likely have resulted in substantial challenges and complexities under even the best of circumstances. The fact that these developments have occurred in combination with a misguided reform that threatens to reduce teaching to a "culture of compliance"[40] while simultaneously creating significant impediments to the achievement of its own objectives has resulted in challenges that are unprecedented in American public education.

This book was conceived as a vehicle for exploring these challenges and the means by which they may be most effectively addressed. There is no shortage of debate, discussion, and research about how best to equip teachers to manage the range of complexities embodied in their job. Historic levels of funding from both the public and private sectors support these efforts, fueled by the conviction that a high-quality teaching force is critical for the nation's continued prosperity. Federal efforts such as the Race to the Top grants and a multitude of philanthropic initiatives—most notably those sponsored by the Bill and Melinda Gates Foundation—exemplify the outpouring of resources dedicated to enhancing teacher quality and effectiveness.

But while we engage many of the issues that currently dominate policy debates about teachers and teaching, this volume adopts a distinctive approach. First, as detailed in the foregoing discussion, we frame the challenges facing teachers with reference to a series of core complexities that have arisen over the past half century, most notably those that stem from the growing diversity and inclusiveness of schools and the impact of the standards and accountability movement. We maintain that these complexities must be identified and made explicit if the challenges teachers currently face are to be fully understood. Policies designed to re-create the practice of teaching that fail to recognize the centrality of these complexities and how they are manifested in the work that teachers do are likely to fall short in aiding teachers or improving the quality of public education.

Second, we believe that initiatives targeting teachers must be grounded in the empirical realities that have shaped teaching in the past and that will continue to do so in the future. We need to understand what the teaching occupation has looked like in recent decades, how it looks today, and, based on this information, what it may look like going forward. To its credit, the quality of education research has improved dramatically in the past two decades, owing largely to richer sources of data, more sophisticated analytic methods, and a professional ethos that emphasizes rigor and replicability of results. Indeed, in the final chapter of this volume, we draw on this expanding research base to inform our recommendations for how teaching can best manage its current and incipient challenges.

Yet even the best research, when applied in a vacuum that fails to take into account the changing characteristics of teachers and teaching, is of limited value. To construct a picture of the realities surrounding the teaching occupation over the last fifty plus years, we rely in large part on a wealth of data derived from surveys of teachers administered by the National Education Association (NEA) during this period. As described in detail in the following chapter, responses to the NEA surveys paint a dynamic portrait of the American public school teacher over time, from the era of *Sputnik* to the age of iPads.

These surveys, combined with a framework emphasizing the complexities of the job, are the canvas on which leading voices in the debate about the future of teaching in America cast their arguments, predictions, and recommendations. Initially, we prepared a summary of the key challenges facing teachers and teaching today (parallel, in many respects, to that presented above), along with data tables documenting trends in teaching from 1955 to the present. We then invited a cross-section of scholars, education and business leaders, policy makers, writers, and teachers to review the materials and write commentaries exploring the implications of the trends revealed in the survey data. Thus, while our topic and the span of time covered were broad, the charge to the commentators was straightforward: with the survey data as a backdrop, interpret and engage the central challenges and efforts to reform the practice of teaching in America.

We were fortunate to assemble a diverse group of commentators who, in turn, chose to tackle a variety of topics. From academia, we present commentaries from Pam Grossman and Michelle Brown, Eric Hanushek, Richard Ingersoll and Lisa Merrill, and Susan Moore Johnson. Grossman is an acknowledged expert in teacher training and the ways in which teachers build their knowledge base. Hanushek is perhaps the best-known economist addressing issues in public education, especially teacher compensation and the teacher labor market. For the past decade, Ingersoll has shed new light on the magnitude of teacher attrition and the factors that influence whether teachers stay in the classroom. Johnson has examined multiple aspects of teaching as a career, ranging from the role of unions to teacher preparation and mentorship. Michelle Brown and Lisa Merrill, respective coauthors of the commentaries by Grossman and Ingersoll, are doctoral candidates in two of the country's leading graduate schools of education, Stanford University and the University of Pennsylvania.

From the world of public policy, we include commentaries from Arne Duncan, James Hunt Jr., and Brad Jupp. Duncan, the current U.S. Secretary of Education, elevated the discussion about teacher quality and training to national prominence immediately on assuming office in 2009. Hunt, the former governor of North Carolina, presided over dramatic reforms to teacher pay in his state and was an early champion of professional certification. Jupp, a senior program adviser at the U.S. Department of Education, has unique insight into education reform policies garnered from his experiences as a classroom teacher, union leader, and school district administrator.

Commentaries from Joseph Aguerrebere, Dennis Van Roekel, and Randi Weingarten present the varied perspectives of leaders of several key education organizations. Aguerrebere heads the National Board for Professional Teaching Standards and is a leading proponent of advanced teacher certification. Van Roekel, president of the nation's largest teachers' union, the NEA, has been an advocate for teachers and public education for over two decades. Weingarten is president of the American Federation of Teachers (AFT) and has overseen that union's efforts to spur improvements in urban schools.

Debate about the future of teaching would be incomplete without the voices of those who practice their craft in the classroom. Dan Brown currently teaches at a charter school in Washington, DC, and entered the teaching ranks through an alternative certification program in New York City. Like Brown, Jason Gipson-Nahman also teaches in Washington, DC, but comes from a technology background and has training in mechanical engineering. Renee Moore, a former Mississippi Teacher of the Year, is an active member of teacher licensing and standards organizations. Barbara Stoflet, a sixth-grade teacher from Minnesota, was awarded the Presidential Award for Excellence in Math and Science Teaching in 2008.

Other commentators include Michael Dell, Jay Mathews, and Andrew Rotherham. Dell remains CEO of the computer company he founded over a quarter-century ago but has also become a leading figure in education philanthropy. Mathews, a *Washington Post* columnist, is one the nation's preeminent education journalists. Rotherham, co-founder and partner at Bellwether Education Partners, columnist for *Time* magazine, and former White House adviser, is one of the most prominent analysts of American education.

Interspersed with the commentaries are the voices of current and former teachers describing their victories, challenges, and frustrations within and beyond the classroom. These personal vignettes provide a glimpse of teaching "on the ground," offering a real-life counterpoint to themes explored by the commentary authors. Among them are invited contributions from Daniel Domenech, a former teacher and superintendent, who currently serves as executive director of the American Association of School Administrators, and Jody Smothers-Marcello, a National Board certified teacher and mentor from Sitka, Alaska. In addition, we selected fifteen other vignettes from those submitted in response to a nationwide solicitation to more than a million educators.

In the next chapter we present data describing the evolving status of the American public school teacher over the past half century, drawing on the NEA surveys and information from other sources. Following that, we present the commentaries, each accompanied by a teacher vignette. Reflecting the range of issues facing teachers and public education, as well as the wealth of data available to interpret these issues, the commentators engage a variety of topics. Their discussions cut across multiple themes and defy easy categorization. Consequently, rather than attempt to organize their contributions thematically, we present them alphabetically. In the final section of the volume, we review the themes that have emerged from the commentaries and interpret them in the context of both the complexities of teaching and the current policy environment. Informed by the cross-current of ideas generated by our commentators, we offer our own perspective on how these complexities might be most effectively managed to create a teaching profession prepared for the twenty-first century.

2

A Statistical Portrait of the American Public School Teacher, 1955 to 2010

IT IS EASY TO FORGET the effort, time, and resources that were once involved in conducting survey research. In years past, most surveys were administered either in person or by mail through a highly labor-intensive process, and completed forms were, by necessity, tabulated by hand. Today, surveys can be designed, administered, and analyzed with a few clicks of a mouse. With the advent of modern technology, information gathering on a multitude of issues has become nearly ubiquitous; and with the rise of education to the top of the nation's policy agenda, few other topics are studied as extensively. In 2010 alone, two polls of Americans' attitudes toward public education—sponsored by Phi Delta Kappa/Gallup and Education Next—made headlines in newspapers across the country.[1] These were accompanied by a third poll commissioned by *Time* magazine as part of a cover story on the nation's public schools.[2] Education surveys directed toward *teachers* have become even more pervasive than those aimed at the public. Between 2009 and 2010 no fewer than five organizations released findings from national surveys of teachers, including MetLife, Scholastic/Bill and Melinda Gates Foundation, Public Agenda, the National Center for Education Statistics, and the National Education Association (NEA).[3] In the saturated world of survey research, it may be hard to imagine a time without seemingly endless streams of data about schools, teachers, and the state of public education. Yet that time was not so long ago. Indeed, for most of the latter half of the twentieth century, valid and reliable information about America's teachers came from just one source: the *Status of the American Public School Teacher* surveys administered by the NEA.

The Research Department of the NEA first undertook a national survey of public school teachers in 1955.[4] The project coincided with the NEA's centennial celebration in 1957 and was intended to "serve as a [benchmark] for further progress by the teaching profession."[5] But rather than restricting the survey to a single snapshot in time, the NEA went on to conduct it at five-year intervals for the next fifty years. The most recent administration (in 2005) represents the eleventh wave of data collection for what has become the nation's longest-running survey of teachers.[6] Although some of the content has evolved to reflect changes in the American educational system, many questions have remained the same over time, and today the survey provides an invaluable resource for historians, educators, and researchers interested in tracing the development of teachers and teaching in America.

For nearly thirty years, the NEA's *Status* project was the only recurring national survey of teachers. MetLife began polling teachers in 1984, and the National Center for Education Statistics inaugurated the first *Schools and Staffing Survey* (SASS) three years later. Both are ongoing, with results from the MetLife study released annually and SASS administered on a four-year cycle. Nevertheless, the NEA surveys are without peer as a living record of the teacher workforce for much of the past half century.

The information gathered in these surveys would be of little importance if the NEA had not also attempted to ensure that the respondents accurately reflected the population of American teachers. Fortunately, since the first administration in 1955, the NEA Research Department has followed carefully prescribed procedures to achieve representative sample estimates. In brief, the design of the survey involves a two-stage process: first, districts are sampled proportionate to their size; next, teachers within the sampled districts are randomly selected.[7] Key to the success of this strategy is obtaining comprehensive lists of teachers in sampled districts from which the final study sample is drawn. The NEA's state and local affiliates have been integral to this task, as has the American Federation of Teachers, which has worked closely with its affiliates to supply teacher lists to the NEA at each administration of the survey.

Excluding the first wave of data collection in 1955, which sampled more than five thousand teachers, the NEA survey comprises responses from an average of fifteen hundred teachers per administration. Mirroring trends in national polls, response rates have fallen over time, especially in the past two cycles (see table 2.1).[8] Yet the broad range of questions and the meticulous sampling method continue to provide valuable insights into teachers' work and professional identity.

At present, the only other recurring, nationally representative survey of public school teachers is SASS.[9] This study, administered by the federal government, draws on a much larger sample size (more than thirty thousand teachers in the most recent cycle) but has typically adopted a focus different from that of the NEA survey. While both collect a wealth of teacher background information—sex, race/ethnicity, and educational attainment—the NEA survey examines the supports and resources available to teachers as well as aspects of their lives

TABLE 2.1

Sample sizes and response rates for the *Status of the American Public School Teacher* survey, 1955 – 2005

Year	Sample size	Response rate
1955	5,602	46.3%
1960	1,881	92.6%
1965	2,344	92.7%
1970	1,533	84.3%
1975	1,374	66.3%
1980	1,435	75.0%
1985	1,291	72.4%
1990	1,354	73.7%
1995	1,325	72.5%
2000	1,467	67.4%
2005	1,000	37.8%

Source: Status of the American Public School Teacher, 1955–1956 through 2005–2006 (Washington, DC: NEA, 1957–2010).

away from school. For example, it asks teachers a series of questions about the types of professional development they have completed, their perceptions of teaching resources, areas in which they need more training, and their affiliations with social and political groups. Taken as a whole, the data collected by the NEA help illustrate the lives of teachers beyond the hours they spend in the classroom, providing insight into the larger triumphs and challenges of being a public school teacher in the United States.

The American Public School Teacher: Continuity and Change

In this chapter we draw on the wealth of data captured in the surveys administered by the NEA, as well as other sources, to compose a kind of broad-stroke statistical portrait of the American public school teacher. This depiction serves as a springboard for the wide-ranging perspectives on teachers and teaching voiced in the commentaries featured later in the book. Our intent is to describe the characteristics of America's teachers and their jobs from 1955 to the present. The use of the word *describe* is quite intentional. We tasked the commentators with *interpreting* the trends depicted in the tables and figures and framing the import of the patterns revealed by the data within the current landscape of education policy. Although we reflect on the commentators' interpretations and contribute our own insights in the concluding chapter of this volume, here we limit ourselves to describing the results of the analyses portrayed in the data displays. Some of the issues that emerge from the data are well-known and commonly discussed among teachers and researchers; others shed new light on the occupation and its organization.

The displays that follow are by no means an attempt to exhaustively record every facet of teachers and their jobs over the years covered by the NEA surveys. Instead, we used the following rules to guide the presentation of tables and figures. First, we identified a small group of measures essential for characterizing teachers and their work—who teaches, how many people teach, and how the job compares to other occupations. Beyond these basic measures, the selection of displays was driven by the commentators' interests. We provided each contributor with a set of analyses organized by the following topical areas: characteristics of teachers and the teaching job; teacher education and training; teacher experiences and satisfaction; and making a living as a teacher. These categories are also used to frame the data displays. We asked the commentators to review the analyses and provide an interpretation of the trends and their implications for the present and future of the teaching occupation in the United States. The tables and figures we included reflect those aspects of the data that resonated most strongly with the volume's contributors and are referenced throughout their commentaries.[10] Reflecting the diversity of the commentators, the displays cover a wide range of topics, most of which are central to ongoing public debates about the role of teachers and teaching in the twenty-first century.

In selected tables and figures, both the NEA surveys and SASS are identified as sources. Where both had the same measures (e.g., teacher race and ethnicity), we took advantage of the larger sample sizes of SASS and report the results from that source. Except where noted, all other analyses utilize the data derived from the NEA surveys.

Characteristics of Teachers and the Teaching Job

Public school teachers constitute the largest college-educated occupational group in the United States (figure 2.1). The number of public school teachers is greater than the number of postsecondary teachers, social workers, doctors, and lawyers combined. Put another way, in a country of approximately 310 million people, more than one in every 100 Americans is a public school teacher.

Figure 2.2 shows both the number of U.S. school-aged children and the number of public school teachers from 1960 to 2010. To aid in interpreting the trends over time, the figure's two vertical axes are proportionate; the left-hand axis, showing the number of children, is forty times greater than the right-hand axis, which shows the number of teachers (e.g., 20 million children corresponds to 500,000 teachers, 40 million children corresponds to 1 million teachers, etc.). The figure

FIGURE 2.1   Employment in selected occupations, 2009

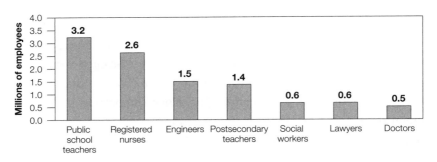

Source: National Education Association, *Rankings & Estimates*, 2009–2010; U.S. Department of Labor, Bureau of Labor Statistics, *National Occupational Employment and Wage Estimates*, May 2009.

FIGURE 2.2   Number of school-aged children and public school teachers, 1960–2010

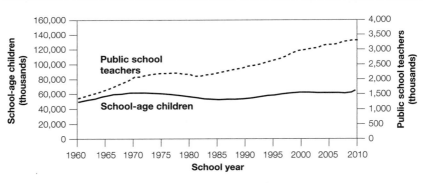

Source: T. D. Snyder and S.A. Dillow, *Digest of Education Statistics*, 2009 (NCES 2010-013), National Center for Education Statistics, Institute of Education Sciences (Washington, DC: U.S. Department of Education, 2010); T. D. Snyder, *120 Years of American Education: A Statistical Portrait* (NCES 93-442), U.S. Department of Education, National Center for Education Statistics (Washington, DC: U.S. Government Printing Office, 1993); *Projections of the Population by Age and Sex for the United States*, 2010–2050 (NP2008-T12), Population Division, U.S. Census Bureau.

reveals an uneven rise in the number of U.S. school-age children, from approximately 50 million in 1960 to just over 60 million in 2010. Over the same period of time, the teacher workforce expanded at an almost linear pace, from under 1.5 million to approximately 3.25 million.

The period covered by the NEA surveys also coincides with the growth of collective bargaining in K–12 education, which began in the 1960s and gained full momentum in the 1970s. Figure 2.3 shows both the total number of members in the nation's largest teachers' union, the National Education Association, as well as the proportion of all U.S. public school teachers with NEA membership. The two lines track one another until the early 1980s, when the proportion of teachers who are NEA members begins a slow but steady decline. Concurrently, the overall number of NEA members continues its upward trajectory. Thus, at the same time NEA membership was growing— thanks to the expanding teacher workforce—the proportion of all U.S. educators who were NEA members was shrinking. Some may have joined the nation's second-largest teachers' union, the American Federation of Teachers, which, according to the NEA survey, saw a slight increase in membership—from 10 to 15 percent of all teachers— between 1980 and 2005 (data not shown). Alternatively, new teachers

FIGURE 2.3 NEA membership and proportion of all teachers who are NEA members, 1958–2005

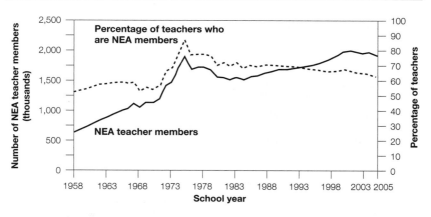

Source: National Education Association, *NEA Handbook,* 1958–1959 through 2006–2007; T. D. Snyder and S.A. Dillow, *Digest of Education Statistics,* 2009 (NCES 2010-013), National Center for Education Statistics, Institute of Education Sciences (Washington, DC: U.S. Department of Education, 2010); T. D. Snyder, *120 Years of American Education: A Statistical Portrait* (NCES 93-442), U.S. Department of Education, National Center for Education Statistics (Washington, DC: U.S. Government Printing Office, 1993).

in jurisdictions not governed by collective bargaining laws may have elected not to join a teachers' union.

Where do teachers work? Figure 2.4 shows that over half work in schools located in cities (26 percent) or suburbs (35 percent); 25 percent are employed in rural schools and 14 percent in towns. By school level, 50 percent of all teachers are assigned to elementary grades (kindergarten through sixth grade), 10 percent to middle school grades (seventh and eighth grade), and 28 percent to high school grades (ninth through twelfth grades). The remaining 12 percent of teachers are employed in schools with other combinations of grade levels.

Teaching has long been a feminized occupation, and trends over the last thirty years indicate that the proportion of women in the classroom is on the rise. As illustrated in figure 2.5, 73 percent of all teachers were women in 1955, dipping to a low of 66 percent in 1970 and rising to a high of 76 percent in 2007.

The predominance of women in elementary schools has been a feature of the teacher workforce for decades, but the data reveal a growing trend toward feminization in middle and secondary schools. Secondary schools were once more evenly split between the sexes. In 1955 half

FIGURE 2.4   Percentage of teachers by locale and school level, 2007

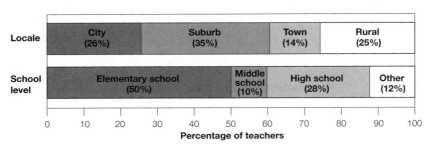

Note: Locale definitions are those used by the U.S. Census Bureau. School level was calculated using teacher reports of the grades they teach within a particular school. Teachers in schools housing only grades Kindergarten–6 were coded as teaching in an elementary school, grades 7–8 as a middle school, and grades 9–12 as a high school. Teachers in schools where grades overlapped the elementary, middle, or high school categories were classified as teaching in an "other" school.
Source: U.S. Department of Education, National Center for Education Statistics, *Schools and Staffing Survey,* 2007–2008, and *Teacher Follow-Up Survey,* 2008–2009.

FIGURE 2.5   Percentage of female and male teachers, 1955–2007

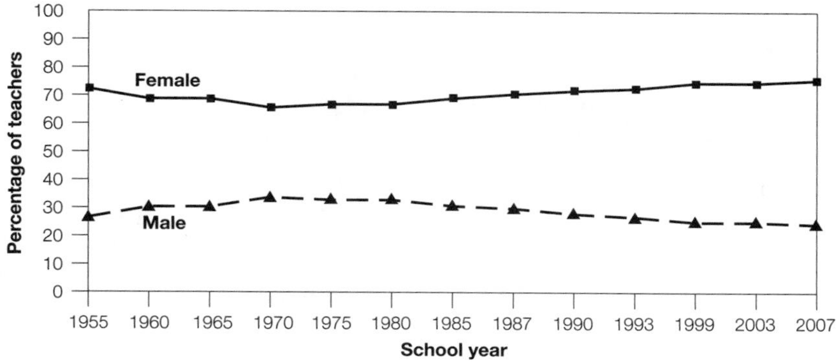

Source: National Education Association, *Status of the American Public School Teacher,* 1955–1956 through 1985–1986; U.S. Department of Education, National Center for Education Statistics, *Schools and Staffing Survey,* 1987–1988 through 2007–2008.

of public secondary school teachers were women and half were men (data not shown).[11] By 1987, as indicated in figure 2.6, high schools were still equally divided between male and female teachers, but middle schools were staffed by slightly more women. Twenty years later, the percentage of female teachers in middle and high schools has continued to rise, with women occupying the majority of teaching positions across all levels of schools.

Just as teaching has long been a female occupation, it has also been overwhelmingly white (figure 2.7). Although the percentage of teachers who are white has dipped over the past two decades, white teachers in 2007 accounted for over 80 percent of the teaching force. Mirroring national trends, the percentage of teachers included in the "other" racial/ethnic group (largely Hispanic and Asian teachers) has increased in recent years. In 2007, for instance, 7.1 percent of teachers were Hispanic, compared with 2.6 percent twenty years earlier (data not shown).[12]

Figure 2.8 shows that, after beginning an upward climb in 1975, average teacher age plateaued at around forty-two years in the mid-1990s. Yet the average masks important differences in the makeup of the teacher workforce. Since the early 1990s, the percentage of the youngest (under age thirty) and oldest (age fifty and older) teachers has

FIGURE 2.6   Percentage of female teachers, by school level, 1987 and 2007

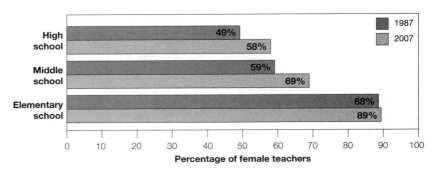

Note: School level was calculated using teacher reports of the grades they teach within a particular school. Teachers in schools who taught only grades K–6 were coded as teaching in an elementary school, grades 7–8 as a middle school, and grades 9–12 as a high school. Teachers in schools where grades overlapped the elementary, middle, or high school categories are omitted.
Source: U.S. Department of Education, National Center for Education Statistics, Schools and Staffing Survey, 1987–1988 and 2007–2008.

FIGURE 2.7   Percentage of teachers, by race, 1970–2007

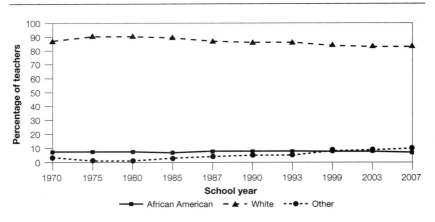

Source: National Education Association, Status of the American Public School Teacher, 1955–1956 through 1985–1986; U.S. Department of Education, National Center for Education Statistics, Schools and Staffing Survey, 1987–1988 through 2007–2008.

FIGURE 2.8   Distribution of public school teachers, by age group and average age, 1965–2007

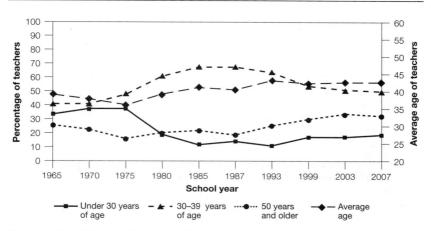

Source: National Education Association, *Status of the American Public School Teacher,* 1965–1966 through 1985–1986; U.S. Department of Education, National Center for Education Statistics, *Schools and Staffing Survey,* 1987–1988 through 2007–2008.

trended upward, while the percentage of teachers between these groups (age thirty to forty-nine) has declined.

Analyses shown in figures 2.9 and 2.10 (contributed by Richard Ingersoll and Lisa Merrill) shed further light on the transformation in teachers' ages. Figure 2.9 shows the distribution of teacher age in both 1987 and 2007, revealing a single peak in the former year and two peaks in the latter. In 1987 the modal teacher age was approximately forty-one; in 2007 the distribution is bimodal, and modal *ages* were twenty-eight and fifty-five.

Figure 2.10 illustrates how a basic characteristic of teachers, years of experience, changed between 1987 and 2007. Over these two decades, the modal years of teaching experience dropped from fifteen years to just one year. The dramatic downward shift in experience raises numerous questions about teacher preparation and retention, especially in a policy environment defined largely by accountability and rising expectations for teachers and schools.

FIGURE 2.9   Number of teachers, by age, 1987 and 2007

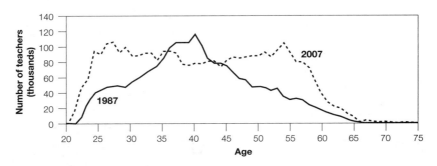

Source: Richard Ingersoll and Lisa Merrill, original analyses of *Schools and Staffing Survey*, 1987–1988 and 2007–2008, National Center for Education Statistics, U.S. Department of Education.

FIGURE 2.10   Number of teachers, by years of experience, 1987 and 2007

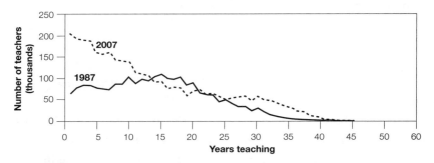

Source: Analysis of U.S. Department of Education, National Center for Education Statistics, *Schools and Staffing Survey,* 1987-1988 and 2007-2008 by Richard Ingersoll and Lisa Merrill.

Teacher Education and Training

The past fifty years have also seen a significant increase in teachers' educational attainment. Bachelor's degrees were once the norm among teachers, but since the early 1980s the percentage holding bachelor's degrees and the percentage holding advanced degrees has been roughly equal. In 2007 the percentage of teachers with a master's degree or higher (52 percent) marginally exceeded the percentage holding bachelor's degrees (47 percent) (figure 2.11).

FIGURE 2.11 Percentage of teachers, by highest degree held, 1955–2007

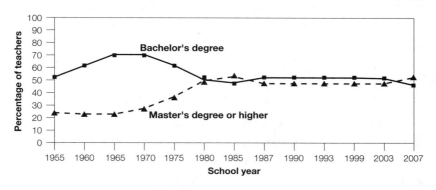

Source: National Education Association, *Status of the American Public School Teacher*, 1955–1956 through 1985–1986; U.S. Department of Education, National Center for Education Statistics, *Schools and Staffing Survey*, 1987–1988 and 2007–2008.

FIGURE 2.12 Percentage of teachers, by sex/highest degree held, 1955–2007

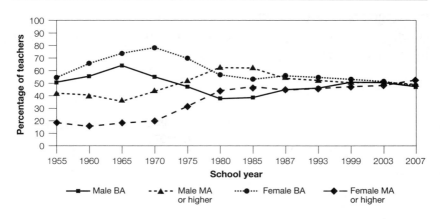

Source: National Education Association, *Status of the American Public School Teacher*, 1955–1956 through 1985–1986; U.S. Department of Education, National Center for Education Statistics, *Schools and Staffing Survey*, 1987–1988 and 2007–2008.

Disaggregating educational attainment by sex reveals similar long-term patterns for both men and women. Figure 2.12 shows that, while the percentage of men with advanced degrees once outpaced the percentage of women with such degrees, the gap between men and women has now entirely disappeared. In 2007 approximately half of both male and female teachers held a master's or other advanced degree.

Not only do more teachers seek education beyond a bachelor's degree, but they also begin their pursuit of advanced degrees earlier in their careers than in the past. In 1987 less than 20 percent of teachers with four or fewer years' experience held a master's degree or higher. By 2007 that figure had risen to nearly 30 percent (figure 2.13).

Beyond their formal training in colleges and universities, teachers also pursue professional development on the job. As figure 2.14 demonstrates, the last thirty years have witnessed an expansion in the role of school districts as the primary providers of professional development opportunities. Between 1980 and 2005 the percentage of teachers who completed development activities sponsored by a school district increased nearly twenty-five percentage points, from 57 to 81 percent. In contrast, the proportion of teachers who received in-service training from another provider—a college or professional association—remained largely the same. Overall, the percentage of teachers completing professional development from any of the three sources—district, college, or professional association—increased from 68 percent in 1980 to 87 percent in 2005 (data not shown).

FIGURE 2.13   Percentage of teachers with an MA degree or higher, by years of experience, 1987 and 2007

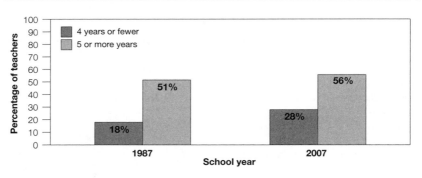

Source: U.S. Department of Education, National Center for Education Statistics, *Schools and Staffing Survey*, 1987–1988 and 2007–2008.

FIGURE 2.14   Percentage of teachers who completed professional development, by provider, 1980 and 2005

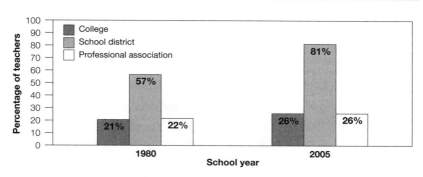

Source: National Education Association, *Status of the American Public School Teacher,* 1980–1981 and 2005–2006.

In 2005 nearly all teachers completed at least some in-service training (table 2.2). On average, teachers attended six sessions that lasted approximately five hours each. Thus, over the course of the school year, teachers completed around thirty hours of professional development. Sessions most typically focused on issues related to curriculum and instruction and to a lesser extent on diversity and using data to inform school improvement. Despite the implementation of the No Child Left Behind Act (NCLB) in 2001, less than one-third of teachers indicated that they completed in-service training on standardized testing. When asked about the areas in which they needed more training, approximately half of all teachers pointed to two areas: integrating technology into classroom instruction and teaching students from diverse (cultural, language, or learning disability) backgrounds.

Figure 2.15 takes a closer look at the relationship between the types of professional development teachers complete and their reported needs for further instruction. Among those who attended sessions on teaching students of different racial/ethnic backgrounds and providing instruction for students with limited English skills, 23 percent and 34 percent indicated that they needed additional training in these respective areas. Results for sessions on the use of technology in classroom

TABLE 2.2

Professional Development Among Public School Teachers, 2005

Percentage of teachers who completed some professional development during the school year	94
Percentage of teachers who completed professional development with a focus on:	
Curriculum and instruction	75
Managing diversity in the classroom	39
Use of data to support decisions about school improvement	45
Standardized testing	30
Percentage of teachers expressing a need for professional development with a focus on:	
Teaching methods	26
Curriculum implementation	14
Balancing of testing with curriculum needs	36
Student assessment	24
Diversity in the classroom	47
Integrating technology into instruction	51
Average number of professional development sessions per year	6
Average hours per session	5

Source: National Education Association, *Status of the American Public School Teacher*, 2005–2006.

FIGURE 2.15   Percentage of teachers who completed professional development and who reported they need additional training, by topic, 2005

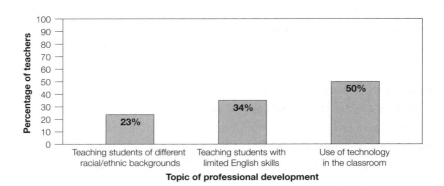

Source: National Education Association, *Status of the American Public School Teacher*, 2005–2006.

instruction were more dramatic: *one in two* teachers who completed professional development in this area in 2005 asserted that they needed additional training.

Teacher Experiences and Satisfaction

The NEA data portray shifting trends in the classroom experience of teachers with regard to class size, hours worked, and distribution of those hours. One of the most striking changes in the teaching job over the past half century has been the shrinking number of students per class, especially in elementary schools. In 1960 the average size of an elementary classroom was about twenty-nine students, and half of all elementary teachers had more than thirty students. Secondary school class size averaged twenty-seven students (data not shown).[13] While direct comparisons between the 1960 averages and those for subsequent years are not possible, SASS surveys reveal a precipitous drop in elementary class sizes over the past two decades: from twenty-six students in 1987 to twenty-two students in 2007 (figure 2.16). Middle and high school class sizes, however, have remained relatively stable over the same period.

While some class sizes have shrunk, the number of hours teachers put into their jobs has not. Looking solely at *instructional* hours, figure 2.17 shows that American public school teachers put in long work weeks, spending thirty hours a week teaching in class, seven additional hours in school on other instruction-related activities (e.g., planning, preparation, and committee work), and ten hours on instructional activities at home. The amount of in-class teaching time for U.S. teachers stands in marked contrast to that of their counterparts in member countries of the Organisation for Economic Co-Operation and Development (OECD), who spend an average of twenty-one hours per week on classroom instruction and an additional ten hours at school outside of class on instructional activities. Indeed, the U.S. average for in-class instructional time ranks highest among the twenty-six OECD countries that reported data—four more hours per week than the closest-ranked countries.[14] In addition to time spent on instruction inside and outside the classroom, in 2005 American teachers reported that they

FIGURE 2.16   Average students per class, by school level, 1987 and 2007

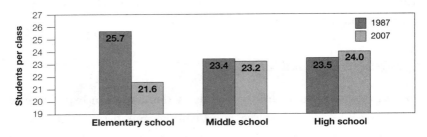

Note: Elementary school includes grades K–6, middle school includes grades 7–8, and high school includes grades 9–12. Special education teachers are excluded from middle and high schools in 2007.
Source: U.S. Department of Education, National Center for Education Statistics, *Schools and Staffing Survey*, 1987–1988 and 2007–2008.

FIGURE 2.17   Average number of teaching and other instructional hours per week by U.S. and OECD teachers, 2005 and 2009

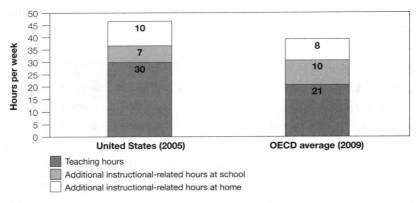

Note: The OECD average for additional instruction-related hours at home is the difference between total statutory working hours and the sum of teaching hours and additional instruction-related hours at school.
Source: National Education Association, *Status of the American Public School Teacher*, 2005–2006; OECD, *Education at a Glance*, 2009.

worked five hours a week on *noninstructional* tasks, such as coaching, sponsoring clubs, and doing bus duty (data not shown).

The proportion of time that teachers spend in the classroom has raised questions among some observers as to whether they have adequate opportunities for professional development and consultation with colleagues. According to at least one measure, the time available for nonclass activities has increased for some teachers. Between 1985 and 2005 the percentage of teachers with seven or more contractual nonteaching days—days that could be used for planning, training, or meetings, for example—increased from 25 percent to 44 percent (figure 2.18). However, whether these additional days are used to address instructional issues or for professional development and collaboration cannot be determined from the survey.

One of the most significant changes in public education over the past two decades has been the expansion of standardized testing of students, which increased in prominence following the implementation of NCLB in 2001. The 2005 survey asked two questions about the use of standardized tests: one concerning the use of such tests in teachers' performance evaluations and the other pertaining to teachers' use of test-score data to improve instruction. Fifteen percent of teachers reported that student test scores were factored into their evaluations; approximately 25 percent indicated that they used the scores to tailor instruction (figure 2.19).

FIGURE 2.18   Percentage of teachers with contractual nonteaching days, 1985–2005

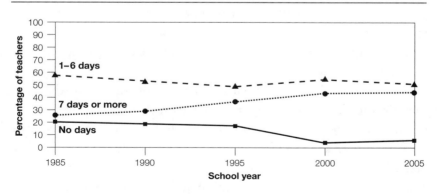

Source: National Education Association, *Status of the American Public School Teacher,* 1985–1986 through 2005–2006.

FIGURE 2.19   Percentage of teachers reporting use of student standardized test scores, 2005

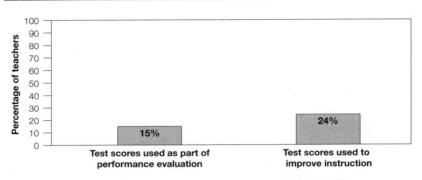

Source: National Education Association, *Status of the American Public School Teacher*, 2005–2006.

Despite changes to the job within and beyond the classroom, teachers' attitudes toward their occupation have remained remarkably consistent. The 1970 survey was the first to ask respondents to identify their top three reasons for becoming teachers. Starting with the five highest-rated reasons listed in 2005, we calculated the average percentage of teachers reporting each reason between 1970 and 2005. The results, shown in figure 2.20, indicate that the most powerful factor motivating teachers to enter the classroom is a "desire to work with young people." Teachers overwhelmingly identified this as their top reason in each survey conducted over the four-decade period, followed by the "value or significance of education in society" and "interest in subject matter field."

Since 1980 teachers have also been asked to note the factors that *keep* them in the classroom. As figure 2.21 shows, the top three responses, based on average percentages from 1980 to 2005, correspond directly to those that motivated teachers to enter the field of education in the first place. Beyond the reasons shown, teachers also point to "job security" and having "too much invested at this point" as key motivating factors.

Another trend question included in the NEA surveys concerns those factors that help teachers achieve their full potential in the classroom.

FIGURE 2.20   Percentage of teachers reporting top reasons for becoming teachers, 1970–2005

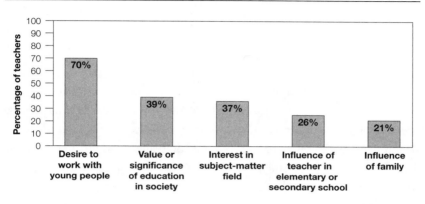

Note: Percentages reflect the average response for each reason from 1970 to 2005. Responses were selected on the basis of their ranking in the 2005–2006 survey.
Source: National Education Association, *Status of the American Public School Teacher*, 1970–1971 through 2005–2006.

FIGURE 2.21   Percentage of teachers reporting top reasons for remaining as teachers, 1980–2005

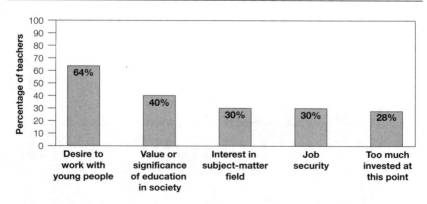

Note: Percentages reflect the average response for each reason from 1970 to 2005. Responses were selected on the basis of their ranking in the 2005–2006 survey.
Source: National Education Association, *Status of the American Public School Teacher*, 1980–1981 through 2005–2006.

Figure 2.22 plots the top five ranked "helps" in 2005 over time, revealing slight shifts in the factors identified by teachers as most important to their work. Access to "cooperative and competent colleagues" has emerged as the most important factor in recent administrations of the survey, eclipsing other helps such as "interest in children and teaching" and "training, education, and subject matter knowledge."

Fewer fluctuations appear when teachers are asked to report the top hindrances to doing their job. As figure 2.23 reveals, teachers have long cited "lack of support from administrators" as a prime hindrance, although in 2005 an equal proportion of teachers identified "testing demands/teaching to the test." In the five-year span from 2000 to 2005, the percentage of teachers who pointed to testing issues as a hindrance increased from 4 to 13 percent.

Figure 2.24 plots two different measures of satisfaction with a career in teaching: one concerns whether teachers would choose this occupation if they were starting over, and the other assesses the likelihood that they will stay on the job until retirement. The percentage of teachers who would elect to teach again reached highs in the 1960s and early

FIGURE 2.22   Percentage of teachers identifying top "helps" in doing their job, 1975–2005

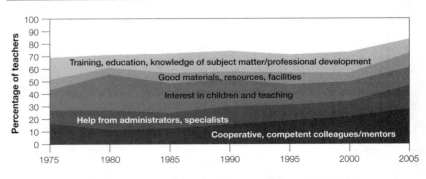

Note: Responses shown are top selected responses reported in the 2005–2006 survey. Respondents were allowed to select up to three "helps."
Source: National Education Association, Status of the American Public School Teacher, 1975–1976 through 2005–2006.

FIGURE 2.23 Percentage of teachers identifying top hindrances to doing their job, 1975–2005

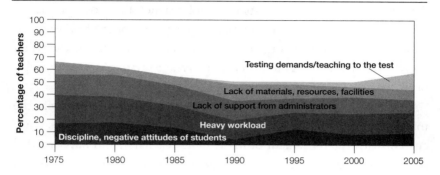

Note: Responses shown are top selected responses reported in the 2005–2006 survey. Respondents were allowed to select up to three hindrances.
Source: National Education Association, *Status of the American Public School Teacher*, 1975–1976 through 2005–2006.

FIGURE 2.24 Percentage of teachers who would teach again and who plan to keep teaching until retirement, 1955–2005

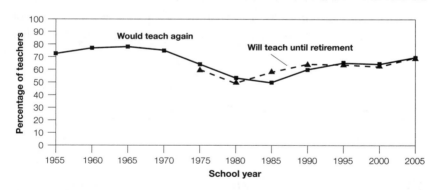

Source: National Education Association, *Status of the American Public School Teacher*, 1955–1956 through 2005–2006.

1970s, dipped dramatically in the 1980s, and has rebounded in recent years. As shown in the figure, the percentage of teachers who anticipate teaching until they retire, which was first asked in the mid-1970s, tracks almost perfectly with the first measure of career satisfaction.

Making a Living as a Teacher

The average salary for a public school teacher in 2005 was nearly $50,000 (figure 2.25). When compared with a number of other occupations that require a college degree, teacher salaries were higher than those for social workers but lower than average salaries for nurses, engineers, postsecondary teachers, lawyers, and doctors.

Average inflation-adjusted salaries for teachers rose between the mid-1950s and 1970, declined during the remainder of the 1970s (concurrent with the retirement of many older teachers), and have trended slightly upward over the past three decades (figure 2.26). The average household income of teachers has followed a similar pattern since it was first reported in 1970. In 2005 the average household income for public school teachers was approximately $93,000 (in 2009 dollars), up from a low of approximately $70,000 in 1980.

In another trend, the percentage of teachers supplementing their contract salaries with pay from other sources—school-related or not—increased between 1980 and 2005 (figure 2.27). In 1980, just over one-quarter of teachers reported earning additional income during the school year, a figure that rose to nearly half of all teachers in 2005. Over this

FIGURE 2.25 Average salaries in selected occupations, 2005

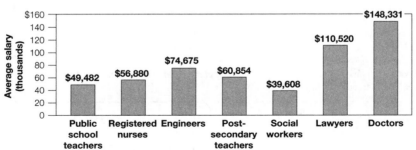

Source: National Education Association, *Status of the American Public School Teacher*, 2005–2006; U.S. Department of Labor, Bureau of Labor Statistics, *National Occupational Employment and Wage Estimates*, May 2005.

FIGURE 2.26   Average contract salaries and household income for teachers in 2009 dollars, 1955–2005

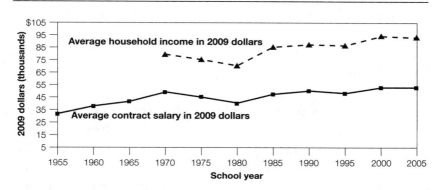

Source: National Education Association, *Status of the American Public School Teacher*, 1955–1956 through 2005–2006.

FIGURE 2.27   Percentage of teachers earning additional income beyond their contract salary, 1980 and 2005

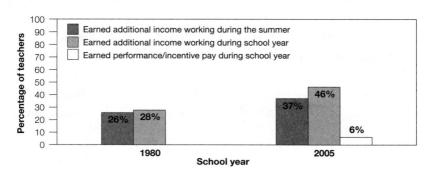

Note: Totals for additional income earned during summer and school year include both school and non-school based jobs, excluding performance/incentive pay. Question about performance/incentive pay was not asked in 1980.
Source: National Education Association, *Status of the American Public School Teacher*, 1980–1981 and 2005–2006.

same period, the percentage earning additional income during the summer increased from 26 to 37 percent. Few teachers (6 percent) in 2005 indicated that they had received performance-based or incentive pay.

Conclusion

Analyses of teachers and the job of teaching over the past half century reveal both remarkable stability and extraordinary change. In some ways—for example, with respect to race—teachers look much the same as they did in the 1950s. Yet teachers in the first decade of the twenty-first century are better educated than their predecessors, are both younger and older, and appear more satisfied with a teaching career than in the recent past. The structure of the teaching job has also evolved. Class sizes, especially at the elementary level, are far smaller than they once were, and the locus of professional development rests firmly with school districts. The next generation of teacher surveys will likely examine the impact of these and other emergent issues on teachers and the teaching occupation, especially those related to the standards and accountability movement.

In the pages that follow, a distinguished and diverse group of commentators provide their interpretations of the meaning behind the numbers. Offering more than a simple interpretation of the data, each frames his or her argument within the context of key issues facing teachers, policy makers, and others with a stake in public education.

Perspectives on Teachers and Teaching

3

Greater Coherence and Consistent Standards for the Teaching Profession

JOSEPH A. AGUERREBERE

President and CEO, National Board for Professional Teaching Standards

Each year more than two hundred thousand aspiring teachers graduate from one of the nation's more than twelve hundred teacher preparation programs. Many complete their entire training in programs housed in regular four-year colleges and universities (sometimes including a year of postbaccalaureate study), others spend the first two years in community colleges and then transfer to university-based programs, while still others participate in a growing number of alternative pathways.[1] My remarks here are driven by one overriding concern: What can be done to develop and support teachers preparing for the classroom in a variety of settings to meet the needs of all children? In addressing this question, I call for greater coherence and consistency across teacher training and career development programs based on what we know about high-quality teaching and the conditions that support effective learning outcomes for all students.

Variation with Negative Consequences

Education stands alone as a profession in allowing individuals to practice independently before they are licensed and to circumvent traditional preparation through alternate routes. According to NEA and SASS data, between 6 and 13 percent of teachers in the nation's public school classrooms received their training through such an alternative pathway.[2] While these practices have been allowed in order to address teacher shortages and attract new teachers to the field, we must recognize that they make education an outlier among professions.

When I look at the state of teaching today, I see a profession that is dominated by variation. Variation is not in itself a bad thing; in fact, it can provide opportunities for innovation, experimentation, and creative approaches. However, variation without rationale, or evidence that an adopted approach is justified and yields better results, is problematic. In the case of teacher preparation and career development, variation in design has resulted in variation in quality and results, a critical problem this country must address. The consequence of not doing so is that we will continue to have great discrepancies in student outcomes, with poor and minority students faring the worst.

What is the evidence for my statement?

First, let's look at the state of educating and preparing teachers in this country. On the one hand, we have never known as much as we do today about effective teaching with children at different levels, backgrounds, and under various conditions. The cognitive sciences are shedding light on teaching practices that, when used appropriately, can yield improved learning. The last decade has produced a number of research compilations leading to conceptual frameworks that synthesize our knowledge about teaching and learning.[3] This growing knowledge, however, is not applied or clinically developed on a consistent basis in teacher preparation programs and school systems across the country. Currently, there are no sound mechanisms for consistently ensuring the transfer and utilization of knowledge about effective practice across all settings.

On the question of the quality of prospective teacher candidates, national trends show some similarities overall. In the last decade, those preparing to enter teaching have slightly higher grade point averages and SAT scores than in the past.[4] The average teacher today has taken more college classes than in the past. A master's degree is now required for permanent certification of teachers in most states, and, as the NEA data show, the number of public school teachers holding a master's has doubled over the last forty years (figure 2.11).

Prospective teachers take most of their courses in the liberal arts and subject-matter disciplines. Elementary teachers take more education courses at the undergraduate level than do secondary teachers. The pattern of preparation usually includes a state-approved course of study in a state college with a normal school history, a large regional public university, a small liberal arts college, or a private university. Most programs include supervised teaching.

However, while NEA data show that 88 percent of public school teachers hold a regular or standard state teacher certificate, licensure requirements and the resources available to prepare and support prospective teachers vary greatly.[5] In a system where each state determines its own educational regulations, states like to believe that their standards are better than those of other states and that their needs are different. Some states require a written competency examination testing basic math and English literacy skills. States often administer other exams—such as the Praxis or a customized assessment—to assess content and pedagogical knowledge. Issues of variability arise in the application of these tests. Even if states use the same exam, they may set different passing scores, which can vary widely. Therefore, with an identical score, a prospective teacher could pass comfortably in one state and fail the same test in another.[6]

A contributing factor to divergent licensing requirements is that states have very different governance models for making policy decisions. The distribution of power within a state is influenced by whether policy makers are elected or appointed and by whom. The result of these many approaches to educational governance is a political process that produces a range of regulations, from very loose to very prescriptive, and very different educational rules and resulting outcomes.

Policy makers seem to operate as if potential teachers will reside and teach permanently in their state. The reality is that teacher graduates go where the jobs are. The differing requirements mean that these teachers may have great difficulty in transferring their credentials.

Adding to the variability issue is the rise of alternative routes to teacher certification, which come in different shapes and sizes and provide a backdoor entry for teacher candidates. Alternative routes have grown because of concerns about the quantity and quality of candidates from traditional teacher preparation programs. Some methods have attempted to address the shortcomings of traditional training by providing more practical and usable knowledge and skills that new teachers desperately need, such as the development of basic teacher routines and classroom management competencies. Others move novice teachers into the classroom before they are truly ready to meet the needs of all their students. To complicate things further, traditional providers, including universities, often deliver these alternative programs, which may raise speculation about whether there are qualitative differences between these offerings.

It is unfair to generalize about these approaches, since some are well designed and do provide improvements to the way teachers are prepared. However, many others are less well thought out—built on a view of teaching that does not recognize the complexities of effective practice and implying that anyone can teach.

The bottom line is that students across the country are being taught by teachers who have an uneven set of knowledge, preparation, and skills that may not serve all students well, given the wide variation in contexts and needs.

Characteristics of a Strong Profession

The challenges outlined above lead me to suggest a more systemic way to think about teaching as a profession. Other professions have evolved a consensus about the key education and standards that must be achieved by all who choose to enter the field. For example, medicine has developed a body of knowledge and a set of protocols that, honed by extensive clinical practice, lead to skilled professional judgment. The same move toward consensus around training and practice is needed in the teaching profession. This would involve a more consistent and rigorous preparation program, with a clinical training component in which teacher candidates are guided by skilled and experienced practitioners before they get their own classrooms. A thoughtful program should have useful assessment measures at various career stages, along with a supportive and ongoing professional development program that acknowledges as well as promotes teachers' progress.

A key characteristic of other professions is that they are accountable for their own development and standing. The education community will need to take the difficult but necessary step of coming to an agreement on what constitutes effective practice in the field. In the case of teaching, the profession should take responsibility for the appropriate and necessary training. The quality of the preparation process will make it possible for states and localities to have complete confidence in the profession's commitment and ability to hold itself to high standards for the public good.

Trends over the last twenty-five years hold promise for positive movement. Attempts to work collectively toward some agreement on professional goals have resulted in reports advocating reforms that called for a more systematic approach to preparing teachers, such as those by the National Commission on Teaching and America's Future and the Holmes Partnership.[7] Various higher education networks and organizations have made progress in identifying a common curriculum and training experience for prospective teachers. The American Association of Colleges for Teacher Education has produced seminal works on the knowledge base for the beginning teacher.[8] And the Interstate New Teacher Assessment and Support Consortium (INTASC) also has worked toward common agreement across states regarding standards and assessments for licensing those entering the profession.

At the institutional level, the most logical lever for improvement is the accreditation process. Students of other professions would not consider going to an unaccredited school, but this has not been the case for the teaching field. An institution that offers a state-approved teacher preparation program need not be nationally accredited, and many districts will readily hire graduates of unaccredited schools. In fact, whether an institution is accredited is not a question that is normally asked by employers.

In other professions there is usually an independent body that draws from the best thinking and research in the field to develop a set of standards and assessments that will ensure some level of accountability to the public. In the same way, a single national accreditation body could develop stringent, consistent standards for institutions. Having all involved in teacher training supporting one accreditation system would go a long way toward gaining common consensus around a code of institutional standards.

Likewise, one can envision an autonomous, national association like the National Board of Professional Teaching Standards (NBPTS) engaging practitioners and scholars in an effort to build a professional consensus on a set of standards coupled with fair assessments that measure practice at various stages of a teaching career. These professional requirements would be updated and validated based on the most current knowledge on cognition, brain research, and effective pedagogical approaches for different contexts and particular populations. For such standards to be professionally and publicly acceptable, the process for determining them must be credible and the assessment of practitioners linked to performance outcomes. The processes that NBPTS currently uses meet this standard.

In the same way that other professions make sure that their programs are aligned with the latest benchmarks and assessments, it would be expected that all teacher preparation and development programs would be consistent with this new knowledge so that their candidates could be successful. Once such processes were in place, all states could then defer with confidence to these national professional bodies as a basis for determining the competency levels of their teachers.

Conclusions

New knowledge about practice is continually advancing, but there is not a well-constructed mechanism for transferring this information into a consistent training program for educators. Just as a majority of states are moving toward common learning standards for students, a logical next step would be for states to move toward consistent and coherent requirements for the preparation and development of teachers. The challenge is how to link these efforts with other reform initiatives that are taking place in isolation around the country. The newly created Council for the Accreditation of Educator Preparation (CAEP) and NBPTS, as national bodies, together could serve as mechanisms for this knowledge transfer, linking the practitioner and research communities in ways that inform and support practice in schools.

The goal is to attain a more coherent and cohesive knowledge base for teaching that is credible, defensible, organized, and codified in a manner that is accessible to practitioners and scholars and built on an open architecture that allows for expansion and revision as our knowledge of good practice grows.

We are at a critical point in the development of the profession. The bottom line is that the education community itself needs to take responsibility for its growth and development rather than reacting to government mandates and policies that vary from state to state and change depending on the politics of the moment. It is the path that other professions have taken, and it is the path that teachers need to take to be seen as strong and respected practitioners. More importantly, it will go a long way toward positioning the teaching profession to be more responsive to the public it is designed to serve.

∽∾∽ A Voice from the Classroom ∽∾∽

Sometimes the most important lessons are the simplest. I was a teacher's aide in a first-grade classroom. My first job. My mentor must have sensed my nervousness when we met early in the school year. "Richard," he said calmly, "just have fun with it."

As an early twenty-something, I was not deeply impressed. Nobody needed to remind me to have fun. I promptly put the advice into my Duh! file.

Flash forward. Now I was a first-year teacher. My very own classroom. My very own twenty rambunctious first-graders. My very own set of demanding parents.

I became a very serious teacher. Like many new teachers, I took the old saying "Don't let the students see you smile until after winter break" to heart. I felt that the key to success as a teacher was complete control of my classroom. Any misbehavior would immediately result in students' cards on my classroom flip chart being turned to yellow or, for repeat offenders, to the dreaded red.

And then came a particularly stressful day. The kids were especially noisy; they all seemed to be tipping their chairs and falling backward; there were a lot of arguments and a lot of tears. There were several impatient messages waiting for me from parents. And just as I was about to begin a math lesson, a little boy in my class dared—Dared!—to call out without raising his hand, "Hey everybody look! I'm Mr. Schaen!" The boy had placed a pencil behind his ear, like I usually did.

For several moments there was silence. During those moments, my very brief teaching career flashed before my eyes—and something inside me changed. I thought about how my students came to school every day laughing, some of them even running because they were so excited. I looked at my bulletin board with the misspelled, enthusiastic notes my students had written to me—"Mr. Shan Is The Bast!" and "Scool Rocks!" I thought about how my students already seemed to be better readers than they were when the school year had started.

Then I did something the students had never seen before: I laughed. And, as more and more pencils began going behind boys' and girls' ears, we all laughed together.

Maybe teaching philosophies have changed since my days as a teacher's aide. But I have never forgotten the advice of my mentor. Just have fun with it. I still come to school with a smile.

—Richard Schaen
  Elm Avenue Elementary School
  Wyoming, Ohio

4

Rocket Fuel

Teacher Support for Energized Classrooms

DAN BROWN

The SEED Public Charter School of Washington, D.C.

—∞∞∞—

Dear Mr. Brown,

I have always loved reading and brainstorming, but I haven't always loved my English classes. This is my first English class that I truly enjoyed. This class has taught me so much. I feel like it has changed me into a new person. As a Pakistani Muslim, I have always been taught to never commit a sin and to hate and stay away from sinners. I have always hated so many people, probably because I was forced to be the "perfect" person and follow rules, more than half of which aren't even a part of my religion (and make no sense to me) but rather are part of the Pakistani culture.

One set of these people I truly have hated are "prostitutes." I thought they were the lowest of all people. But after reading In Search of Our Mothers' Gardens by Alice Walker, I realized something. No one wakes up and decides that they want to commit a sin today. Walker considers the African American women she writes about to be saints instead of sinners. These women were forced into prostitution and were kept from reading, writing, or expressing their creativity. Like Nick's dad tells him in the beginning of The Great Gatsby, don't be too quick to judge someone because you may have something that person may not have had.

Realizing this made me so thankful that in my religion (and in many other religions) the first thing a kid should be taught is that God is the kindest, most understanding, and most forgiving. God is not someone who punishes hate with hate, death with death, evil with evil. Just being able to understand this one thing has made all the difference to me. I am so thankful that you gave me those passages to read. I am even more thankful to you for making us write in our notebooks.

I have always been a person who loves to think about why life is the way it is, why there is so much hate and pain, why there is so much anguish in the world. I don't play a major role in my family. I keep to myself and love to think while I am alone. And it felt great to write those thoughts out and have someone else read them; it meant the world to me to have someone else "listen." Thank you for all you have done.

Sincerely,

—Leena B.
DeWitt Clinton High School
Bronx, NY

Why Choose the Classroom?

I don't want any other job.

Count me among the majority of teachers (almost two-thirds, according to NEA data [figure 2.21]) who intend to stay in teaching mainly because we want to work with young people. Letters like Leena's are rocket fuel. When I get a note like this, an after-class visitor, or even an appreciative nod from a student on the way out the door, I am reenergized. I want ten more. I buzz.

Positive feedback from a student renews my commitment to the marathon work of teaching. It keeps me coming back for more. I know I'm not alone. Public education is, at its core, a complex system of person-to-person interactions. Educators and students often spend more time with each other than with their own families. Those long hours shared in relatively small classroom spaces can create pressure cookers, for good or ill. When either side is frustrated from achieving its potential, a ripple effect of cynicism can easily spread, diminishing student achievement and accelerating teacher turnover. But when all parties have the requisite skills to succeed together, the potential for rocket-fuel moments is limitless.

America's teaching force is aging. As the survey data (figure 2.8) reported in this volume indicate, nearly 35 percent of today's public teachers are over fifty—an all-time high. In the next decade we need to recruit two million new teachers. Many will be hungry for letters like Leena's, drawn to the profession by a love of students and a chance to contribute to society (the two most commonly cited reasons for entering teaching, according to the NEA data [figure 2.20]).

Nurturing these idealistic neophytes into experts and then retaining them are major challenges. It is a battle we're currently losing. More than one-third of teachers who expect to leave the profession before retirement cite factors associated with system-related stress as the underlying reason, while another quarter name low pay. Only 5 percent of teachers cite student-related reasons for leaving.[1]

The three school experiences I describe below are emblematic of the crushing failures, great triumphs, and evolving efforts—both systemic and individual—in the battle to support teachers motivated by idealistic goals and their vulnerable students.

Hindrances to Good Teaching: Why Teachers Leave and Students Lose

Straight out of NYU Film School, I joined the New York City Teaching Fellows, an alternative certification program. Following seven frantic weeks of summer training, I was leading a volatile fourth-grade class at P.S. 85 in the Bronx.

My class teetered into chaos with unnerving ease. I was putting in well above the national average of class and prep time (fifty-two hours per week, according to NEA findings), and even so I struggled to keep up with the job's demands. (Think about that number: the average teacher works *six-and-a-half* traditional eight-hour days each week).[2] Most days I rode the subway home in a stupor, exhausted and dismayed. I scratched out little, but important, victories: starting a peer-tutoring group and a Visual Arts Club, engaging in meaningful heart-to-hearts with several students, observing palpable progress in some. Still, I was ground down by the 210-minute instructional blocks I had to plan, prepare, and deliver; by stinging reprimands from an ambitious assistant principal; and, most of all, by the struggle to manage students' explosive behavior without administrative support.

Furthermore, a fixation on standardized test scores put a chokehold on my ability to experiment with lesson planning; many would-be creative classroom possibilities never materialized for lack of time. Such experiences are increasingly common: the number of teachers citing testing requirements as the top hindrance to good teaching has more than tripled from 2000 to 2005 (figure 2.23).

Because P.S. 85's faculty had split into acrimonious factions, peer support and mentoring were not available. I relied mostly on myself to improve my practice, gravitating to other rookies, my comrades-in-arms, for venting and encouragement. While I can't say we made each other into better practitioners, they did keep me from quitting midyear.

The effects on my students were devastating and made for an unnecessarily turbulent fourth-grade year. I clung to isolated positive moments, but rocket fuel was in scarce supply, and I was more often overcome by distress. At year's end the administrators opted not to offer me a classroom position for the following term, and, after June, I resigned.

My flailing at P.S. 85 is a familiar narrative, illustrating the teacher attrition crisis in American public education. My lack of experience certainly hindered me. However, my classroom was also an embodiment of the top-reported teaching hindrances (figure 2.23): heavy workload, demands of teaching to the test, discipline problems, uncooperative or unsupportive administrators. These factors inevitably fostered both personal and classroom disorder that undermined any potential I may have had to succeed at P.S. 85.

Support for Excellent Teaching:
Everything in Its Right Place

A year away from the classroom reaffirmed my interest in working with young people, and I enrolled at Teachers College, Columbia University, to train as a high school English teacher. My experience as a student teacher at DeWitt Clinton High School in the Bronx could serve as a case study for how, under the right conditions, new teachers can succeed.

The NEA data cite "cooperative, competent colleagues and mentors" and "help from administrators and specialists" as the two most valuable supports identified by teachers (figure 2.22). I had both. I conferred daily with Ray Pultinas, a seventeen-year veteran. He observed my classes and provided actionable feedback in the form of longhand letters, which we later discussed. Our structured opportunities for reflecting on past lessons and collaborating on upcoming ones were invaluable in arming me with the strategies and skills—many of which were less than intuitive—to lead a classroom successfully.

As a student teacher, my workload accommodated this growing process. To teach my sixty-five students split between two classes, I spent about thirty hours per week planning, teaching, grading, and going to meetings. Only ten of those hours were spent in actual instructional periods—markedly fewer than the national average for regular full-time teachers, according to NEA survey data (figure 2.17). Each night I came home tired but not exhausted, and I looked forward to seeing my students the following day.

The teachers' lounge at Clinton was a bustling center for exchanging ideas and reflections. Two teachers invited me into their classrooms, where I picked up on different styles for engaging glazed-out students. The administrator supervising Clinton's forty English teachers observed me twice, and I used her feedback to good effect. I felt supported, not under attack. Clinton's community spirit and competent, cooperative colleagues fostered positive moments—the kind that facilitate quality classes and energize teachers.

This is how it's done! I wanted all classrooms to be as positive as the two I led at Clinton. I wasn't a master teacher; I had simply been provided an opportunity to own my class and to work with great colleagues without the common obstructions. The results were excellent learning experiences for my students and a sustained boost to my confidence, capability, and enthusiasm for staying in the profession. And one enduring, tangible reward—Leena's letter.

Making It Work: Teaching in Imperfect but Evolving Environments

A move to Washington, D.C., prevented me from accepting a full-time teaching position at DeWitt Clinton. However, I now have a world-class teacher education degree under my belt and a job I love. At the SEED Public Charter School, I hold a few aces that most public teachers do not. My classes range from ten to nineteen students, far below the national average of twenty-four pupils per high school class (figure 2.16). This is a blessing, and the individualized attention I can provide my students during class is essential. Also, I enjoy tremendous flexibility in crafting my curriculum, provided I hit the state standards. My principal knows my students and supports me. SEED also has allowed me to attend teaching conferences out of state and to partner locally with organizations like the PEN/Faulkner Foundation and the Shakespeare Theatre Company to bring authors and teaching artists to my classroom. These opportunities inspire me and my students.

SEED participates in an excellent professional development program called Take One! I count myself lucky; many teachers are crying out for useful programs like this. On average, teachers receive a mere six days per year of professional development, and one-quarter get no such support related to curriculum and instruction (table 2.2). The sustained support of Take One! has elevated my performance and put me on the road toward National Board for Professional Teaching Standards certification. Nationwide, less than 10 percent of teachers have attained or are working toward this accreditation.[3]

Still, I often struggle. What prompted Leena's letter was her appreciation that I listened to her through her writing. In her class I was scrupulous about returning student assignments, festooned with comments, the next day. In my current job, such quick turnaround is often impossible. A recent batch of exams took me upward of sixteen hours to mark. The workload of planning and leading my classes uses up virtually all of my time in the eight-hour school day, and I usually stay an hour or two after school to keep things afloat. Then I commute home, eager to spend time with my wife and baby daughter. But many evenings my folder of ungraded papers yanks at my brain like a kite string. I love my students and respect my colleagues, but the physical and mental exhaustion takes an insidious toll.

I'm working to find the balance of rigor and reality. According to colleagues, it's a lifelong search. The relentless workload haunts teachers, to their students' detriment. Chronic budget shortages tend to press teachers to cover more students and more classes, practices that represent steps backward in the campaign to retain strong teachers for the long haul. As enthusiastic as I am about teaching, I can't imagine carrying my current workload for the next three decades.

Recruiting and Retaining a New Generation of Strong Teachers

We can't count on an innate magic in America's 3.2 million public teachers to unlock the potential of our students. Leena's letter to me was not predestined; it was an outgrowth of a well-supported learning environment. The P.S. 85-style trial by fire—a gauntlet of the most common hindrances to good teaching—is clearly unacceptable; it burns through the precious human capital of teachers and students. The status quo of sink-or-swim teacher initiations will only perpetuate the revolving door of teacher attrition. Yet, if all incoming teachers could receive the DeWitt Clinton treatment—individualized support, mentoring and co-planning opportunities, and a manageable, reduced teaching load as they get up to speed—we'd find more confidence, longevity, and positive results for the profession.

Each year I get better, and there are more of these forward leaps. However, the long hours conspire against millions of teachers and students across the country to prevent an unknowable volume of breakthroughs from ever surfacing. At SEED those victories do happen, and when they come I still feel that renewing burst of enthusiasm and energy. In order to empower teachers to be their best, a new level of respect for the teaching profession must be a bedrock for modifying teachers' workloads, providing substantive opportunities for professional development, fostering a greater sense of ownership, and, inevitably, increasing pay.

Indeed, the most common reason given by teachers leaving the profession before retirement (25 percent) is low pay.[4] The most recent NEA data (figure 2.26) put the average adjusted contract salary for an American public teacher at $52,657. Most teachers are the breadwinners in their families; that $52,657 accounts for about 56 percent of the average teacher's adjusted household income.[5] This is not good enough. More competitive pay and opportunities for student loan forgiveness might bring in and retain many excellent teachers who are forced out of the profession by the economic realities.

A recent raft of politically popular reforms mute the screaming need for higher base salaries by emphasizing various models of performance pay. Regrettably, current iterations of performance pay aim for specious goals (ephemeral test-score bumps) and betray a cynical assumption that teachers just aren't trying hard enough. Teachers will take the much-needed extra money, but our country's educational foundation will not be strengthened. The breathing room teachers need to hone their craft and to connect with students will be choked by outsized emphasis on test prep—the anti-rocket fuel.

I have tasted sustained excellence in the classroom. It happened at DeWitt Clinton when I developed my craft among encouraging, reflective veterans. It happened when my job didn't consume my nights and weekends. It came when I was able to take time to focus intensively on the top reason that I, along with a majority of America's teachers, joined this profession—to work with and inspire their students.

It would be silly to define excellence solely by tabulating heart-lifting letters. But seeing the positive impact of my work is crucial to maintaining the enormous energy required to plow through each epic school year. Quite often teaching is a leap of faith: you work with students for a year and then, uncertain of your influence, usher them forward on their long, winding journeys. Hopefully you've gathered compelling evidence of learning, but you can't expect or quantify inspiration. Yet in teaching, a thoroughly human endeavor, these points of connection are critical.

Imagine an American school system in which teachers taught fewer classes with fewer students and carved out significant time within the school day for collaboration. Consider a corps of teachers emboldened to hone their craft, not crippled by inadequate training and mind-bending stress. Envision schools where administrators are not under a crush of pressure to deliver stats, wedged into an unending series of conflicts between their bureaucratic directives and the genuine needs of students.

Classrooms come alive with quality teaching; the tools to foster that caliber of teaching are before us, unambiguously identified. I've seen and felt their powerful effects. The reflective, highly engaged response from Leena's class could be the norm, not the exception. The costs of not heeding teachers' on-the-ground needs are many; the rewards of zeroing in on what matters most are extraordinary. You get schools where teachers and students alike are inspired. You get classrooms powered by rocket fuel.

A Voice from the Classroom

When I was sophomore in college, I joined a tutorial program in a midwestern city. There had been race riots in the district, and I was a bit apprehensive as I rode a bus to my first meeting. Arriving at the school, I was escorted to a room in the basement of the building. A fourth-grade boy came over to me; he wore a white shirt, its collar soiled from several days' wear. His curly, black hair was cut close to his head, and his round brown eyes met mine. He carried a yellow number-two pencil in his hand. "You my teacher, Mr. John?"

I nodded, took out a reading book from the inside of the desk, and introduced myself: "My name is John, and I am a student just like you. I am going to be your tutor." And I began the tutorial session. Every week, I ended each session with, "Next week—same time, same place." And he would say, "See you next week, Mr. John."

These initial tutorial sessions with my first student had a profound effect on my future teaching. Being called "Mr. John" resonated to my core. A simple act of respect. He saw me as a teacher. I dedicated myself to helping him become a reader. We shared a common goal. He never called me by my last name; he just called me Mr. John. That was fine for him and even finer for me.

Times do change. That same natural, mutual respect for student and teacher often seems irreclaimable. In my first year of teaching, administration advised me to establish student-teacher boundaries. Never become a friend to the student; be his teacher. Establish social boundaries. Never allow the student to know personal details. The student will learn, and you will gain professional satisfaction.

My students appear to be cleaner and better dressed than students were when I first began that tutorial session so many years ago. Their hair now is gelled and stands up like porcupine quills dyed red, pink, blue, green, and purple. One student wears an earring through his nose, while another plays with a gold stud that pierces her tongue. It is difficult for me to see through to the windows of their souls, since their eyes are obscured by thick mascara and blackened bangs. Instead of one student needing help with reading, fifteen students lack proficient skills in literacy.

At the beginning of every class, my students and I gather as a group to discuss our goals for the day. Then for twenty minutes we silently read books of our choice, the silence broken only by the turning of pages or the voices of professional readers on students' iPods. When the reading period ends, a third of the class works on the computer, improving their independent reading strategies; another third writes in their reading skill books, and the rest proofread a persuasive essay. A student aide meets with small groups to reinforce reading comprehension. I work individually with students on their writing while another assistant meets with students to discuss quarterly goals. Students are intent on the development of their skills, and as they travel through the three rotations, it is clear that they are becoming more responsive, more confident, better students.

At the end of eighty minutes, the hallway bell signals the end of class. Books are placed in their cubbies, the computers are shut down, and the chairs are pushed beneath the group desks. As students file out, a cacophony of shouts is heard: "Have a good day, Mrs. G. See you tomorrow, Ms. C. So long, Mr. F. Good-bye!"

I smile, place my hands behind my head, and tilt back in my chair, feet on the desk. Lifetimes of students pass through these classroom doors. The times change, and the styles reflect a new generation. Yet there are still constants—that children are my students and that I am their teacher. That natural, mutual respect still exists, and while "Mr. John" has become "Mr. F," there is still the belief that there is something honorable in being a teacher.

—*John J. Fulco*
Killingly High School
Danielson, Connecticut

5

Time, Teaching, and Technology

MICHAEL DELL

Chairman and CEO, Dell Incorporated

I WAS FORTUNATE to have been mentored by some outstanding teachers who helped spark my curiosity about science and mathematics and a lifelong desire to learn. My junior high math teacher, for example, spent countless hours after school with a group of us who demonstrated a deeper interest in the subject. She brought in our school's first teletype computer terminal, which was a great source of inspiration for me. No one could have guessed how impactful those sessions—and that teacher—would be in my life.

Today, demands on teachers' schedules are tougher than ever. From NEA data (figure 2.23) we know that teachers now have even less time to teach because they have to focus on disciplinary actions, increased paperwork, testing demands, and meetings. We also know that classrooms are increasingly made up of students with unique learning styles and from diverse backgrounds—so much so that nearly half (47 percent) of teachers want more training to help them manage diversity in the classroom (table 2.2). Given this spectrum of students and styles, one teaching approach will probably not work for the class as a whole. I believe that technology has the power to address this problem by helping teachers spend more time meeting their students' individual needs.

This assertion seems logical coming from a technologist like me. However, when it comes to technology and education, the discussion too often segues immediately to computers in the classroom: How many computers should schools invest in? Is it one computer per student? Is a single computer lab enough? As many districts have learned, these are not necessarily the right questions to ask when considering how to use technology to improve teaching and learning.

I had a discussion along these lines last year with a group of school superintendents gathered at our Texas headquarters. One of these administrators told me that his district had purchased a computer for every student but hadn't really seen improvements in student performance. That's not surprising. The point is that computers on their own, absent the right training, curriculum, and measurement, won't make a difference. It's what people—teachers and administrators—*do* with technology that has the power to transform lives.

Using Technology to Get More Personal

The NEA data tell us that 45 percent of teachers want to understand how to use data in their decision-making processes regarding school improvement (table 2.2). I have a few suggestions. Imagine a classroom where the teacher has a comprehensive history of students' educational careers—how they performed in previous years, what subjects they excelled in or struggled with, how often they missed school. All of this information close at hand would not only free up time for educators but would also enable them to focus more closely on lesson plans that have the greatest potential to impact the class as a whole. How about a classroom in which teachers get real-time feedback on how students are doing as they work through each six weeks' worth of material? This is where technology can help drive personalization—and ultimately success—in education.

But the technology must first be applied to assemble the needed data. While a vast amount of information on students is generated every day, these resources are not easy to access, analyze, and ultimately act on. They often reside in fragmented, incompatible district databases—even in file cabinets—that prevent meaningful sharing of information.

And thus, too often, the beginning of a school semester is more like the beginning of each student's educational career: the slate is essentially wiped clean from year to year. As much as they want to know their students, it's simply not possible for teachers to go on a fact-finding mission for each and every one before the school year begins.

But that doesn't have to be the case. Progressive districts are demonstrating that it's possible to centralize data so that, with a few clicks of a mouse, teachers can get the background information they need to plan ahead for how to help students improve in areas where they need specific attention. With the right data, aided by technology, teachers have the power to tailor education for every student.

Let me share a real-world example. The Michael & Susan Dell Foundation worked with the New York City Department of Education to implement the Achievement Reporting and Innovation System (ARIS). ARIS gives teachers a holistic view of students' test performance, grades, attendance, special programs, and discipline records. All of this information is compiled into one online database. When teachers log on, they see an intuitive dashboard they can use to get information on their students. For example, a teacher can click on the "My Students" tab on the dashboard and view each student's profile to see where similarities or differences exist in the students' records and then use that data to create specialized lesson plans.

Through this technology, a teacher already knows what actions she can take to move students forward before they've even started the school year. She's able to flag emerging issues before they become problems. She can devote more time to teaching to her students' strengths and focusing on the subjects in which they need help. And, most important, the students benefit from this personal attention because they're able to learn in a way that is unique to their circumstances.

This application of technology can also help make a difference to students preparing for college. In both Dallas and Chicago schools, principals use dashboards to monitor their students' college readiness.

These tools identify trends in attendance, test scores, and grades so that teachers can intervene quickly and put a personalized plan in action to prevent students from dropping out or failing their classes.

For example, students with an excessive number of absences are flagged for attendance intervention before school starts the following year. Principals, counselors, and teachers share these reports online through the attendance tracking database. Teachers share information and take action, such as adjusting class schedules when they recognize a group of students who are distracting one another. They have in-person counseling sessions with students to help them understand how they can improve their own performance by attending class regularly.

Just one year after the plan was put in place, one Chicago school reported that 69 percent of ninth graders were on track to graduate on time, up 10 percent over the previous year. Imagine extending this results-oriented concept beyond the individual school to an entire district, or even a state.

By using online dashboards and Internet-based applications to understand students' backgrounds, administrators can more quickly identify where to invest funding and boost teaching resources. Teachers can identify groups of students with special needs or advanced skills in order to develop specialized curricula. They can use Web-based technology portals to search for state-approved courses that meet their specific needs. They can even participate in online communities to share their challenges and collaborate with other educators district-, state-, and, ideally, nationwide. What's more, all of this information can be available at anytime from any location with Internet access.

A perfect example of this occurred in 2009 when American Reinvestment and Recovery Act funding was made available to schools. In many cases, the application process for these grants was complex, and districts needed help getting through all the paperwork. Dell helped bring these educators together with people who gave them the advice they needed to optimize their chances for receiving the funds. This did not happen at a conference or an event; this work took place in an online community. I continue to be encouraged as I see more and more teachers embracing the Internet and social networking as ways to inspire each other to integrate technology into their classrooms.

Just Like Teaching, Technology Is Not One-Size-Fits-All

For technology to be effective, each district or school needs to assess its goals, gaps, and measures of success. It must have a plan that will work within its unique circumstances. What systems are currently in place and where are the gaps? How do teachers use technology at present, if at all? We know from the NEA data that almost all educators have their own computers and access to the Internet and use e-mail regularly, but more than half of them want training on how to use technology in the classroom (table 2.2). As part of any plan to implement technology as an effective teaching tool, teachers and administrators must be offered professional development that will give them the skills to better integrate technology into instruction. There also should be milestones set to track progress and reinforce accountability.

Obviously, all of this requires strong leadership and commitment from school and district administrators, from planning to implementation to measurement to continuous improvement and maintenance. It's only when everyone is aligned and moving toward one goal—empowering teachers with the data and technology they need to improve the quality of education for our youth—that they can truly realize success.

I am grateful for the opportunity to share my passion about how technology can help teachers personalize their students' education. And I thank teachers across the United States for their selfless dedication. For me, technology has always been about enabling human potential. For teachers, this potential is embodied in how they can use its capabilities to best prepare our students to achieve their dreams.

A Voice from the Classroom

It was 1972 when I first heard the Eagles' "Witchy Woman." Thirty-eight years later, I've started humming that song again. I can't help it. Every day, I arrive at school and turn on my computer, and—Woo-hoo!—I am "Wiki" Woman! After sixteen years of teaching, I am newly bewitched by the power of technology.

This year I decided to teach my sophomore English students Franken-stein using a wiki. We have a great media specialist who helped me get started, and now I am hooked. The wiki enables students to discuss lit-erature by posting comments and access resources related to the text. I can incorporate links to YouTube, movie clips, text files, e-text versions of the book, enrichment materials, and writing prompts—you name it, you can link to it, find it, or interact with it. These wide-ranging sources are col-lected in one place that the wiki members—my students—can access from any computer at any time.

The wiki was the bait I used to lure my sophomores into a new way of doing homework and practicing online discussions in a controlled, aca-demic setting. What could be more perfect than teaching a book about the risks of science outpacing ethics by using a new technology that requires students to confront this exact same dilemma? If students made irrespon-sible comments about another's interpretation or posted an inappropriate answer to a question, these comments would be public. As with Victor Frankenstein, sending a creation out into the digital world without think-ing it through could lead to harm. I think the unit was a success. Many students said they preferred doing homework this way, and, as with Google, wiki was quickly turned into a verb—"Let's wiki tonight at 7:00." More importantly, everyone held to our standard of appropriate language and interaction.

Under the category of unintended consequences, the wiki was meant to change the way the students did their Frankenstein homework, but instead it changed the way I do mine. Now when I prepare or teach a lesson, I work from the wiki, linking in clips to Boris Karloff's film, Mel Brooks's spoof, that great site on romanticism . . . Wordsworth and the Romantic poets . . . the Monster Mash . . . the Visual Thesaurus . . . the possibilities are endless.

We literature teachers are often frustrated by having to compete with technology for our students' attention, so it's particularly satisfying to be able to wed a classic text to this alluring beast. We need to encourage stu-dents to integrate the best of both worlds—classic literature and innovative technology. However, we need ongoing development programs and quali-fied support personnel to keep us on top of evolving Web 2.0 capabilities. And as various writing communities—blogs, tweets, texts, social networks, and self-publishing sites—increase, the number of "dialects" students are expected to master also increases. My responsibility as a writing teacher is to stay fluent so I can help my students become flexible writers, able to be successful in all paths of communication—even those yet to be created.

We also must instruct this new generation of Frankensteins to use the Web responsibly. There is uncertainty in this burgeoning world, and we should heed Shelley's warnings about technology leading to irresponsibility and destructiveness. Reports of cyberbullying and teen suicide show the consequences of failure to address the ethical use of these new technologies.

But still I revel in this new world. Teenagers can and will learn how to adjust their language to suit the audience and make responsible choices. Most do so already, and if they don't, isn't that what teachers are for—to help them learn this essential communication skill? Yes, there are more modes of writing now, but the basics are the same: knowing when to use the lingua techna and when not. And even with the risks, these new avenues of writing—and new ways of teaching writing—are intoxicating for me. I will admit that sometimes I'm concerned about the cacophony of unfiltered voices on the Internet. But the only solution is to arm this generation with even stronger writing, thinking, and communication skills—that's where I come in. Woo-hoo, wiki woman, she's got the moon in her eyes—and another wiki under construction.

—Patricia O'Connor
   Brookfield High School
   Brookfield, Connecticut

6

A Vision of the
New Teacher in the
Twenty-First Century

ARNE DUNCAN

U.S. Secretary of Education

FIFTY YEARS OF NEA DATA chart dramatic changes to our nation's education system. Today's students represent a range of racial, cultural, linguistic, and socioeconomic backgrounds unthinkable when the survey began. The ultimate aim of public education was once a high school diploma; today the goal is some level of postsecondary education or training, along with the skills and credentials to ensure a fulfilling career, a living wage, and productive engagement in all the benefits and responsibilities of civic life. And today's job-seekers confront advances in information, technology, and globalization unimagined by earlier generations.

All these changes are challenging schools to rethink strategies for instruction, assessment, teacher collaboration, and accountability and to ensure that students' experiences in the classroom keep pace with the reality of their lives beyond the school doors. What competencies and conditions might characterize the work of the high-performing twenty-first-century teacher? And if we could accomplish all that we hope for, what might the teaching profession look like in the future?

In addition to providing a chance to rethink what it means to be a teacher, these trends also invite consideration of the future form and role of America's teachers' unions, with the potential to begin to blur traditional labor-management distinctions in favor of a focus on more shared ownership for student performance and school results.

Teachers as Leaders for a New Framework for Learning

Diverse learners are now the norm. Soon they will dramatically change the face of our classrooms. According to Census projections, minority populations will be the majority by 2042. This change will be most apparent among children. By 2023 more than half of all children are expected to be minority. By 2050 that proportion will climb to 62 percent.[1] First and foremost, then, I envision all teachers having the skills and supports they need to help these learners excel and to develop their cultural awareness and ability to negotiate an increasingly complex and diverse society.

In this vision, teachers help their students to be much more self-directed—more responsible for their own learning—and the environments and opportunities for learning have expanded. The teaching experience regularly incorporates methods like interdisciplinary and project-based learning, work-based learning, and service learning. By rethinking how they use time and technology, schools offer a blend of face-to-face and online education, along with more self-paced, personalized, independent courses of study for students. And face-to-face instruction may deploy educational teams with a range of experience and skills—for example, one or more teachers focused on large-group instruction as well as teacher-residents focused on small-group instruction and online support—that coordinate daily to monitor student growth and prepare and implement instruction.

In addition, with the help of a wide range of community stakeholders—from civic and cultural organizations to area business and labor partners—teachers use multiple methods to engage students in academically rigorous, real-world experiences and offer multiple learning environments (including online environments) that are supportive and safe.

Since this ideal future includes equitable broadband connectivity for teachers and students—in schools, throughout the community, and at home—teachers can better personalize learning, increase relevance, and expand students' opportunities to achieve. Examples range from customized lesson "playlists" that respond to individual students' demonstrated competencies, skills gaps, and learning preferences to tools that help disadvantaged learners or learners with special needs—from low-income early learners to English language learners to learners with disabilities—to excel.

My vision is of teachers who are adept at assessing what students have learned, addressing gaps in learning, and charting students' progress. No longer limited to standardized, fill-in-the-bubble tests, teachers in this scenario have multiple tools to diagnose students' strengths and weaknesses in the course of learning, offer immediate feedback and interventions to increase student performance, and help drive continuous improvement for the school and district. I envision teachers employing assessment *systems*, including new types of evaluations, multiple measures, and new data and statistical tools. In addition to administering assessments, teachers may also help to review and score them, as now happens with Advanced Placement exams.

I picture these teacher-led, learning-driven environments shifting the emphasis away from a traditional course-and-class model, which measures *time spent* in learning, toward a model that measures *value gained* in learning. Rather than logging seat time, the focus is on determining whether students know the content and can demonstrate the necessary skills. Students can place out of a class if they have mastered the skills to advance beyond it.

In this scenario, teachers are skilled at using data for decision making and accountability, and they play an active role in keeping their communities informed about student and school results—both gaps and gains. In my vision, teachers know how to communicate clearly about standards and expectations with students, parents, and other stakeholders, helping them understand the data and buy in to school performance plans.

As teachers play a stronger role in defining and measuring student progress and achievement, this may lead to a broadening and deepening of content standards. I see these future teacher-leaders playing a powerful role in driving an ongoing conversation around creating and updating world-class standards in subjects that promote a well-rounded education while maintaining an emphasis on and excellence in the science, technology, engineering, and math (STEM) skills. This conversation increasingly focuses districts, states, and the nation on standards that reflect both U.S. priorities and the demands of the global marketplace.

A Vision for the Twenty-First-Century Teaching Profession

In keeping with our diverse student population, my vision for the teaching profession begins with an equally diverse teaching workforce. While the teaching force has undergone a dramatic expansion in the last fifty years—doubling from 1.5 to 3.2 million teachers—the composition of the workforce has remained relatively constant (figure 2.1). Over the past thirty-seven years, the percentage of minority teachers has increased to 17 percent, up only five percentage points (figure 2.7). And the proportion of male teachers in the workforce has declined slightly (figure 2.5). I envision a teaching workforce more diverse in terms of race, ethnicity, language background, socioeconomic background, and disability, as well as in the pathways through which these individuals are prepared for career excellence.

I envision a future where there are multiple, equally effective ways to join the profession. What will matter is how teachers are prepared and what skills and qualities they exhibit. The new teacher preparation model involves rigorous training and real support for those entering or transitioning into the profession. It will be built around a combination of academic and hands-on experiences, mirroring the rigor and relevance of, for example, training for the medical profession. Teachers benefit from year-or-longer residencies that include intensive observation, mentoring, and coaching by master teachers. These programs intentionally equip participants to teach *and* lead effectively, enabling them to fully embrace the scientific and research-based aspects of the profession and to engage in data-driven decision making. This clinical model lays out a clear pathway blending strong, current, research-based theory with intensive practice.

Once in the classroom, new teachers will continue to learn their profession through induction programs. This period will last up to three years, offering a lighter schedule, built-in time for learning and reflection, and the opportunity to team-teach with experienced colleagues. New teachers will not be given the toughest assignments, as happens too frequently today. And, like their students, all teachers, from novice to veteran, will engage in "anytime, anywhere" learning. They will help identify needs and shape professional development both as individuals and as members of the school faculty. Gone are the days when teachers feel isolated in their classrooms: my ideal for the profession includes a broad range of well-known, easily accessible ways for teachers to interact and collaborate. I envision teachers constantly working to boost their own effectiveness, access or publish information and best practices, and energize their careers. My ideal for the profession connects teachers with the tools, resources, and expertise they need to be highly effective and to engage in multiple communities of practice—in their states, across the nation, and even around the globe.

I envision a profession in which teachers share leadership responsibilities in their school buildings and communities. This leadership manifests itself in various forms and combinations, depending on the skills and inclinations of the individual teacher.

One avenue for expanded teacher leadership emerging today is the partnership model of teacher-run schools. A 2003 report by Public Agenda found that the majority of teachers who had been teaching less than five years, as well as half of those who had been teaching for more than twenty years, expressed interest in working in a partnership-based or teacher-run school.[2] And researchers like Richard Ingersoll at the University of Pennsylvania suggest that schools are more effective when teachers play larger roles and exercise more authority in school operations.[3]

There are many variations on this model. In some cases, teachers might have a stronger hand in school governance in partnership with a principal. This principal's role might also have been recast by shifting the administrative functions to a building manager or an administrative team, freeing her to concentrate on serving as an instructional leader and facilitator. In other cases, there is no administrator, director, or principal; instead, a team of teachers handles all decision making for the school. (Some schools' site-based decision-making teams also include parents and community members.) In these cases, in addition to teaching part time, designated teachers handle business or program management functions, public outreach, or other key areas. In another variation, site-based teams opt to contract out administrative functions to service providers that specialize in school operations.

Site-based teacher leadership may also involve teachers helping oversee new models in which schools function as community hubs. Teams of teachers may have specific roles in refashioning their schools as sites that offer integrated academic, social, and health services for students and their families and include extended time for academic and enrichment experiences before and after the standard school day.

Leadership may also take the form of hybrid positions that allow teachers to devote a portion of their time to teaching and a portion to collaborating with other teachers, teaching assistants, content specialists, community experts, and volunteers. Teachers can also serve as on-site or virtual subject matter experts in areas such as literacy coaching or coordination, English language learning, formative assessments, data analysis, family and community relations, or instructional technology.

All these avenues increase teacher empowerment and teacher engagement. But they share one goal: improving student learning. Teacher-led, school-based decision making holds teachers accountable for school and student performance while giving them the authority to affect the factors that will improve that performance.

These multiple possibilities also foster even greater teacher quality and commitment. There is evidence that teachers now entering the workforce expect and value upward career paths and dynamic opportunities to acquire new skills over the career plateaus with job security that their parents or grandparents might have accepted.[4] For the growing number of teachers likely to be dissatisfied with unchanging duties and static career prospects, teacher-led and school-based decision making offers variety and opportunities that extend beyond the classroom without forcing dedicated and talented professionals to choose between a love of teaching and career advancement.

To enable these expanded roles, my vision of the new norm for the teaching profession includes scheduled blocks of nonteaching time for educators to spend completing their own projects, working with the community or creating partnerships with other organizations, mentoring other teachers, or otherwise strengthening the profession. Teachers have time during the day, month, and year—as well as the option to take extended periods over the course of their careers—to work with an area postsecondary institution, nonprofit entrepreneur, or private education firm; serve in curriculum design or policy development at the school, district, regional, or state level; conduct research; or participate in externships in industries related to their disciplines in order to learn about the latest trends and applications of their subjects, particularly in the STEM fields. In short, teachers are expected and enabled to combine strong classroom practice with enrichment work in other aspects of the field. Today some researchers and professional collaboratives are calling this new paradigm the *teacherpreneur.*

In my vision, teacher evaluations are rooted in clear job descriptions and performance standards as well as in consensus about expectations for each position. Schools employ *frameworks* that help define as well as gauge teaching excellence and include multiple measures tied to student performance and other factors. These other factors could include a teacher's content knowledge or skills in lesson preparation, instructional design, student assessment, or classroom management. They could take into account a teacher's use of various teaching techniques or resources in addition to other responsibilities like working with parents and families, pursuing professional development, collaborating with colleagues, or contributing to the school environment. The system might include self-evaluation and feedback from parents and students as well as observation and evaluation by peers and other school leaders. Certainly, teachers participate in designing and implementing these frameworks. They also help ensure that they are fairly administered, that they offer recourse and support for those evaluated, as well as consequences for any who fail to make progress, and that they are transparent and yield useful information for professional development and continuous improvement.

I envision teachers being compensated, in part, based on the impact they have on student and school performance, the value they add to the profession, and the products or services they offer. Student achievement would be a significant factor in compensation, though not the determining factor.

These new compensation systems also would reward teachers working in teams—or as a whole school community—to raise student achievement. The pay systems would also encourage the most effective teachers to take on the most difficult assignments and student learning challenges.

I picture an education system that recognizes what good teaching and school leadership is worth and compensates teachers and leaders accordingly, allowing teachers to build careers that value growth and opportunity and challenging experiences over stability or seniority.

The Evolving Role of Teachers' Unions

Conversations about expanded teacher leadership suggest an evolving role for America's teachers' unions. As teachers (and other school staff) become increasingly involved in school-based decision making, we may be approaching the end of the era of labor-management antagonism and entering a new age of cooperation toward common goals.

Giving teachers greater say in how the school runs and in how learning is handled may imply a shift from traditional union-district contracts toward school-based compacts. It suggests a growing responsibility for teachers in negotiating expectations, schedules, salaries, assignments, and other key aspects of their jobs. In *The Teachers of 2030: Creating a Student-Centered Profession for the 21st Century*, Barnett Berry and his TeacherSolutions colleagues from the Center for Teaching Quality predict a move toward a model that resembles "a professional guild."[5] And in *United Mind Workers: Unions and Teaching in the Knowledge Society*, Charles Taylor Kerchner, Julia Koppich, and Joseph Weeres suggest a new vision for professional unionism, arguing that the industrial model of labor-management relations, with its adversarial approach and narrow scope for negotiations, fails to accommodate the realities of today's standards and accountability movement—to the detriment of districts, schools, and students as well as unions and their members. The authors point out that, while the industrial model worked to improve pay, benefits, working conditions, and security for a definition of teaching as a uniform job, it is less successful as applied to a profession with a large degree of differentiation.[6] The vision I have outlined features a wide range of differentiated roles for teacher-leaders that could render the old labor-management distinctions obsolete.

I picture reinvigorated twenty-first-century unions that have embraced the idea of teaching as a differentiated profession and consequently changed their approach to the way they represent teachers, the way they conduct business with districts, and the wider opportunities they afford for teachers and administrators to work as partners. This may include revising the criteria for selecting union staff and school-based union representatives, the way budgets are allocated and managed, and the way contracts are structured and negotiated.

These changes could call for a reevaluation of such traditional elements of compensation as seniority and single-salary schedules while allowing for a greater recognition of differing levels of skill, experience, and professional goals. Reinvigorated unions could help shift the standard from centrally driven, fixed-year contracts toward more flexible options like "living" (adjustable) contracts or school-based compacts, as we are seeing in school systems as diverse as New Haven and Denver. This would place union leaders in a position to negotiate broader incentives such as improved job responsibilities and differentiated pay for teachers in hard-to-serve schools and hard-to-fill assignments. In return, teachers would accept greater accountability for meeting high expectations for students and schools.

This new paradigm calls for labor and management to adopt shared ownership of the mission and success of public schools, including accepting shared responsibility for improving student learning and closing the achievement gap. In this view, the contract would no longer just protect teachers' job security but instead promote career security. It would move from outlining the rights of individual teachers to capturing teachers' individual interests and affirming the teaching profession's public responsibility. The outcome, as Kerchner, Koppich, and Weeres suggest, would be increased trust and goodwill between the negotiating parties—and, I would argue, with the American public. This is a result to be hoped for and a conversation worth having.

Toward a Revitalized American Teaching Profession

My vision is of a diverse, highly skilled, highly respected teaching workforce that is compensated according to the true value it contributes to our society. It positions teachers as acknowledged educational leaders, with strong decision-making authority for how schools are run. These teachers play multiple roles and exercise a variety of skills—within school settings and beyond them. They take part strategically in advancing the profession. They collaborate together in instruction, evaluation, and administration. A teaching profession like the one I've described is filled with highly visible leaders who have every opportunity to earn the public's respect as effective professionals, as collaborators and partners with their communities, and as entrepreneurial experts helping to further the profession locally, nationally, and even internationally.

In the vision I've outlined, Americans recognize that the twenty-first-century teacher is preparing students to excel in fields and jobs that may not yet exist and value teaching as one of society's most complex, creative, and important ventures. The profession enjoys widespread public recognition that, even as our education system helps all students set goals, stay in school, earn a high school diploma, and secure college and career success, it is also nurturing informed citizens, effective problem solvers, ground-breaking pioneers, and dedicated leaders—in short, generations of life-long learners who are proficient in today's tools and technologies and ready for the challenges of tomorrow.

—ὲέὲ— **A Voice from the Classroom** —ὲέὲ—

Diversity was the first lesson I learned as a teacher. Even in the most seemingly homogeneous classrooms, each student has unique skills and challenges. Thank goodness! It is the differences, the varying personal histories, and the contrasting opinions that create rich classroom experiences. Diversity enriches all of our learning.

My Colorado middle school students are most alike in reading below grade level. But they are a portrait of diversity as well as a collection of challenges. My reading students and classes speak a variety of first languages. A high proportion live at poverty level. Alcohol and drug use, as well as gang involvement, crops up. But diversity comes in many forms and means many different things in a classroom. I have learned to never make any assumption about a student's life outside school and discovered that even though we live in the same place, we often do not live in the same world. To effectively teach these students, I have to let them teach me who they are and what they need.

On one home visit to work with parents and students, I learned that a student could not complete an assignment to cut out geometric shapes because there were no scissors in his home. Crayons, scissors, paper, and glue were taken for granted by my children and their friends, who all colored and cut and made things with paper and paste. But many of my students consider those activities "school things," just as they do reading and writing. Convincing them that "school things" have importance for life outside school is a challenge. This is especially true in middle school, because at this age students share a uniform short-term view of the world—if it does not matter to them today, it does not matter. Period.

Poverty can result not only in a lack of books and crayons at home, but also in a lack of conversation. Some lower-income children start school behind their wealthier peers because they simply have had less meaningful contact with the world of words. One student's mother took in neighborhood toddlers for day care. The babies crawled around and were never talked to—simply handed food or a toy if they fussed. My student said there was no point in talking to babies because they can't talk yet. Did he read to his little sister? "No," he said. "She isn't in school yet so she doesn't need books."

My students who are English language learners [ELLs] also come from diverse backgrounds. Many have lived in the United States all their lives, but seldom heard English until they went to kindergarten; their families spoke Spanish, watched television in Spanish, and live in neighborhoods where English is almost never spoken. Some, even if their parents read or write in Spanish, came to reading only in school and brought home picture books in English. For a number of ELLs, this was the first of many disconnects between home and school. For some, English becomes another "school thing" that is unimportant in their life outside school.

An additional set of challenges is faced by ELLs who are newcomers to the United States, to English, and even to school itself. Some are literate in their first language, which is a great advantage. Others have to learn the mechanics of written language at the same time they are learning that language itself. I need to be cognizant of everyone's stage of language learning. This includes their listening, speaking, reading, and writing ability. I have to present learning in an understandable manner for all students to enable them to each have equal access to learning and to achieving the standards of all students.

Providing my diverse students, including the native English speakers, with the skills to read at grade level before they reach high school is a challenge. Many walk into middle school with the absolute belief that they cannot be successful at school. The only way to meet the challenge of reaching and teaching this diverse group is to recognize that regardless of their background, the stress in their lives, or their feelings about school, they all want to feel skilled and successful. Very, very much.

—Nancy K. Hahn
    Everitt Middle School
    Wheat Ridge, Colorado

7

Making a Place for Technology in Our Schools

JASON GIPSON-NAHMAN

The Next Step Public Charter School, Washington, D.C.

FIFTY YEARS AGO, very few people could have fore-seen how much the landscape of American public education would change. Some of the most drastic changes can be seen in the tools that teachers use to do their jobs. For instance, to my knowledge, the school in which I recently taught has no chalkboards, all grades are kept and submitted electronically, and most classrooms are equipped with ceiling-mounted LCD projectors. Some schools even provide teachers with interactive SMART Boards that are electronically synced with the teacher's computer. The NEA data indicate that most teachers in American public schools have access to computers in their classrooms (although one-to-one school computing programs are still rather uncommon). The district I taught in issues laptops to all teachers, and at the high school level this privilege extends to the students as well.[1]

These tools have evolved to reflect society's universal embrace of technology. To some, technology itself is an equalizer, providing anyone with an Internet connection access to a wealth of educational resources. And to many, integrating these new tools into classrooms serves to prepare students to be active participants and leaders in a world driven by technology. Since the days of Horace Mann, one of the main goals of public schools has been to raise and educate young people to be productive members of society. Today, many jobs require at least basic computer skills, and this trend will only increase. If we are to prepare our students for the working world, their education must include basic computer literacy.

These skills are already being taught in schools with the resources to provide the instruction and equipment. In many districts, however, students from low-income families attend poorly resourced schools. These inequalities between schools and school districts contribute to a technology gap. Many students, predominately those from less-advantaged backgrounds and minorities, do not have the same exposure to technology as their peers in wealthier school systems. But even resource-poor schools are finding ways to catch up. Many school districts—and, in some cases, private organizations—are working to reverse this trend, providing equipment and technology grants to teachers and schools in low-income areas.

However, funding and equipment resources are just the starting point. To take full advantage of technology at the instructional and professional levels, teachers must be given the resources and training to (1) understand students' computer literacy needs and foster their practical skills; (2) apply well-thought-out technology to enhance the classroom experience; and (3) learn and adopt technology to save time and enhance lesson planning, grade preparation, and communication.

Fostering Student Computer Literacy

A common misconception is that all young people are computer literate and that they are experts at anything computer related. From my work with students, I know this is far from the truth. Although many American youth are very comfortable adopting technology and using it for social purposes like texting and social networking, they may have only limited experience with common tools like spreadsheet programs, word processing, and presentation software. For example, when I first began teaching physics in my previous school, I mistakenly assumed that my students would quickly pick up the necessary skills to analyze lab data in Microsoft Excel. I ended up spending almost an entire ninety-minute period just getting students comfortable enough to enter data and format the rows and columns of the spreadsheet.

A significant percentage of students still have limited computer access outside of school, so exposure to and training in basic computing are crucial if they are to be on even footing with their peers upon graduation from high school. This lack of experience is even more of an issue with recent immigrants from poor communities in developing countries. With such students, the classroom teacher's use and incorporation of technology is even more important for their development.

If society expects that students will acquire such skills, schools have to provide meaningful opportunities for learning and applying them. One implication is that teachers who have access to technology and regularly incorporate it into their teaching practices can more easily create opportunities for students to learn and demonstrate their understanding of the same kinds of tools used by professionals in the working world. For example, high school students who must use a spreadsheet program to analyze data from a lab experiment and then summarize those findings in a report will be better prepared for a career in business, which might require them to analyze and summarize financial data. For many students, school is their first opportunity to learn such skills.

I am not implying that content teachers should be responsible for teaching their students computer skills. While technology-savvy teachers can help their students become computer literate, it is not a realistic expectation that a content teacher will teach students fundamental computer skills like word processing. Content teachers should focus on teaching the material outlined by their state standards. If students enter the classroom with a set of basic computer skills, then the teacher has more flexibility and more options when creating practical opportunities for the students to apply their skills.

One way to meet this need is to create a basic computing class that all students are required to take. Such a course would provide a foundational skill set that students could enhance and develop through application in their content courses. However, adding any extra course requires time and money, so if a school has a limited budget, it might consider letting upper-level or advanced students teach such a course.

This would achieve the goal of creating a computer-literate student body without increasing the teacher workload while at the same time allowing some students an opportunity to develop their leadership skills.

My previous school took a similar approach by creating a Student Technology Assistance Team (STAT). Advanced students made themselves available to assist other students—and even teachers—with various computing issues. One specific limitation of this solution, however, was that it did not provide all students in the school with a minimum set of skills as a mandatory class would. But while this approach is not as thorough as the creation of a separate course, it was beneficial to many students and reduced some of the workload of the regular school technology support staff, giving them more time to resolve other issues. Involving students in the solution is just one of the many innovative ways in which schools are helping students become tech literate.

Using Technology to Enhance Teaching Efficacy

Ways of presenting and communicating information, creating assignments, and managing a classroom are all determined by the tools a teacher uses. Although many of the newer tools available are designed to help teachers both maximize their time and enhance their current practices, learning to use some of these tools requires time. Also, for some veterans, adopting new technologies may require a change in teaching style altogether. Such a huge investment of time and resources must be justified by concrete outcomes. This is happening in some places but not in others. Technology alone will not lead to higher student achievement. Only with proper planning, implementation, and training can teachers use technology to help education become the great equalizer.

Technology as a Teaching and Learning Tool

We teachers may not be responsible for giving students basic computing skills, but the potential for technology to dramatically impact student learning does lie primarily with us. Presenting content and helping students access and navigate that content to develop understanding, ideas, and skills is our job. There are a number of tools available that are designed to help teachers do this more effectively. For example, some students are more completely engaged when a teacher presents information using a PowerPoint presentation with videos and animation, as opposed to relying solely on a chalkboard or whiteboard. This is definitely true of the students I teach. Moreover, I am able to post slides on a secure Web site with links to supplemental materials that students can access during or outside of class. And while I do still work through physics problems on a whiteboard, I often find it useful to work out solutions on an interactive notepad that allows me to save a digital record of my work.

There are also tools to allow students to collaborate, communicate, share, and critique ideas. Students may create a blog to respond to course readings or to document their progress on a class project. Or they may work collaboratively, using a wiki to complete a group activity. There are many ways that teachers can use technology to create engaging learning opportunities.

Time Management and Other Activities

Technology is equally useful outside of the classroom. For example, calculating and submitting grades for 150 students takes much less time with a grading software program than doing so by hand. And communication with other teachers, administrators, and some parents can sometimes be more convenient for all parties when done via e-mail. Less time spent calculating grades and calling parents means that there is more time for teachers to spend developing lessons and reflecting on their practice.

The Need for Professional Development

Implementing technology in schools can involve a steep learning curve. Teachers need to know what's available and the most effective ways to apply the best tools and programs in varying contexts. A significant number of teachers are encountering these technologies for the first time, while new technologies emerge every day. If teachers are to use technology effectively, professional development that addresses these new issues must be available.

Computer Literacy Training

In some schools, the expectation is that teachers will use technology as a tool in their everyday teaching practices. In others, teachers are actually evaluated on how well they integrate technology into their classes. While for many this is a nonissue, as they feel extremely comfortable using technology, half of the respondents in the NEA survey indicated that they needed help learning how to integrate technology into their instructional practices (table 2.2). And the need for professional development focused on technology is ongoing: among teachers who had completed training on the use of technology in the classroom, half indicated a need for additional training (figure 2.15). The average American schoolteacher is in her early forties, so most did not grow up with computers at home, and many may not have used computers until adulthood. This does not necessarily imply that older teachers have more difficulty learning to manage technology in the classroom; but the lack of early exposure can contribute to an initial level of discomfort with these new tools.[2]

As a result of this challenge, many teachers are requesting—and districts are offering—more technology-focused professional development opportunities. Some schools have gone so far as to appoint staff (called technology integration specialists in the district where I recently taught) who help teachers better utilize technology to enhance their teaching practices. These people provide both group and individual training sessions on the various technology resources available to staff. As they all have teaching experience, these specialists focus on the *use* of the tool as a means of achieving a specific educational outcome instead of just on the tool itself.

But in difficult economic times, such positions are a luxury, and many districts simply cannot justify including them in their budgets. An alternative solution is to have a number of teachers become designated technology specialists who can dedicate a small portion of their time to helping other teachers who need assistance. Providing a stipend to teachers who assume this role would be much more cost-effective than hiring additional full-time staff. Regardless of the method by which training is offered, some level of support is clearly needed, especially if a school district is going to evaluate its teachers on how well they use technology.

There are many wonderful uses for technology in education, but a school should have a clear reason for encouraging or requiring teachers to use a particular tool. Ideally, teachers should be required to adopt a new technology only to address the particular needs of their classrooms. Unfortunately, some schools can get caught up in the race to acquire the latest and greatest gadgets. Sometimes they do this because they see a certain technology or program used at another school, or they may just be trying to enhance their own image. This is less of an issue in difficult economic times, however, since many districts have to pinch pennies and justify every expense, but it still occurs.

Planning for Technology

In addition to offering computer literacy training, schools should have a clear plan for the implementation, management, and support of any new technology they adopt. Not having a plan could lead to discontented teachers, distracted students, and wasted resources. For example, without proper monitoring, computers can easily become classroom toys instead of classroom tools. Students can use computers to play games, visit social networking sites, or even shop online during class instead of being involved and engaged in the lesson. I have dealt with these issues in my own classroom. Before my former school gave teachers the tools to manage students' use of technology, we teachers were spending inordinate amounts of time trying to keep our classes on task. Students and teachers were wasting both time and resources. Some students' grades dropped, and teachers, parents, and administrators all became frustrated. Many schools are still learning how to maximize their use of technological resources for the benefit of students, and in the process they are helping students make tremendous academic progress.

Conclusion

Technology holds great promise for our students. For many it means greater learning opportunities and a richer academic experience. For all it is a key to the future. Without a basic understanding of technology, today's students will be extremely limited tomorrow. And without the ability to use technology as a productive tool, they will never move beyond being consumers of products and ideas to being creators. The key to making technology work in schools lies in properly training and supporting teachers, equipping them with the skills to effectively manage these new tools, and understanding and nurturing students' computer literacy. Without this support, and without a vision for technology in schools, we will just waste the time, resources, and talent of both students and teachers.

A Voice from the Classroom

As a junior high school teacher during the 1970s, when desktop computers first became available to local public schools, my assignments included an Apple Computer class and a Commodore 64 Computer class, with small labs for each. The program included graphics and sound, with a reward (fireworks graphic with appropriate sounds, for example) for correct responses and correction and reteaching for incorrect responses. Humor and creativity had a definite place in this program, and students often gave each other tips based on their own discoveries. The sharing was wonderful. One program by a student from Saudi Arabia taught us all about his Muslim religion. These experiences were a great basis for future learning in every subject, since the students used logical thinking and creativity.

When my teaching assignment changed to a local high school, I was assigned to teach in a computer reading lab. Initially the students learned basic computer skills, then some word-processing skills with an emphasis on creative writing. Later the district dedicated the lab to an expensive, highly structured reading program. Within a short time central office administrators purchased even more expensive software that used short reading selections followed by exercises to test comprehension. A great deal of money was spent on computers and on this software—which was lauded as a technological breakthrough at the time—as well as on in-service training that equipped teachers in the district to teach the program. Such programs are probably still in use in many school systems because of the illusion that this modern technology is better than older methods of teaching reading and writing. Some software developers make a great deal of money when districts adopt their programs for their computer application labs.

But these high-tech programs fail to challenge the majority of students who use them. Out of boredom, some students use their creative skills to outwit the software, devising ways to access the final answers without even reading the selections. Other students mark random answers just to appear busy throughout the period, without concern for grades.

The problem lies not in the technology itself but in the utilization of these ever-evolving avenues for learning. Moreover, many adults have a fear of technology. Adults feel more in control when the software used has specific answers for every question, complete with an answer key, whereas a desire to discover and to learn new skills is built into a child's nature. If avenues for discovery and exploration are blocked, youngsters may work at outwitting the technology itself.

The optimum learning environment would include individualized classroom teaching and full utilization of libraries as well as the use of high-technology programs. In other words, the technology should be one more resource from which the educator draws in order to meet the needs of each student. Whatever methods are chosen should encourage student exploration and creativity. Let us hope our educational systems will achieve this balance soon.

—*Nancy Lyles Durham*
Terry High School
Richmond, Texas

8

Developing Professional Expertise

Rethinking the MA Degree for Teachers

PAM GROSSMAN AND
MICHELLE BROWN

School of Education, Stanford University

ALMOST TWENTY-FIVE YEARS AGO, reports such as the Holmes Group's *Tomorrow's Teachers* and the Carnegie Corporation's *A Nation Prepared: Teachers for the 21st Century* issued a call for greater professionalization in teaching.[1] This same period saw the formation of the National Board for Professional Teaching Standards (NBPTS). Attaining professional status for an occupation requires a range of factors, including restricted entry, a recognized professional knowledge base, and the license to exercise professional discretion and judgment during the course of work. The argument for professionalization contends that teachers' work is both consequential and complex. As such, it requires an investment in professional preparation that combines clinical and theoretical foundations with ongoing support and development. The Holmes Group suggested that professionalization be partially reflected in a more differentiated profession, one in which those committed to teaching would be given additional training and greater responsibility in the school organization.

The need for such training is more urgent as teachers increasingly are held accountable for student learning. While some argue against assessing teachers on the basis of their students' achievement, accountability for client outcomes is a hallmark of professions. A professionally oriented graduate program, designed to help teachers improve both their own practice and their students' learning, could help teachers address accountability demands and make the investment in graduate education worthwhile. Yet the Holmes report also warned against the pitfalls of credentialism, whereby people are unfairly excluded from the profession and where those credentials are not backed up by improved classroom results. In this caution, the report identified the twin motivations behind the push to professionalize: improved status and conditions for members of the profession and better outcomes for students.

Current Trends

The NEA survey data presented in this volume offer some indication that the movement to professionalize teaching has had an effect. They show a significant growth in the proportion of teachers holding master's degrees—from 24 percent in 1955 to 52 percent in 2007—which is evidence of a movement toward professionalization (figure 2.11). Further examination reveals that women account for almost all of this rise. Over the fifty-two-year period, the proportion of men holding master's degrees increased from 42 percent to 51 percent, while the proportion of women with master's degrees nearly tripled from 18 percent to 52 percent (figure 2.12). This trend may reflect women's expanding career and earning ambitions, but it also indicates more stringent requirements for professional or continuing state certification as well as an increase in postgraduate alternative route certification.

We find significant growth in the rates of degree attainment for both new teachers (those with four or fewer years of experience) and more experienced teachers, but the proportion of new teachers with master's degrees has increased particularly quickly: from 18 percent to 28 percent between 1980 and 2007 versus 51 percent to 56 percent among more experienced teachers (figure 2.13).

Although the number of teachers holding master's degrees has clearly increased, it is less clear what this means for teachers' status or for student learning. Master's degrees are commonly rewarded with a pay bump for teachers; in light of the rising numbers of teachers with a master's degree, the associated salary increase represents a substantial investment for districts. The added financial burden has attracted an examination of the performance of teachers with advanced degrees, particularly in terms of associated growth in student achievement.[2] In one study, data aggregated at the school level suggest there is little difference between student progress in schools with a higher proportion of teachers with MAs and those with lower proportions.[3] This finding aligns with earlier studies by Dan Goldhaber and Dominic Brewer that conclude that, on average, master's degrees are not associated with gains in student achievement.[4] While Goldhaber and Brewer find that a discipline-specific master's degree in math is associated with significant positive growth in student achievement, Marguerite Roza and Raegen Miller discount the importance of this positive finding by countering that "90 percent of teachers' master's degrees are in education programs—a notoriously unfocused and process-dominated course of study."[5] Goldhaber and Brewer also note that many studies of the outcomes related to master's degrees do not make distinctions between different types of degrees or between degrees from institutions of varying quality. Such critiques seem to justify the warning the Holmes Group issued more than two decades ago: "credentialing can ultimately erode the public's trust in the quality of a profession."[6]

But before we declare the investment in graduate degrees a failure in the effort to professionalize teaching, we should pause to consider what more rigorous graduate programs aimed explicitly at honing professional knowledge and skills might look like. Such a reconsideration could also address the increasing pressure to hold teachers accountable for student learning, where accountability might be seen as a double-edged sword. While teachers rightly protest that they do not control the conditions under which they work, and cannot by themselves ameliorate the effects of poverty on educational attainment, accountability for the outcomes of practice is a defining feature of professions. If a professionally oriented graduate program can be designed to help teachers improve both their own practice and the learning of their students, it would help teachers address accountability demands and make the investment in graduate education worthwhile.

At what point in their careers would teachers invest in further education? The NEA data show that many teachers have earned master's degrees within the first few years of teaching. Since these teachers are still relatively new to the field, graduate study is not serving as an opportunity to refine an already solid skill set but is instead being undertaken while teachers are still "getting their sea legs." In fact, many programs have developed entry-level master's programs in which students receive both an MA and certification. However, there is little evidence that new teachers with graduate degrees are any more successful than teachers who enter without them; at the point of entry, the MA probably adds little to professional practice.

This is not to say that teacher preparation should be completed solely during the undergraduate years; developing multiple pathways into the teaching profession may help attract a wider range of talented candidates. However, the MA can be developed so that it signals a specialized expertise and skill in an aspect of the practice of teaching.

The authors of *A Nation Prepared* argued for a differentiated entry into the profession, one with greater responsibilities tied to further education.[7] In their vision, novice teachers with relatively minimal preparation would enter and teach for two years. During this time they would not be asked to take on the full load of curriculum development or other professional duties and would work under the close supervision of an experienced teacher. At the end of this probationary period, these entrants could either leave or choose to undertake further professional education to become "career teachers." Some might then opt to become "career professional teachers," a level that would require still more study. In many districts such a model already exists in the guise of alternative-route programs; teachers are increasingly entering the profession through programs that require relatively minimal preservice education. The high attrition rate in teaching in the first five years also suggests that many new teachers are opting out at the beginning of their careers. While new teachers leave for a variety of reasons, some may leave, in part, because they feel unsuccessful in the classroom.

Given the negative impact of teacher turnover, how might the profession create master's programs that are explicitly designed to improve teaching and learning and retention?

Shaping the Advanced Degree Toward the Development of Clinical Expertise

One possibility for improving the efficacy of graduate study is to design MA programs that are closely tied to developing clinical expertise. Since the start of the push toward professionalization, NBPTS has presented a way to identify common standards for teaching excellence and to distinguish accomplished teachers. This performance-based credential has been found to serve as an effective means of development for those seeking certification, and a number of studies find that National Board Certified teachers' performance is stronger, as reflected in improved student achievement.[8] Some master's programs are already designed around preparation for National Board Certification.[9] Such programs focus intensively on helping teachers document and reflect on their practice and on evidence of student learning. They also are explicitly tied in to a professional community that has laid out expectations for expertise in teaching and a consequential assessment.

One might imagine other programs that prepare teachers for expertise in particular approaches that have proved effective in supporting student achievement, such as complex instruction or Reading Recovery. Such programs must demand more than credit hours or seat time, however; they will have to require teachers to demonstrate the quality of their practice in using such methodologies and to document changes in classroom practice and student learning. Another version of a professional master's program could focus on building teachers' content knowledge. Bread Loaf, the well-known professional development program for English teachers, provides one such example.[10] While graduates receive an MA in English, the coursework and professional community are centered around the demands of teaching. Following this example, schools of education could create MA programs in, say, mathematics pedagogy, in which teachers spend their time investigating student ideas and developing an understanding of how best to respond to non-standard explanations. Elementary teachers might return to specialize in biology for the elementary school curriculum, deepening their understanding of both the content and how best to teach it. Such programs could also require a culminating assessment that demonstrates both growth in content knowledge and the impact of that knowledge in classroom teaching.

Learning from Other Professions

What would it take to create a course of study focused on specialized expertise rather than the accumulation of credits—to make mastery of practice the norm rather than the exception? For guidance we might look to similar efforts at reform in physical therapy, another "helping profession." Teaching and physical therapy share some key characteristics that challenge their claims to professional status, including a predominantly female workforce and weak control over working conditions. The American Physical Therapy Association's (APTA) Vision 2020 agenda stands out as an example of a coordinated and successful effort to shift the status of the profession.[11] Vision 2020's call for the gradual increase in entry requirements for physical therapy has led to the current state of the profession, where most newly minted physical therapists are doctors of physical therapy, a degree that includes a major emphasis on clinical practice and expertise.[12] Remarkably, this shift has taken place in just the last ten years. It is important to note, though, that this was made possible in part by the centralized structure of the physical therapy field. In an interview with a trade publication, a member of the APTA explained that in making the move to a doctoral-level entry, it was necessary to "ensure that the educational programs were there, that the universities accelerated their education to that level."[13] A major advantage in meeting this challenge is the fact that the APTA both creates the long-term vision for the field and appoints the commission responsible for accrediting institutions. The world of teaching, teacher education, and professional development is far more subject to external dictates. While this means that coordinated, systemic reform is unlikely, there is space for experimentation. As programs prove their merit, the ideas and practices at their core will gradually spread.

Conclusion

To support true professional status, master's degrees need to demonstrate the development of professional knowledge and expertise. The incentives for advanced degrees must be more than monetary; as envisioned by the reports mentioned earlier, such programs could be tied to differentiated responsibilities and the development of specialized skills and roles in educational settings. The increased focus on teacher accountability provides the opportunity to create programs that foster teachers' effectiveness, and developments in the technology for measuring teacher effectiveness could allow programs to track the progress of their graduates across multiple dimensions, including growth in knowledge, classroom practice, and outcomes for students. If such programs are successful in producing demonstrably more effective teachers, the demand from both individuals and districts would be great. Only when master's degrees are tied to the development of professional expertise will they advance the professional status of teaching.

──── ∞∞∞ ──── **A Voice from the Classroom** ──── ∞∞∞ ────

We often expect that a child's path to the future is well lit by others who have influenced him or her. In today's schools, too often the teacher is the only light there is. Robert was a troubled student when he arrived as a new fifth grader in my social studies class. He came defiant and angry, and he didn't change much over the year. His goal was to see how worked up he could get me. He had already made up his mind he was not going to be "saved" by me or anyone else. His goal in life was to show the world how bad he had it by driving his future into the ground. I was glad to be rid of him at year's end.

The next year I was mortified to read my new sixth-grade class list for homeroom. Robert's name was right at the top! But at open house, I was all smiles and told him nothing but how excited I was to have him in my class. He shockingly flashed a timid smile. As the school year progressed, I took Robert's late work and minor misbehaviors in stride, drawing little attention to them. This somehow seemed to make their occurrences rarer.

From the home front, we would hear horror stories of his violence toward animals and his siblings. I knew that he kept his anger and brutality under control at school partially because of the relationship we'd built and the welcoming environment he found there.

One beautiful spring Friday, all the kids were talking about their exciting afterschool plans. But Robert had fallen significantly behind in his work, so I told him he had to stay. I saw the anger fall over his face immediately. Surprisingly, though, he went to his seat and got started, and I worked at my desk. But a few minutes later, I glanced up—and he was gone. I raced into the hall, asking where he'd gone. Other students had seen him head out the door. I had two choices. One was to let his negative behavior slide once again and deal with it Monday. This would give us both time to cool down. My other option was to go after him. I took off—I was not going to let this kid ruin everything we'd built with one enormously bad decision!

I ran with all my might. I knew the neighborhood where this kid lived. I knew the route he would take. And I was steaming mad! As I rounded the turn to his block, I saw him just as he saw me. I saw shock—and then fear. From a half-block away, I shouted, "You are coming back with me!" I pointed my finger from him to school dramatically.

I'd like to say Robert followed me back willingly, apologizing all the way. Instead, he barricaded himself in his house. But I couldn't back down now. What message would that send? That he'd beaten me and that he could do it again any time he wanted? As I stood out front, I took everything in—the sagging porch, the shabby curtains sagging in the windows, the trash littering the yard, the four young kids playing out front, unbathed and unsupervised.

Soon a sister came out: their mother was on the phone and wanted to speak with me. I had more to take in as I made my way through the house. It was literally patched together in places. It was filthy—laundry, dishes, and bugs everywhere. I also knew that two adults and five kids lived in this three-room house. Robert was nowhere to be found.

When I got on the line, Robert's mom apologized on his behalf and told me to put him on the phone. That made him crawl out from his hiding spot. When his mother told him to return with me, he started bawling. It was looking bleaker by the minute. There was no way this kid was coming back unless I threw him over my shoulder and hauled him. It would have to wait until Monday.

But as I walked away from the house, I felt an odd sense of accomplishment. I hadn't succeeded in getting him back to school, but a few important things had happened that afternoon. For one, Robert knew I cared enough to run after him. He knew he would be held accountable for his actions. For another, his younger siblings realized that the crazy red-headed sixth-grade teacher was nuts enough to chase students home! I figured that would make my years ahead with them a little easier. More important, I'd gained an appreciation for what this kid had accomplished, considering what he went home to every day. I now saw what was behind the evasive eyes and the sullen looks I got when I attempted to connect with him.

On Monday, though, a smiling Robert came through the door. "Hey, Mrs. Reed," he said without missing a beat. I said hey, patted him on the back, and breathed a sigh of relief. I couldn't believe my luck. After trying so hard to reach this kid and teach him a valuable lifelong lesson, he had taught me instead. He taught me I can run a quarter of a mile in flip-flops! He taught me the importance of patience and building strong relationships with kids. He taught me to never assume I understand a kid and where he comes from until I see it with my own eyes. He taught me you can never care too much for kids.

Robert will be moving on to middle school next year. He's worked hard and had a better attitude since that day. I just hope that the foundation we've established this year will be strong enough to last. Middle school years are vital to kids like Robert—that's often when they decide which path they will take in life, the dark one they've been set on or the bright one that lies right before them. I know I was only one ray of light shining on Robert's path. I just hope it's bright enough to guide him down that path for the rest of his life.

—Erin Reed
Arlington Public Schools
Arlington, Nebraska

9

Paying Teachers Appropriately

ERIC A. HANUSHEK

Hoover Institution, Stanford University

THERE IS A SIMPLE STORY which describes our schools that, on the surface, just does not make sense. It goes like this: teachers are the most important element of schools; we value high-quality schools and want to improve their performance; yet we are unwilling to ensure that teachers' pay keeps up with pay elsewhere in the economy.

The changes in the teacher labor market, particularly as they involve the wage path for teachers, are very obvious to both policy makers and the public. Teachers' wages have not kept pace with those for other occupations (see figure 2.25). The trend in wages almost certainly affects who does and who does not think about teaching as an occupation. And this has been going on for a long time.

Interestingly, the NEA data suggest that over the last fifty years, most teachers entered the profession motivated not by money but by a desire to work with youth (figure 2.20). And just a quarter of those contemplating leaving before retirement cited low salaries.[1] Yet it is difficult to rely on the good intentions of teachers when the temptations of other occupations and jobs loom as large as they currently do.

This commentary builds on the salient parts of this history in order to discuss a range of proposed policy options. An underlying theme is that the current pay structure—based on the single-salary schedule—acts to turn policy makers away from any substantial increases in teacher pay. As a result, any efforts to improve our schools through attracting and retaining effective teachers are handicapped by eliminating use of monetary incentives.

In the current system we tend to underpay effective teachers while overpaying their ineffective peers, again avoiding use of any monetary incentives to improve the teaching force. We are thus left to hope that the goodwill and strong drive of effective teachers is sufficient to keep them in the classroom and that the poor performance of the ineffective teachers will not be too damaging.

The Central Importance of Teachers

Hundreds of research studies have addressed the question of how important teachers are to the educational process. These studies have approached the issue from a variety of vantage points, but the most relevant involve relating teachers to student outcomes. Two findings emerge. First, teachers are very important. In fact, no other aspect of schools—spending, leadership, curriculum, etc.—is nearly as important in determining student achievement. Second, it is not possible to identify specific characteristics of teachers that are reliably related to student outcomes.

It is important to understand both of these findings, because they relate directly to the subject of teacher salaries. The general finding about the importance of teachers comes from the fact that the gains in learning across classrooms, even classrooms within the same school, are very different. Moreover, year after year, some teachers produce larger gains in student achievement than others. The difference can be radical: some teachers have been found to get one and a half years of gain in achievement in an academic year, while others with equivalent students have been found to get only a half year of gain.[2] In other words, two students starting at the same level of achievement can know vastly different amounts at the end of a single academic year. No other attribute of schools comes close to having this much influence on student achievement.

The related issue is what makes for an effective or ineffective teacher. Extensive research has found little that consistently distinguishes among teachers in their classroom effectiveness. Most well-documented has been the finding that master's degrees bear no consistent relationship to student achievement. But other findings are equally interesting and important. The amount of classroom experience—with the exception of the first few years—also seems to have no relationship to performance. On average, a teacher with five years' experience is as effective as a teacher with twenty years' experience. But this general result goes even deeper: there is little evidence that conventional teacher certification, source of teacher training, or salary level are systematically related to the amount of learning that goes on in the classroom.

The exception, as noted, is that during the first one to three years of classroom experience, the typical teacher will get better—developing the craft, learning the tasks, and finding ways to help students learn. The existing evidence does not suggest any clear way to provide this experience before entry into the classroom or to alter significantly the adjustments that should be made once that teacher is in the classroom. For example, changes in teacher preparation or more extensive induction and mentoring programs, while plausible policies, have yet to be shown to significantly alter teachers' early career learning.

This quick and necessarily cursory overview of the importance of teacher quality has some direct implications for the pay of teachers. The most important implication to an economist is that we want to pay salaries that are sufficient to ensure that there are high-quality teachers in all classrooms. Salaries are viewed as a way of providing incentives to attract and retain the teacher force that we need as a country. This conclusion, however, is not as straightforward as it sounds given the current structure of schools and labor markets for teachers.

The Pattern of Salaries

Perhaps the most noticeable aspect of teacher salaries is how dramatically they have fallen over time, in relative terms. Teaching has always been a highly skilled occupation, with teachers among the most educated of the population in most localities. It has also, particularly in the post–World War II period, been a female-dominated occupation. The status of teachers was clearly reflected in salaries at the beginning of World War II. Compared with the earnings of other male college graduates, the average male teacher's salary was slightly above the fiftieth percentile in 1940. That of the average female teacher was close to the seventieth percentile of other college-educated females. But then came the fall. Male teachers' salaries dropped precipitously to the bottom third of the earnings distribution for male college graduates over the next several decades, and those of female teachers were below average during the 1960s and close to the relative male position by 1990.[3]

This trend in salaries is mirrored by other metrics. While it is somewhat difficult to trace general measures of achievement and ability over time, it appears that teachers are drawn from the lower tiers of college graduates, and that the best are not the ones going into teaching.[4]

How could we simultaneously place high value on teachers and their role in society and yet let their pay slip so badly against others in the economy?

Two factors are important in answering this question. First, by most accounts, the skills needed to be an effective teacher are not necessarily those needed to be successful elsewhere in the economy. This statement is difficult to document with any precision, in part because we do not have any clear description of what skills are needed to be an effective teacher. Nonetheless, we do not find that pure measured achievement or ability of teachers, although closely related to earnings elsewhere in the economy, is all that closely related to student outcomes.[5]

Second, the current structure of teacher pay—the single-salary model that pays all teachers with the same experience and degree level the same amount—almost certainly works to hold down teachers' salaries. As described previously, the factors that determine pay are unrelated to effectiveness in the classroom, as are individual teachers' salaries. According to the NEA data (figure. 2.27), very few teachers report an opportunity to earn more for teaching in a shortage subject area, for working in a more challenging school, or for improving student performance.[6] These facts, which defy most public and policymaker sentiments, act as a drag on overall salary increases.

Policy Alternatives

Most people in society believe that salaries are roughly related to the economic value put on different workers. While the salaries of some professional athletes or celebrities may keep us from accepting this as a universal truth, it is nonetheless the case that the overall compensation pattern across the economy seems reasonable to most people. Economists interpret this alignment of salaries and productivity of individuals as a natural outgrowth of a competitive economy. The logic is straightforward. If one firm does not pay a worker a salary that matches her value in terms of output, a competing firm will. If the firm pays the worker too much for her value, it will not be competitive with other firms and will risk going out of business.

Teacher labor markets, however, differ. Salaries are determined by collective bargaining between teacher organizations and their employing school districts. School districts will not go out of business if they pay the wrong amount. But, being public organizations, schools are always subject to political forces, and the goals for quality of schools depend on governmental decision making. As a result, teacher salary decisions are only partially driven by the economic forces that underlie salary determination in private, competitive industries.

The political nature of the teacher salary process also invites a wide-ranging discussion about the appropriate way to determine teacher pay. Some would argue from basic principles of fairness. Others would attempt to relate salaries to other, competitively determined wages. Still others would focus first on the overall quality of schools that is desired and use that discussion to suggest what is needed in terms of teacher salaries.

This discussion follows from the perspective of an economist whose primary interest is the role of quality education in determining outcomes—both individual outcomes and outcomes for the nation. One overarching theme is that individuals gain considerably from high-quality education, in terms of college completion, occupational attainment, lifetime earnings, and overall health, among other things. A second theme is that the nation as a whole benefits in terms of a well-functioning democracy, a civil society, and a wealthy society that enhances the well-being of individuals.

One implication of the economist's perspective is that many policies—including those that enhance teacher pay—can be justified if they improve the quality of schools, because both individuals and society gain. This really describes a simple benefit-cost framework in which gains from improvement can be weighed against the costs of any change. The other side of this model, however, is that policies that do not improve educational quality will confer no benefits and thus, if they cost something, will yield costs that exceed benefits.

With this perspective in mind, it is possible to consider a variety of policy ideas that have received some currency.

Restore the Relative Pay of Teachers

Given the previously documented drop in teacher salaries over the past half century, an obvious starting point of many policy discussions is how to reverse some or all of this decline. This discussion is most typically framed in terms of average teacher salaries, and the policy option in large part involves a percentage increase in pay to close the gap with former earnings levels.

The policy arguments are generally phrased in terms of attracting new people into the teaching profession: if teaching salaries were as competitive today as they once were, similarly talented people would be attracted to the profession. This argument rests heavily on assumptions that may or may not be true: that the new people attracted to teaching would have skills that are better than those recently employed in the profession and that schools will choose and retain the better teachers from the expanded pool of applicants.

But this raises a deeper issue. The policy discussions generally presume that *all* teacher salaries, not just those of new teachers, will be raised. It is unlikely that the existing teachers will teach any differently if paid a higher salary. They might stay in the profession somewhat longer, although the rate at which teachers with five or more years' experience exit teaching is already quite low. Yet if the policy is meant to attract better teachers in the future, reduced exit rates of current teachers make the process of upgrading teaching staff slower and more expensive.

Without some assurances of improved achievement—and, more particularly, improved achievement commensurate with the expenditure—this type of policy has little political appeal and little likelihood of even partial enactment.

Compare Salaries to Those of Other Professionals

A variant of the previous policy discussion argues that the right way to set the salaries of teachers is to use the market salary for professionals in the open economy. At its heart, this is simply one notion of how to determine a salary level, but it is generally unrelated to any arguments about the relative advantages and disadvantages of alternative occupations. To the extent that the overall compensation levels of teachers would be raised by this policy, it is subject to the same discussion as the previous arguments about restoring relative pay.

There is one aspect of this approach that does have specific relevance, however. It is unclear precisely which professional occupations would provide an appropriate comparison. If the standard is privately employed professionals—say, lawyers, doctors, and accountants in private employment—a feature of the comparison is the overall structure of employment. Most private professionals have their salaries set much more in line with their individual productivity, and, consequently, these occupations have much larger discrepancies in earnings and noticeably higher employment risks than are found in teaching. Thus, even if the comparison set of alternative professions were clear, the appropriate way to compare salaries under different employment conditions is not.

Differentiate Salaries by More Characteristics

Going in a different direction, another set of proposals addresses the single-salary structure itself and considers how different teachers are paid. The politics of pay currently prevent large salary increases that

are unrelated to performance. Better alignment between teacher salaries and performance would likely open the door to overall increases in
teacher compensation.

The version of this policy that is very commonly discussed, and
found in a range of existing contracts, proposes to broaden pay from
the traditional experience and degree matrix to include details of a
teacher's preparation, professional development, and other objective
measures of teachers. The strength of this approach is that objective
differences are used to set differentiated salaries. The weakness is that
the characteristics typically discussed have not been reliably validated
against classroom effectiveness. Thus, this approach does not surmount
the basic stumbling block to overall increases in teacher salaries.

Pay for Specialties or Location

The labor market for teachers works against the backdrop of the rest of
the economy. Many teachers can easily find employment outside of
education, and the external demand for individuals with particular
specialties affects the ability of schools to hire those with specialized
knowledge. For example, the impact on hiring math and science teachers has been recognized since the launching of *Sputnik*. Filling certain
specialties—notably math, science, foreign languages, and special education—is perennially difficult when schools pay all teachers the same.
If schools are concerned about having high-quality teachers in shortage
areas, they must recognize the competitive environment that exists. At the
same time, simply paying higher salaries to recruit staff in these shortage areas does not necessarily ensure that effective teachers will be
attracted.

A similar concern relates to staffing specific schools. Schools serving
concentrated disadvantaged populations tend to be located in worse
neighborhoods than those serving more advantaged students, generally
provide more challenging teaching experiences, and have a number of
other characteristics that adversely affect working conditions. Yet
teachers in these schools are paid the same as teachers in schools with
superior environments. As a result, teacher turnover in the most needy
schools is greatest.

Pay for Performance

History teaches us that there are few easily measured factors that correlate with classroom effectiveness. If we are interested in classroom performance, there simply are no real alternatives to making judgments about the ability of individual teachers to raise student achievement. Clearly, this conclusion is not one that has been embraced by teachers' unions, largely because it introduces a subjective element into the retention and pay of teachers.

Herein lies the big trade-off. If parents, taxpayers, and politicians cannot be convinced that increasing salaries will yield improved student outcomes, the political process will consistently yield minimal pay increases. Teacher salaries will likely continue to fall relative to earnings outside of teaching. This is a consequence of insisting that ineffective teachers be paid the same as effective teachers. Reversing this outcome, however, will require teachers to backtrack on the long-held principle that "a teacher is a teacher is a teacher."

There is a compromise position. The evidence today indicates that the typical teacher is quite good. At the same time, there is little disagreement that a small proportion of teachers in the current workforce is unacceptable. It turns out that those at the bottom of the teacher quality distribution—consistently and accurately identified as such by everybody in the schools—cause real damage.[7] Moreover, if they have tenure, they are frequently allowed to stay in the classroom, something that does not happen in high-performing school systems around the world.[8] A compromise position would be to remove ineffective teachers from the classroom and pay the remaining effective teachers substantially higher salaries.

Conclusion

The nation's future very much depends on maintaining and improving the quality of its teaching force. It is hard to imagine that this can be accomplished without using salary and compensation as a central policy tool. But avoiding the use of salary to inform policy is exactly what we have done for several decades.

The consequence of a teacher labor market in which salaries do not respond to performance is a political outcome that is neither in the best interest of most teachers nor the nation. The economic benefits of having a good teacher show that we can afford to pay effective educators substantially more than we do now. The idea of standard six-figure salaries for good teachers is quite feasible today when the value of their impact on students is calculated. But such salaries are not feasible if ineffective teachers must be paid the same. Thus, we find ourselves in a bad equilibrium in which good teachers are underpaid, and, as a result, our public schools end up with less effective teachers than is desirable.

Political forces are currently pushing to introduce more pay for performance, and there is widespread recognition that some differentiation of teacher quality is necessary. The problem is that this approach introduces a subjective element into teacher evaluation and raises a variety of practical questions concerning implementation. We cannot overcome salary problems and problems of teacher effectiveness without developing fair and effective evaluation policies.

Pay for performance has, of course, become a very contentious issue, dividing teachers, unions, policy makers, and the public. It should be recognized that it is not necessary to go to a highly differentiated pay-for-performance system to reap most of the gains. A simple compromise would be a commitment to remove the small number of teachers who fall below a minimum level of effectiveness. If this is done systematically, regardless of tenure, achievement could be dramatically higher, and there would be much less political difficulty in paying teachers an appropriate salary that recognizes their contribution to society.

A Voice from the Classroom

I will never forget the night I walked out on my shift at the restaurant. I had been waiting tables there for three years while working toward a master's in education as a full-time graduate student. I never had a problem balancing my time. Working forty hours a week, I still managed to excel in all my courses and keep my stress to a minimum, even during my time as a student teacher.

When I was first hired as a teacher, I had every intention of keeping my waitressing job. I needed something to supplement my teaching income. From August until mid-October I was both a first-year middle school social studies teacher and a server. My teaching schedule was rigorous. I'd wake up at 5 A.M., then commute fifty miles to school. I'd prep for the students' arrival from 7 to 8, teach from 8 to 3, attend meetings and answer e-mails until 4, make the hour commute home and then plan lessons from 6 to 11. On the weekends, I'd put in seventeen hours at the restaurant, working Friday, Saturday, and Sunday nights until closing. After my Friday shift, I was usually so exhausted that I would end up sleeping in until 3 or 4 P.M. on Saturday, which only gave me a couple of hours until I had to be back at the restaurant. I planned lessons Sunday mornings, then continued into the late hours after my Sunday shift ended.

I was stressed. The economy was struggling and, as a consequence, business in the restaurant was slow. I started coming to the restaurant with papers to grade during the down times. My general manager would reprimand me. "You're on the clock," he would say. "Put that stuff away." Whenever I would argue that business was slow and I wasn't making any tips, he would find menial chores for me to do. I grew increasingly vexed as I found myself sweeping floors and cleaning windows when I was well aware that I had seventy-five tests to grade and a lesson to plan.

Then, one night, everything came to a head. I was one of the supervisors of the Outdoor Club at school and we were going to explore a bike trail on Sunday. I had been trying for a week to get my Sunday-night shift covered, but no one would pick it up. I had asked each of the other servers, called everyone on the phone tree, and begged management to give me the night off. I had no luck. When I walked into my shift on Saturday night, I was already in an unpleasant mood. I asked my manager one last time if I could have the next night off. Though I had been working there for three years and had never missed a single shift, he still said no. Around 7 o'clock, during the dinner rush, I was back in the kitchen and my manager reprimanded me for my negative attitude. That was when I snapped. I put down the tray of food I was carrying, walked out of the kitchen and continued to walk right out the front door. Needless to say, I was able to attend the bike excursion with the Outdoor Club the next day.

I ended up going back into the restaurant a few days later and quit the professional way. I put in my two weeks' notice. In my letter of resignation, I told my manager the simple truth—that I needed to concentrate on my teaching career. I had come to realize that trying to juggle two jobs as a first-year teacher was not fair to me, nor was it fair to my students.

—Annmarie Noonan
   Signal Knob Middle School
   Strasburg, Virginia

10

A Governor's Vision

Reforming Teacher Salaries and Standards

JAMES B. HUNT JR.

*Governor of North Carolina (1977–1985, 1993–2001)
and chair of the James B. Hunt, Jr. Institute for
Educational Leadership and Policy*

IN 1995, as I was preparing to run for my last term as governor of North Carolina, I learned that my state was ranked forty-third in average teacher salaries according to the NEA average salary rankings of all fifty states. It was a wake-up call for me and, I determined, for the state of North Carolina.

I have always had a high regard for teachers, a view that goes back to watching my own mother teach. She was patient and knowledgeable, as all good teachers are, but what made her outstanding was her determination that *every* student who came into her charge would learn. That belief was fierce and focused and felt by all her pupils. Then I married an excellent teacher who had those same qualities, and I watched and learned from her as well.

I pursued that interest in teachers into my public life. In the mid-1980s I worked with the Carnegie Corporation to found the National Board for Professional Teaching Standards (NBPTS). For ten years I chaired the board and learned how complex—and demanding—good teaching is. I came to see that really high standards could be set for the teaching profession and that teachers across America would rise to those standards if given the opportunity.

In 1994 and for some years thereafter, I also chaired the National Commission on Teaching and America's Future (NCTAF). From NCTAF's creator and first executive director, Linda Darling-Hammond, and the members of the commission—including many excellent teachers—I gained many insights and expanded my knowledge of the profession. I came to appreciate the continuum of teaching and where we needed to place more emphasis so we could get and keep the best teachers. And I was convinced that there was a need to provide extra incentives along the salary schedule that would reward more than just experience.

As I shaped my vision for reforming the salary and standards for North Carolina's teachers, I encountered many of the issues addressed in the NEA survey—issues that are of concern to the profession nationwide: the need to provide salaries that enable a reasonable standard of living; the thorny issue of tying salaries to student achievement; and the value of professional development.

Campaigning on an Issue

It was John Wilson, then the executive director of the NEA's state affiliate, the North Carolina Association of Educators (NCAE), who first told me about our teachers' low salary ranking. John and I had a history of agreements and disagreements and a mutual respect for one another, so I listened carefully when he brought me the information. The NEA statistics indicated that teacher salaries across the U.S. public school system are far lower than those for other professions, so that a ranking of 43 was even worse than it sounded (figure 2.25). Moreover, the NEA data revealed that an increasing number of teachers supplemented their teaching salaries with school-related or non-school-related jobs after class hours (figure 2.27). I determined that I would focus my attention on doing something about the economic plight of teachers in North Carolina.

I set forth in my 1996 gubernatorial campaign to make higher standards and higher salaries the focus of my message to the people of North Carolina. I ran on the promise of taking our teacher salaries to the national average by 2001 and of tying those higher salaries to higher standards at every significant step on a teacher's career continuum. I ran on a commitment to teachers and our public schools, and I planned to govern on that commitment.

In that campaign I traveled the state speaking about the importance of our public schools and the need to do something for our teachers. The public, as virtually every poll shows, trusts and supports teachers. That was confirmed by the questions I was asked as I campaigned, the electorate's enthusiasm for raising salaries for teachers, and their belief that teachers would reach high standards set for them.

There were skeptics, of course, and there's much to be learned from them. As I pushed the message of higher teacher standards and salaries, I was hit by parents, business leaders, and others. Some asserted that the NCAE was supporting me and my message only for selfish reasons. Many pointed out that there were bad teachers, that tenure was making it impossible to get rid of them, that test scores were low—problems that beset our schools across this nation. All of us who seek to reform public schools have to be respectful of the concerned people who raise such issues. I didn't always have the answers, but listening to the questions gave me a lot of the information I needed to craft the plan I would use to keep my promise to North Carolina if reelected.

I could point to the beginning of a rise in our state test scores. I could dismiss the accusations against NCAE by offering a broad list of supporters of my message as well as my belief that only collaboration across a diverse group of stakeholders would produce the results we wanted for our schools. As to underperforming teachers and tenure, I reiterated my message of high standards and the effect they would have on the entire profession. And I reminded voters that in North Carolina, tenure—or "career status," as we call it—was based on a system of fair employment and due process, not a rigid law guaranteeing a job for life.

I won that race by a substantial margin, which I took as confirmation that the people of North Carolina really did want to do something about improving teacher salaries and raising professional standards. So after Inauguration Day in January 1997—held at a public high school in our capital city—I began the work of governing and keeping my promises to the people, especially the students and teachers.

Governing on an Issue

During my campaign, I gave considerable thought to what action would be needed to carry out my promises. I wanted a comprehensive bill that would accomplish both increased salaries and improved standards over the course of four years. The bill would be complex in its implementation but simple in its message. I called it the Excellent Schools Act.

This act laid out the career continuum of a teacher: entering a school of education, qualifying for an initial license to teach, gaining a continuing license, achieving career status, and advancing in the profession through obtaining a master's degree and National Board Certification. At each of these key career steps, a teacher would receive a "bump" on the state salary schedule after starting at a much-improved base salary.

To make the salary increases palatable to the legislators, I had to ensure that teachers met measurable standards, which would be demonstrably higher than in the past. I began by looking at our requirements for hiring candidates who had gone through the traditional route of a school of education. I learned that we used the Praxis exams for both entrance into a school of education and obtaining an initial license. I also noted that we had, and needed to keep, our high cut scores. I discovered that even though the latest NEA data showed that teachers rate cooperative and competent colleagues as the most helpful factor in their teaching, we did not pay teachers to mentor (figure 2.22). I reviewed our tenure act. I examined the data on when teachers were most likely to leave teaching, so we could add a salary boost at those years, and scrutinized our expectations for professional development and ways for teachers to advance without leaving the classroom—a complicated task, since, as NEA data show, teachers nationwide already feel that heavy workload, extra responsibilities, and paperwork hinder their best teaching (figure 2.23). With this knowledge, I worked with my staff to craft the Excellent Schools Act, an act I would need to convince others to support.

In 1994 Republicans had gained the majority in the state House of Representatives and had elected a Republican Speaker for the first time since Reconstruction. The state Senate still had a Democratic majority and controlled the leadership. And the fiscal note on the Excellent Schools Act was going to be very high. This was the setting for the work I needed to do.

The question the media most frequently asked was about the price tag. The press always pointed out that it would cost at least a billion dollars and seemed primed for me to back down on the program. My response from the beginning and throughout the effort to pass the act was, "Actually, it will cost one and a quarter billion dollars, but it will be worth every penny of it." I knew I'd need to put together a formidable coalition if I were going to succeed. I started with the Republican Speaker and the Democratic president pro tem of the Senate. I wanted to be able to announce their support in my State of the State address, which would have the Excellent Schools Act as its centerpiece. The key to winning their support was the focus on standards. This was true, too, of the next group I approached to gain support, our state's business leaders. They proved invaluable in the first legislative hearing on the bill, when nearly a dozen business and industry heads came to Raleigh to speak on behalf of the act.

The key to winning support is always personal contact. By meeting individually with these key government and business community leaders, explaining the proposed legislation, and answering their questions, I was able to get them on board. It takes time, but if any leader really wants to have the backing needed to do something of consequence, it's time well spent. The other key to getting and keeping the support of this group of people and the public was to make the clear connection between education and the economy. That was not a new message. I'd been making that case since the late seventies and early eighties, when I first served as governor. I believe that the best—perhaps the only—way for my state and our nation to improve its economy is to improve the education of all our citizens. I also believe that the best way to do that is to ensure that every child has a competent, caring, and qualified teacher.

The Excellent Schools Act was introduced early in the 1997 legislative session. I found that I needed to spend time with most legislators, members of the higher education community, administrators and school boards, the state superintendent of public instruction, the chair and members of the state Board of Education, and, of course, teachers and the leaders of the NCAE. I also found that, as the session continued into the summer, I had to broker compromises. I expected that and didn't mind it—as long as the foundation of higher standards and higher salaries remained the focus and the time frame for reaching the national average by 2001 was intact.

I was committed to personal contact as the most effective means of hearing concerns and addressing them. To that end, I invited key players to come to the Executive Mansion to sit at the round table in the library, where we could look each other in the eye, talk plainly, work out details, and resolve issues troubling anyone. These informal meetings proved to be one of the best uses of my time and theirs.

The turning point for legislative passage was when I recruited CEOs of North Carolina's top fifteen companies to come to the Joint Legislative Appropriations Committee meeting in Raleigh and testify to the value of the bill, including the money involved in paying for it. When those fifteen CEOs walked out of the Legislative Building, the bill's passage was assured.

One of the great successes of the act was a direct result of bringing together a broad coalition. The NCAE and the North Carolina School Boards Association (NCSBA) collaborated to dramatically streamline the process for dismissing incompetent teachers. NCAE and NCSBA attorneys reworked the state's Fair Employment and Dismissal Act to the satisfaction of both organizations, gaining even more legislative support. We also had agreement from NCAE and NCSBA, as well as the North Carolina Association of School Administrators, on performing more teacher evaluations in the first three years and increasing the time needed to gain professional status from three years to four.

One of the compromises all of us in the coalition had to make—and one that could have derailed the bill—was allowing a key Republican member of the House to insert language on testing teachers. Teachers were concerned about stories of the harshness of such efforts in other states, and some legislators were insistent on more stringent testing because teachers' salaries were being raised significantly. By listening to both sides, working on language that was not punitive, and pointing out the advantages of the bill, we were able to keep moving forward.

No one in the broad coalition working with me was completely happy with this compromise, but no one wanted to scuttle the bill by demanding no changes. Our common goal was the eventual passage of the bill. As it turned out, no practicing teacher in our state was tested under the compromise terms of the bill, and we raised the bar by keeping very high standards for entry into the profession and by increasing the number of required teacher evaluations.

One more compromise had to be made regarding master's degrees. I recommended that the holders of master's degrees receive 10 percent more than base pay, but the business community saw little value in such an expenditure. The state's higher education community, to its great credit, agreed to rework its graduate education programs over four years to reflect the higher standards of the National Board for Professional Teaching Standards with the understanding that the new salary schedule for master's degrees would go into effect at the end of that period.

One aspect of the Excellent Schools Act that was never seriously questioned was the plan to pay National Board Certified Teachers (NBCTs) 12 percent more than base salary. In 1994 North Carolina had put into place support for teachers seeking and achieving National Board Certification and had the highest number of NBCTs in the nation in 1997—as we do today. We had strong anecdotal evidence—testimonies of teachers and administrators—as to the difference the process made and a number of researchers undertaking studies that would later confirm that evidence.[1] Today, of course, there are scores of studies showing the positive effects of National Board Certification on student achievement, teacher retention, teacher leadership, and more.

Lessons Learned

The Excellent Schools Act was signed into law in the summer of 1997, "six months and 60 degrees warmer" than when I'd spoken of it in my January inaugural address.

What difference has the law made? North Carolina climbed the ladder of salary rankings to get to the national average—though it has slipped in recent years. In addition, our test scores on both state and national tests climbed. During the 1990s North Carolina made greater gains on the National Assessment of Educational Progress (NAEP) math tests than any other state. We also had higher-than-average retention of our NBCTs. At the time the act was passed, the state had among the highest cut scores for the Praxis exams, ensuring that the teachers we hired and set on the career path toward becoming NBCTs were knowledgeable in their content areas and ready—with the help of paid mentors created by the act—to work toward continuing licenses after year three and career status after year four. Finally, as our state continued to grow and win awards for best business environment and best place to live, the public maintained strong support for its public schools.

While the major components of the Excellent Schools Act were still intact in 2010, parts have been deleted. For example, the portfolio requirement for teachers to obtain continuing licenses was ultimately abandoned. But this was done because administrators didn't want to "trouble with it" not because of teacher opposition. Some additions to the language of the law have been made to keep up with changes in the economy and the needs of the schools. However, the essence of the act remains and can be seen in the salary schedule still in place: additional pay for teachers with master's degrees and for those with National Board Certification; mentors provided for new teachers; and a stream-lined Fair Employment and Dismissal Act.

Why did I spend so much time on accomplishing the goals of the Excellent Schools Act? I'm convinced that the bedrock of our economy is a quality workforce, and that can be achieved only through high-quality schools. What makes a high-quality school? My answer has always been good teachers. I think others joined with me in this effort because they believed the same thing.

The lessons I can pass on from those two years of campaigning for and passing the Excellent Schools Act are that bettering our schools depends on focus, collaboration, and leadership. If we want to improve education in our states and across our country, governors, chief state school officers, legislative leaders, and business leaders will have to aim toward this common goal, funding initiatives audacious enough to make a real difference, even if it costs "a billion dollars." They will have to collaborate despite differences and learn to compromise to reach the common goal. And someone has to lead. For public education, I think the primary someone must be the governor of the state. Our governors have the biggest bully pulpit in their states and can implement bold, even unprecedented, moves to improve schools—if they focus and are willing to take risks, collaborate, and really lead.

Teacher salaries in America are still, comparatively speaking, woefully behind those in other countries where teachers are considered key to the nation's success. But we can fix that. This is America. We must again create the best schools in the world—now. And the key to that is having the best teachers.

A Voice from the Classroom

Tomica and Tyfini were best friends in my classroom my first year of teaching. They were the kind of young women I love: scrappy, defiant, strong, intelligent—rebelling against lives full of poverty, drug addiction, and single parents on welfare. They were the kind of students most teachers in the building had battled and dismissed as too much trouble. I gave them my Tupac/Shakespeare challenge: out-rap Ms. Beck on Tupac and you don't have to memorize the Shakespeare sonnet. I have yet to have a student not memorize a sonnet. I introduced them to Maya Angelou's "Phenomenal Woman" and asked them to stand on their chairs, fists high in the air to "Still I Rise." That year, I offered extra credit to any student who attended Nikki Giovanni's poetry reading at the local bookstore. The next day, Tomica and Tyfini approached my desk for their extra credit. "You weren't there," I replied. "Oh, yes we were and we knew you wouldn't believe us, so . . ." and they dropped the brochure for the reading signed, "To Ms. Beck from Nikki Giovanni." I still keep that brochure.

Ten years later, Tyfini is a wife and mother of three working on her master's degree in education. Tomica has two master's degrees and works for the university as a therapist for students.

Other students from that first year of teaching have also been successful. Gideon was the cross-dressing student who wore makeup and safety pins through his ear when I was just a student teacher. He contacted me last month: he is pursuing his law degree and is married with two children (unfortunately, he has lost the safety pins and the skirt). China got pregnant in high school—a beautiful, brilliant young woman with an incredible future. She chose to keep her baby and is now studying nursing. Narquiesha entered my ninth-grade English class with a new baby. I watched her graduate on time with honors, walking down the commencement ceremony carpet with her four-year-old holding her hand. She received academic scholarships to every school to which she applied. Carsteige's mother was murdered by drug dealers the year he was in my class. He tracked me down years later to share with me the joy of the birth of his first son and his successful career.

To say that teachers are underpaid is to state the obvious. Our society pays athletes and entertainers more for one event than most teachers will ever see in their lifetimes. However, the "real" paychecks I receive come more often the longer I teach. They come in the form of past students contacting me or seeing me out in the community and approaching me. They come in the form of these students succeeding in life and then remembering a few lessons I taught them. I am never so delighted as when one of my students greets me and I see them as the mature adults I knew they would become. Their success in life is my "real" paycheck.

—B. Elizabeth Beck
  Crawford Middle School (Retired)
  Lexington, Kentucky

II

The Changing Face of the Teaching Force

RICHARD M. INGERSOLL
AND LISA MERRILL

*Graduate School of Education,
University of Pennsylvania*

IN WHAT WAYS HAS the elementary and secondary teaching force changed over the fifty-year period examined in this volume? More specifically, have the types and kinds of individuals going into teaching changed?

The NEA data are based on the longest-running survey of public school teachers ever conducted and, as such, are uniquely positioned to address these questions. In support of our analyses, we employed data from both the NEA surveys and the U.S. Department of Education's *Schools and Staffing Survey* (SASS).[1] The latter began more recently, in 1987, and has been administered over six cycles since then, the last in 2007. While SASS lacks the impressive historical perspective of the NEA surveys, its advantage is its larger sample—about fifty thousand teachers per cycle. Together, these two data sources provide some interesting, and surprising, insights relevant to the questions posed above. They show that the teaching force has greatly changed over the past several decades and continues to do so. Yet even the most dramatic changes appear to be little noticed by researchers, policy makers, and the public. Below we summarize five of these trends: the teaching force is larger, grayer, greener, more female, and less stable.

What are the reasons for these tendencies, and what are their consequences? We have been able to test and rule in, or out, a number of possibilities. Nevertheless, our objective here is largely descriptive and suggestive rather than explanatory or evaluative; at this point we ask more questions than we are able to answer. Hopefully, in time, further research can rectify that.

Ballooning

Teaching has long been one of the largest, if not the largest, occupational groups in the nation, and the data presented in this volume show it is growing even larger. Figure 2.1 illustrates the size of the workforce relative to that of other occupations requiring college degrees, and figure 2.2 documents the increase in teachers over the past fifty years. Indeed, data from the U.S Department of Education show that the numbers of both students and teachers have grown since the beginning of the twentieth century.[2] These numbers began to soar in the late 1940s with the post–World War II baby boom.[3] By the early 1970s student enrollments peaked and then declined until the mid-1980s. At the same time, the number of teachers similarly peaked and then leveled off. By the mid-1980s student enrollments again began to grow—the result of the baby "boomlet"—continuing to the present. During this period the teaching force has also been increasing, though not at the pace of the baby boom years. There is, however, one large difference. While the overall number of teachers has grown faster than the number of students throughout the past century—resulting in a continuous decline in the pupil-teacher ratio—since the late 1980s the number of teachers has been outstripping student enrollments at an accelerating pace. In short, the teaching force has ballooned.

Our analyses of the SASS data show that over the past twenty years, K–12 student enrollment in the nation (public, private, and charter combined) went up by 19 percent. In comparison, during the same period the teaching force increased at more than 2.5 times that rate—by 48 percent. Why is this?

One possible explanation is that reductions in teacher workloads (class sizes, hours teaching, or classes taught per day) have necessitated an increase in the number of teachers employed. SASS data show that the sizes of regular primary-level classes did go down about 20 percent during this period and that, accordingly, the number of general elementary school teachers increased.[4] Since, according to these findings, primary teachers comprise about one-third of the entire teaching force, this accounts for some of the observed ballooning, but not as much as one might expect, and less than that due to other factors.

In contrast to primary classrooms, our analysis shows that class sizes for typical subject-area courses at the middle and secondary school levels changed little from the late 1980s to present. Moreover, during this period there was a slight increase in the workload of teachers at all school levels, illustrated by a slight increase in the average weekly instructional hours worked per teacher.[5]

These data indicate that an important source of the ballooning is the growth of special education, perhaps linked to changes in the Individuals with Disabilities Education Act. While the ranks of general elementary education teachers rose by 33 percent from the late 1980s to 2008, the number of special education teachers increased by 102 percent. This figure alone accounts for almost one-fifth of the entire increase in the teaching force during the period. The fact that special education class sizes are about half of those typical in elementary and secondary schools also helps explain why growth in the teaching force is outpacing that of students.

Another source of ballooning is a dramatic increase in the number of teachers of elementary enrichment classes—by 111 percent since the early 1990s. These are instructors who teach one subject (predominantly art, music, and physical education) to most of the students in an elementary school.

Besides a ballooning, there have also been significant shifts within the teaching force at the middle and secondary levels. Overall, the number of typical subject-area teachers has increased by a higher rate—50 percent—than general elementary teachers. But there has been a large redistribution of these teachers across fields as well. Non-core areas, such as art, music, and physical education, have seen far smaller increases than special education and the core academic subjects, especially math and science.

A major factor here appears to be nationwide changes in secondary school graduation requirements for core subjects, especially math and science. The SASS data show that, since the early 1990s, students enrolled in math and science classes increased by 69 and 60 percent, respectively. No doubt these developments have played a role in driving the upsurge in the employment of teachers qualified in those subjects: the math cohort has grown by 74 percent and the science cohort by 86 percent. Although there are two and one-half times as many general elementary teachers as math and science teachers, the latter two groups accounted for almost as much of the overall ballooning as did elementary teachers.

Another possible factor behind the ballooning in the number of teachers may be an increasing proliferation of programs and curricula, especially at the secondary level, as schools are continually asked to take on more of the goals and tasks once the responsibility of parents, families, and communities—a process educational historians have told us has been going on for a century.

Implications

One sobering implication is the financial cost of expanding the teaching force, given that teacher salaries are the largest item in school district budgets. How have school systems been able to cope, and who pays for it? How much of the increase in special education staff has been covered by federal, state, or local funding to schools? As fields such as art and physical education in secondary schools have declined relative to core subjects, what are the implications of cutting noncore academic programs? Finally, the large increases in the employment of math and science teachers have implications for the ongoing policy concerns over the math and science teacher shortage, an issue we have explored in depth elsewhere.[6]

Graying

The teaching force has aged. This is a trend we often hear about, and it is true. Analyses presented in figure 2.9 show the age distribution of teachers in 1987 was shaped like a tall peak. The modal, or most common, age was forty-one. This peak has moved as these teachers have aged; by 2007 the modal age of the teaching force was fifty-five. The number of teachers age fifty or older has also increased, from about 527,000 in 1987 to 1.3 million in 2007.

A corollary is that the number of teacher retirements has also increased—from 35,000 in 1988 to 87,000 in 2004. Our analyses indicate that the average age of retirement for teachers is fifty-nine. This suggests that the number of teachers retiring will reach an all-time high in the 2011–2012 school year and probably begin to decline thereafter.

Implications

Certainly, aging has cost implications, given that veteran teachers earn higher salaries and an increased number of retirees require greater spending on pensions (although the greening trend may soften the impact).

Another implication of aging is its impact on the supply of teachers. Conventional wisdom has been that retirements are a major contributor to teacher shortages. But often overlooked is that retirees have always represented only a small portion of all those leaving teaching— less than one-third in recent years. And of all departures of teachers from schools (both those moving between schools and those leaving teaching altogether), retirement accounts for only about 14 percent of the total. In our research on the teacher shortage, we have found that preretirement turnover is a larger factor in school staffing problems than retirement.

Greening

Graying, however, is not the only age trend. As the proportion of older teachers grows, there has been a simultaneous increase in the proportion of the teaching force that is younger (see figure 2.9). The latter movement is driven by the ballooning trend—the huge increase in new hires.

Most of these newcomers are younger, but a rise in midcareer switching has also introduced significant numbers of older, relatively inexperienced teachers. The result is a third trend: a burgeoning proportion of teachers who are beginners—a *greening* of the teaching force.

This trend is illustrated by the distribution of teachers by years of experience. In 1987 the modal teacher had fifteen years' teaching experience, and the shape of the distribution was a single peak (figure 2.10). By 2007 the data show that the modal teacher was not a gray-haired veteran but a beginner in her first year of teaching. In 1987 there were about 65,000 first-year teachers; by 2007 this number had grown to 200,000, and a quarter of the teaching force had five years or less of experience.

Implications

On the one hand, new teachers can be a source of fresh ideas and energy. Yet, on the other hand, for many schools and school systems fewer veterans will be available to provide mentoring and leadership. Financially, this greening trend may ameliorate the costs of the ballooning teacher force and retirement rates, since the newcomers represent a larger portion of teachers at the low end of the pay scale who are contributing to, not withdrawing from, pension systems.

Becoming More Female

The teaching force is becoming increasingly female (figure 2.5). At first this may seem odd, given that many alternative, traditionally male-dominated professions have opened up to women over the past fifty years. But since the early 1980s there has been a steady increase in the proportion of female teachers—from a low of about two-thirds to more than three-quarters by 2007.

The change in the male-to-female ratio is not owing to a decline in men going into the occupation. Following the ballooning trend, the number of male entrants has also grown, by 26 percent since the late 1980s—also a faster rate than that of the student population. But the number of female teachers has increased at more than twice that rate since the late 1980s.

It is unclear why this is so. One reason appears to be a variant of the increased opportunities hypothesis. The influx of female teachers is not spread evenly within schools but has been concentrated at the secondary level, which was predominantly male until the late 1970s (figure 2.6).[7] There have been only slight increases at the elementary level—already long female dominant. Notably, the SASS data show that there has also been a sharp increase in the proportion of female school principals since the late 1980s.

Another contributing factor might be that the proportion of adult women entering the paid workforce as a whole has dramatically increased. Hence, although women have more varied career opportunities than in the past, more women overall are seeking employment, and a portion of those continue to choose teaching as a career. Moreover, the winter and spring breaks and long summer vacations that have traditionally made teaching a more manageable occupation for mothers of young children may still be a factor attracting women to teaching.

Implications

If this trend line continues, by 2012 over 80 percent of the nation's teachers will be female, and an increasing percentage of elementary schools will have no male teachers. This may have negative implications for the stature of teaching as an occupation, since women's salaries and status have not yet caught up with men's in the workplace. If the feminization of teaching continues, what will it mean for the way this line of work is valued and rewarded?

Becoming Less Stable

The SASS data show a rise in teacher movement between schools and an increasing number leaving the occupation altogether. Average annual total turnover rates (including both movers between schools and those leaving the field entirely) have fluctuated but, overall, have increased by 28 percent since the early 1990s—from 13.2 percent in 1991 to 16.9 percent in 2004. In the larger context we have found that, as one might expect, teaching has far higher annual turnover than some higher-status professions (such as lawyers, engineers, architects, professors, pharmacists), about the same as other occupations (police, corrections officers), and less than some lower-status lines of work (child-care workers, secretaries, paralegals).[8]

But these figures mask large differences in turnover among different types of teachers and schools, revealing the need for disaggregation. For example, increases in turnover over this period have been even higher for beginners; rates of turnover for first-year public school teachers rose by 31 percent from 1988 to 2004. Another example is minority teachers. Over the past two decades, from the late 1980s to 2009, the data indicate that minority teachers tended to have higher rates of turnover than white teachers. Moreover, this gap appears to have widened in the last decade; in recent years minority teacher turnover has been significantly higher than white teacher turnover.

The data also show that the flows of teachers out of schools are not equally distributed across regions, states, and districts. The largest variations in teacher turnover by location, however, are between different schools, even within the same district. Our analyses show that in 2004, 45 percent of all public school teacher turnover took place in just one-quarter of public schools and that high-poverty, high-minority, and urban public schools have among the highest rates.

Implications

One negative consequence of teacher turnover is its important role in school staffing problems and teacher shortages.[9] Increases in turnover of beginning teachers may further exacerbate these problems. Minority teachers, who are already underrepresented in the teaching force, have begun departing at higher rates as well.

Conclusion

Has the elementary and secondary teaching force changed in recent years? The answer is yes, in a number of ways. It is larger. It is both older and younger. It is more female. It is less stable. And that answer raises its own questions: What are the reasons for, and sources of, each of these trends? Will they have a positive or negative impact?

We do not know if these patterns will persist. But if they do, we see teaching becoming a very, very large occupation dominated by those trained in core academic subjects and special education. If the ballooning trend continues, teachers' salaries may likely decline in real dollars. And, as the large older portion of the teaching force retires, teaching will become an occupation predominantly practiced by beginners and the young.

Beginners, the largest group of the largest occupation, are also the least stable, and the number of beginners leaving the teaching workforce is increasing. Continuation of these attrition rates will hasten the greening of this occupation.

If the gender trend continues, teaching will become an occupation practiced largely by women. Many students will encounter few, if any, male teachers during their time in either elementary or secondary school. Given the importance of teachers as role models and as surrogate parents, certainly some will see this trend as a problem.

Perhaps there is an irony in all of this. When the public school system as we know it today was invented a century ago, the teaching force was transformed—it quite rapidly became a very large mass occupation that was a relatively low-paid, temporary line of work and predominantly populated by women prior to entering their "real" career of child rearing.[10] Perhaps these changes in the teaching force over the past twenty years reveal not an entirely new face but a return to an old face.

At the same time, we must warn against taking a deterministic view of history. The similarities of this new transformation of the teaching force to the previous transformation should not be considered conclusive evidence that the workforce is incapable of change. The data also suggest unprecedented opportunity: the largest occupation in the nation is being expanded, replaced, and remade. Who will they be?

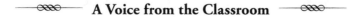

A Voice from the Classroom

I began teaching in 1997—a nervous, yet excited, twenty-six-year-old college graduate assigned to a fourth-grade classroom in a lower-income district in Texas. I was told almost immediately that we did not assign homework to students because they would not return it. I understood that most of them had chaotic lives and that school was sometimes the most stable part of their day. It was difficult to try and teach them things that didn't seem to be so important when matched against their daily worries. Yet at the same time I was told that these students needed to be pushed and challenged; that they would meet my expectations if I made them clear.

After a time, I began working in St. Louis in an inner-city school. I started out teaching second grade and eventually taught special education. I ran into many of the same frustrations as before. Our students were staying with different people every night. They would come to school in the same clothes they wore yesterday, with their backpack left at the house they stayed in two nights before. They hadn't bathed in days; many did not have running water. They were not sure who, if anyone, would be waiting for them when they came home from school. Returning homework seemed to be meaningless, and the state test was a joke—my students would never pass. They were so far behind the state standard that all the modifications and accommodations I could give would not be enough to help. This fact was the reality . . . could my expectations really change that? I became so discouraged with the family lives of my students and the pressures of state testing that I quit teaching until 2000.

I have been teaching special education for almost three years now, and it has been the same thing every year. Students working in second- and third-grade levels are expected to pass a state standardized test that is way beyond their reach. I still have the same struggle: can my expectations really push them to improve that much? I want to believe they can, but sometimes reality is just too harsh.

I have moved often and have taught in seven different schools across three states in my short career. Although the setting and characters were different, the plot and story were not. There has always been dysfunction in the lives of my students that seems to bring into question the appropriateness of what I'm teaching. There has always been a state test that seemed unrealistic for my students to pass. I have always been conflicted about what I should expect and what I should accept. There has always been a relationship built that made these struggles worthwhile and made me go back the next day, and the next, and the next.

I will not stop searching for the answer to what will actually make a difference in their lives, for the balance that will allow my students to be successful if only in their own minds. Isn't that what matters after all— what they believe within themselves? If they ever come to a point where they have expectations of success for themselves, then I will feel my questions have been answered.

—Paige Foreman
   Alderson Middle School
   Lubbock, Texas

12

Two Generations of Teachers Meet in the Schools

SUSAN MOORE JOHNSON

Graduate School of Education, Harvard University

THE PROFILE OF THE U.S. teaching force today is bimodal. At one end of the distribution is an enormous cohort of teachers approaching retirement and at the other a substantial number of new teachers who recently entered the classroom, with relatively few midcareer educators separating these two groups (see figure 2.9). This profile is reflected nationally, locally, and within individual schools.

What accounts for this pattern? The generation of teachers retiring or nearing retirement today is the first to have made teaching a lifelong career. Before the 1960s, teaching was largely a short-term profession: for men, a step to higher-paying, higher-status work; for women, a job until they married and were required to leave the classroom. But by the late 1960s, restrictions on married women teachers had been eliminated, allowing them to stay on the job long-term. Many chose to do so. Despite higher rates of retention through the 1980s and 1990s, demand for new teachers surged due to a number of changes affecting public education, including efforts to reduce class size, the growth of special education, and other factors.[1] These changes, in combination with the need to replace retiring veterans beginning around 2000, have resulted in the current profile of the teaching force. Today, districts, schools, and teachers' unions face both the opportunities and challenges of working simultaneously with these two distinct generations of teachers.

Similar in Purpose and Demographic Makeup

In several key respects, the two generations have much in common. The NEA data show that new teachers today have chosen the profession for the same reasons that their veteran colleagues did forty years ago: to work with young people, serve the public good, and share their knowledge and love of their subject (figure 2.20). Similarly, the data show that teachers of both generations continue to be motivated by the same purposes that originally led them to the classroom (figure 2.21).

The two cohorts also are similar in that they are both predominantly female. Women in the generation now retiring chose the career largely because teaching and nursing were the only professions open to them in the late 1960s and early 1970s. Today, although women have access to virtually all occupations, the cohort of new teachers remains largely female.[2] Teaching is no longer women's default career, but it still attracts far more women than men, especially at the elementary level, where 89 percent of the teachers are women (figure 2.6).

Both generations are also predominantly white. We must remember that before public schools were desegregated in 1954, large numbers of African American teachers headed classrooms in all-African American schools, especially in the South. Following the *Brown* decision, many of those schools were closed or integrated, and many of those educators lost their jobs.[3] Since then, the percentage of African Americans in the teaching force nationwide has remained relatively stable, ranging from 7 to 9 percent between 1970 and 2007 (figure 2.7). Although the percentage of all other minority teachers has increased slightly over the same period (from 4 to 10 percent), the teaching workforce is still overwhelmingly white. The scarcity of minority teachers is cause for continuing concern, given the increasing racial diversity of public school enrollments as well as evidence that students of color benefit from being taught by teachers who share their racial and ethnic background.[4]

Growing Proportions of Midcareer Entrants

Despite the significant demographic similarities of these two generations, there is at least one notable difference: the age at which new and retiring cohorts entered teaching. Whereas the large majority of veterans entered teaching as a first career directly after college, a growing proportion of new teachers—nearly four out of ten—come to the classroom after working in some other profession. These career switchers cite meaningful work and a family friendly calendar and schedule as reasons for entering the profession. Recent U.S. Department of Education Schools and Staffing Survey data reveal that between 1987 and 2003 their numbers nearly doubled—from 20 to 39 percent.[5] Given that the average age of midcareer entrants is approximately thirty-five, while first-career entrants are on average about twenty-six, age is no longer a good indicator of experience. Today it would not be unusual for a forty-year-old novice to have a thirty-three-year-old colleague with a decade of teaching experience.

Midcareer entrants often have experience as parents, Sunday school teachers, or community sports coaches, making them more confident and comfortable as they exercise the authority of their new role with students. Because they are older, many also are expected to bridge the age and experience gap between the new and veteran teachers. Many midcareer entrants also bring with them professional background in the subject they teach. Pharmaceutical researchers run high school chemistry labs, engineers explain geometry, and journalists teach the skills of expository writing. In addition to enriching curriculum and pedagogy, career switchers may help students see how studying in school prepares them for a career in the real world.

This diversity of experience among new teachers also presents challenges for the traditional school structure. Most first-career entrants have been students for the past two decades. Thus, they bring to their new assignments few alternative conceptions of how schools might be organized. The cellular model of schooling—one teacher, one class, one classroom—continues to dominate their sense of what is possible. Career switchers bring a different perspective. Their former workplaces generally paid more, determined compensation differently, offered higher status, and provided more comfortable working conditions than the schools they join. These new teachers may also have had varied roles, responsibilities, and experiences—for example, leading a team of peers to complete a project, being promoted or compensated on the basis of performance, or conducting training or assessment of their colleagues. They report being surprised by the uniform organization of schools and the undifferentiated role of the classroom teacher. Notably, they have changed jobs at least once and could do so again if their school fails to support them in doing the meaningful work they seek.

Single v. Serial Careers

The two cohorts also have different expectations about the course of their employment. In the 1960s professionals tended to choose a career (and often an employer) for a lifetime. Today, entrants in many fields choose their jobs within a social context that supports—even encourages—frequent changes. Unlike their veteran colleagues, many new teachers today view teaching as a short-term occupation.[6] Few first-career novices say that they will remain in the classroom for a lifetime. Often these teachers are impatient with the seniority-based norms and rules that slow the pace of career development.

Still, the NEA surveys show that the proportion of early-career teachers (one to nine years of experience) who report that they plan to teach until retirement was higher in 2005 than in 2000, suggesting that today's teachers are increasingly committed to teaching long-term.[7] However, the survey can only capture the views of current teachers, not those who have left. Data from the Teacher Follow-Up Survey administered by the U.S. Department of Education show that 8.1 percent of teachers with one to three years of experience left teaching in 2004 and 9.1 percent left in 2008. For teachers with four to nine years' experience, rates were also high (7.9 percent in 2004 and 2008), as were those for teachers in urban and rural schools.[8] Further, among those early career teachers (one to nine years' experience) who remained in the field, a substantial proportion move from school to school each year. Therefore, not only must public schools compete with other fields to attract teachers, they must also strive to retain them in particular districts and schools.

Working as Colleagues

Colleagues have become increasingly important to all teachers, but early-career teachers are especially concerned with this aspect of the job. Although veteran teachers acknowledge the importance of colleagues in their own work, qualitative research suggests that the two generations' expectations for colleagues differ.[9] Veteran teachers favor independence and autonomy, while the younger group leans toward interdependence and teamwork. This is not surprising, given that new teachers are more likely to have participated in teams either during their own schooling or in previous work experience. However, few schools are organized to truly support teams, and the isolated nature of teaching remains a barrier to the kind of collaboration new teachers say they want.

Most school districts now provide induction programs, usually featuring one-to-one mentoring. However, given the size of the entering cohort, there often are not enough experienced teachers ready or willing to assume the responsibilities and relationships that good mentoring requires. Also, with tight budgets, few districts allocate sufficient time or stipends to effectively support the program. As a result, mentoring practices are often superficial and fall well short of new teachers' expectations. But even "high-quality" mentoring programs that follow current practice—one-to-one mentoring—have been ineffective in improving student achievement and teacher retention rates. In a recent randomized trial, expectations among policy makers and administrators that schools providing comprehensive mentoring would experience greater student achievement and less attrition among teachers than schools offering traditional programs were not borne out.[10]

Although one-to-one mentoring does not appear to provide the kind of support that new teachers seek, they do report valuing the opportunity to work closely with experienced teachers in what my colleagues and I call an "integrated professional culture."[11] In such a situation, all teachers work together as a matter of course, team-teaching in classrooms and clusters or participating on grade-level teams and school-wide committees. Induction is incorporated into the work of the school rather than set apart as an isolated program. Integrated professional cultures rarely emerge spontaneously. Instead, they require careful planning and concerted effort by principals and teachers.

Moving from a professional culture that is dominated by veteran teachers' priorities and practices to one that engages everyone in providing effective instruction for all students is not easy. It may disrupt the routines and expectations of the veteran teachers, since it involves reassigning courses and classes so that new and experienced teachers work together. Integrating these two groups can be especially hard where the typical national demographic—a large cohort of retiring teachers and a large cohort of entering teachers—prevails.

Evolving Differentiation of Roles

The teacher's role has been remarkably uniform over time; it is often noted that teachers have the same responsibilities on the first and last days of their career. In this regard, new teachers stand in sharp contrast to nurses, who can look forward to specialized assignments and supervisory responsibilities that provide higher pay, status, and influence. Interestingly, the NEA surveys include no questions about roles for teachers as instructional coaches or leaders, suggesting that these opportunities either do not exist or are not important to teachers. And for the most part, veteran teachers have neither sought nor had access to such roles. However, surveys and interviews with new teachers suggest that members of this cohort do consider such opportunities important and that their plans to remain in teaching may depend on having access to them.

Beyond retaining new teachers, there is good reason for schools to develop differentiated roles for teachers. When teachers work full time in separate classrooms and concentrate solely on their own students, there is little opportunity for them to see others teach, get helpful feedback about their own teaching, or work together to improve the school. Periodic grade-level or department meetings, even if they are meant to promote collaborative work, are still remote from instruction. Having effective teachers leave the classroom full time or part time to serve as coaches encourages the exchange of ideas and practices and increases the fund of expertise. In any school, there will always be some less experienced or less effective teachers. If a school is to become more effective in serving all students, the skills of expert teachers must be available schoolwide. Even if new teachers remain in the classroom for fewer than five years, schools with structured roles for expert teachers as instructional coaches can ensure that such entrants will find early, strong support, enabling them to succeed from the start with their students.

When schools plan to have a tiered career structure featuring differentiated roles, it can be challenging to select individuals to fill these positions. One source is the National Board for Professional Teaching Standards (NBPTS), which has certified more than eighty-two thousand teachers as "accomplished." With rare exceptions, however, this pool of potential teacher leaders has been untapped, and their expertise is largely confined to their classrooms. Initially, many thought that veteran teachers would be the most likely candidates for NBPTS certification, which requires applicants to have at least three years of experience and demonstrate expert teaching skills. However, according to the NEA data, 62 percent of those holding NBPTS certification in 2000 and 59 percent of those certified in 2005 had fewer than nine years' experience.[12] This suggests that those in the cohort entering teaching are highly motivated to distinguish themselves and to advance in the profession.

Studies of teacher leaders repeatedly find that such leadership roles for teachers are difficult to implement.[13] Introducing differentiated roles, some of which involve teachers evaluating their peers, often meets with resistance in schools with a strong veteran cohort for whom norms of egalitarianism, autonomy, and seniority still hold sway. However, districts that have implemented peer assistance and review (PAR) programs have found considerable success because the position of consulting teachers is clearly defined, competitively selected, and well supported. As a result, the roles appear to be more accepted, stable, and influential.[14] Yet few districts approach the roles of teacher leaders systematically. Until they do, many in the new generation of teachers will not find sufficient promise and reward in the career of teaching, and schools will never achieve the instructional capacity they might have otherwise.

Compensation

Related to new teachers' interest in differentiated roles is their support for a new compensation system. Teachers have long reported that pay is important not because they hope to get rich but because a good salary allows them to live a middle-class life while doing the work they love.[15] Across all levels of experience, low pay is the reason most often cited in the NEA survey for why teachers would leave the classroom before retirement.[16] The single-salary scale, adopted by states beginning in the 1920s in order to eliminate racial and gender discrimination, bases pay almost exclusively on years of teaching experience and academic coursework. When teachers began to bargain collectively in the 1960s and 1970s, they widely endorsed this standardized salary scale as a fair compensation system, and veterans continue to defend it. However, many new teachers are interested in some form of performance-based pay, which would allow them to be rewarded for their individual contributions and accomplishments.[17] Their veteran colleagues oppose such proposals, as regularly reported by the media.

Two Generations View Teachers' Unions

The generational divide apparent in teachers' views of roles and pay also shows up in their views of unions. In 1980 approximately 71 percent of all public school teachers were NEA members, but by 2005 this number had dropped to only 62 percent (figure 2.3). Within that decline there are notable differences between cohorts. In 2005 59 percent of teachers with one to nine years' experience were union members, compared with 70 percent of teachers with more than twenty years' experience.

An interview study of local union presidents revealed the challenges they face in trying to serve these two large cohorts.[19] As one respondent observed, "We're running a couple of parallel organizations." As with the school environment, the two distinct generations of teachers have conflicting beliefs, needs, and priorities when it comes to their relationship with unions.

Overall, veteran teachers expect their unions to support traditional approaches to pay and autonomy in the classroom. In contrast, new members want the unions to provide ongoing training, pursue innovations in pay, create opportunities for differentiated roles, and refuse to defend underperforming teachers from dismissal. Local presidents find that they must rely on the older cohort, the generation that organized the union and has negotiated contracts over the years, to carry out union work, since few new teachers are active members. In fact, many have no memories of schools before unionization and often think that unions are unnecessary or unwarranted. Yet the future of the union depends on cultivating new leadership among early-career teachers. Therefore, union presidents intensely recruit new members and supplement the traditional bargaining agenda with reform initiatives.

Conclusion

The presence of two distinct generations of teachers in public education today provides both challenges and opportunities. When these cohorts hold divergent views and remain separate, they tend to work at cross-purposes and undermine the effectiveness of their schools and unions. However, by working together, both can benefit. Experienced teachers bring instructional expertise and collegiality that new teachers seek, while novices can offer skills in technology, data analysis, or standards-based instruction, which can enrich the teaching of veterans.

The conventional egg crate structure of schools and the flat teaching career may have been functional forty years ago, but they no longer are. If public schools are to survive and succeed in effectively preparing students to lead productive lives, they must change. The innovations that many new teachers seek—differentiated roles and pay, more teamwork, expanded influence beyond the classroom, and higher standards for teaching performance—are increasingly important not only to support and retain that cohort but also to ensure that their schools meet the demands of today and tomorrow. As public education changes, however, the legacy of effective veteran teachers should not be lost, for their deep instructional knowledge and rich experience are invaluable resources for new teachers. Only if the two generations of teachers work in concert, rather than at odds, can the contributions of each be realized and their students be well served.

A Voice from the Classroom

My first year as a schoolteacher was 2008–2009. For most of my professional career I had dealt with individuals society didn't care for, working as a federal corrections officer, a probation and parole officer, and in corrections for the military. So my first reaction in a school was to keep the students at arm's length. I would hear other teachers refer to the students as "kids" and think, "They are in high school getting ready to graduate and face the real world. You can't think of them as 'kids.'"

So if students had a problem, I referred them to the counselor's office or more experienced teachers. I was blind to the fact that these students were beginning to trust me and wanted to come to me for guidance. I now know that I alienated a lot of the students because of that.

It was not until March that I finally realized why I wanted to become a teacher and how much we (meaning teachers) meant to these students. I got the news that one of my students had died in a motorcycle accident on his way home from school. This student was on an "out program"; mine was his last class before he went home to get ready for his job. I was the last teacher to talk to him, and I remembered telling him to be careful and have a good weekend. I started to feel my heart drop and the tears well up in my eyes and my hands start to shake. What was worse, I could not figure out why I was feeling this way. The jobs I had been in before always had the air of violence just by their nature, and I had seen the violence first-hand, but it had never bothered me before.

On the Monday we returned, in my fourth-period class—the class that student was in—I broke down. The students gathered around me. These were the same students I had scolded for talking in class, whose cell phones I had taken away, whom I had punished for being tardy. Why did they care? Instead, they let me know that I meant something to them, that despite the teacher-student roles we had to play, we were a family: they were no longer my students . . . they were my kids. I realized why teachers referred to the students as kids, because when they succeed we are just as proud of them as if they were our own kids, and when they hurt we protect them like they were our own kids, and when we need help they are there for us just like our own kids.

   —Pedro Jimenez III
     Horizon High School
     El Paso, Texas

13

What Are Teachers in It For?

Money, Motivation, and the Higher Calling

BRAD JUPP

*Senior Program Adviser,
U.S. Department of Education*

"WELL, I'M CERTAINLY not in it for the money."
This is one of the most common answers offered by teachers (especially at the beginning of their careers) when they are asked why they were drawn to the profession. If I have heard one teacher say this, I have heard a thousand. In my more than twenty-five years as a teacher, union activist, and policy leader in public schools, I have never once thought they were telling me anything less than the truth.

This attitude comes through clearly in the NEA's *Status of the American Public School Teacher* surveys. In 1970, when the NEA first posed the question, only 6 percent of the teachers surveyed cited money as the reason they chose this career; by 2005 the figure had dropped to 3 percent (see figure 2.20).[1] And they say the same thing when asked why they remain in teaching: in 1980 9 percent of the respondents said they were motivated by money; in 2005 the number had dropped to 7 percent (figure 2.21).[2]

These strong views are echoed when the question is asked from another perspective: What hinders teachers in doing their best work? In all the years but one since 1975, fewer than 10 percent of respondents pointed to "lack of funds/decent salary" as their top reason; only 7 percent singled it out in 2005 (figure 2.23).[3]

This attitude is not unique to the NEA findings. I have seen it in countless local union surveys, focus group reports, and political polling exercises. Values this strongly held, this consistent over time, and this widely reported form a professional bedrock—a cornerstone in the foundation of teacher self-perception.

The Higher Calling and Other Incentives

These responses demand the follow-up question, "What are teachers in it for, then?" But the answer can be hard to tease out. When teachers are asked why they choose teaching as a career, why they stay on the job, and why they leave, the reasons are complicated, and the subtleties are too often obscured by the overheated debate about the role of financial incentives in teaching. We must think beyond such polarizing rhetoric and come to a more thoughtful, less melodramatic understanding of the profession and the compensation systems that support it.

In 2005 only 3 percent of the teachers responding to the NEA survey cited money as a key reason they entered the profession. The top three reasons cited—the desire to work with young people (71 percent); the value or significance of education in society (43 percent); and an interest in the subject matter (38 percent)—have not changed since the question was first asked in 1970. And the same three responses are among the leading reasons why teachers *remained* in the job (at 64, 43, and 35 percent, respectively, in 2005).[4] It is important to note that teachers were permitted to select more than one response to these questions. Their answers thus include a range of motivations rather than a single most important one, reflecting the breadth of their views.

These data tell us a lot about the character of the profession, revealing a workforce motivated by powerful causes and strongly held ideals. Teachers choose and stick with the profession for lofty reasons: because they want to influence lives, because education matters to their community, and because they love what they teach.

Incentives to Stay or Leave

Beginning in 1995, the NEA added "too much invested at this point" to the list of possible considerations for remaining a teacher. In 2005 26 percent of the sample selected this reason. The phrase leaves a great deal to interpretation. Given the idealism discussed above, the teachers who picked it may be giving voice to a personal investment in the job. Perhaps they made an emotional commitment, choosing to remain because they have put their hearts into it. But the teachers who select this answer could also be doing so because they have made an economic investment in the job. They have worked for fifteen or twenty years, and the value of their pension package is beginning to loom large, holding them in a job they might otherwise want to leave. So the reason they are staying in the job could, in part, be the money. Neither of these interpretations is definitive, but neither should be discounted.

While money does not rate high among reasons that people choose to become or to continue on as teachers, the NEA data point to money as a critical factor in decisions to quit the field. Beginning in 2000, teachers who were planning to leave their jobs before retirement were asked to name the single most important reason for this choice. Low salary was cited by 37 and 25 percent of the respondents in 2000 and 2005, respectively.[5] In both years, this option was by far the most frequently chosen. (The large percentage difference may owe in part to changes in the questionnaire rather than teacher attitude: the 2000 questionnaire gave ten choices of reasons, whereas the 2005 questionnaire provided fifteen.) Most other choices—like working conditions, lack of prestige, and lack of opportunity for advancement—rank in the low teens or single digits.

This question is posed differently from those that asked about reasons for becoming or remaining a teacher—and it gets a very different result. By forcing respondents to select only one answer, complexity is replaced with certainty. Instead of multiple competing values, the answer reflects a single, dominant value: the overriding reason why teachers leave before retiring is the money.

The NEA has been asking these questions for at least ten—in some cases, up to thirty-five—years. Changes in responses from survey to survey, even across the entire period the questions were asked, rarely extend beyond a couple of percentage points and never exceed fifteen percentage points. Thus teachers' views regarding compensation as a reason for entering and leaving the profession, while complex, are remarkably consistent over time.

Incentives and Teachers' Educational Attainment

From its inception, the NEA survey has asked teachers to report their highest level of educational attainment. Unlike the teacher attitudes discussed above, which have been largely consistent over time, the data here reveal a dramatic change. The portion of the teaching workforce that had not received a bachelor's degree went from 22 percent in 1955 to 0 percent in 1980 and subsequent years. Meanwhile, the portion with a master's degree or higher has grown steadily—from 24 percent to 52 percent in the last fifty-plus years (figure 2.11).[6]

Keep in mind that while this change occurred, the size of the public school teacher workforce grew from 1,141,000 to 3,166,000.[7] That means the number of teachers with a master's degree or higher has increased almost sevenfold, from approximately 274,000 in 1955 to 1,646,000—a total larger than the entire teaching force when the NEA introduced the survey.

Such a significant shift in behavior is noteworthy. The survey data do not provide insights into why it took place. Certainly, the trend toward college and advanced degrees is not limited to teachers. But for teachers in particular, part of the motivation can be attributed to two major policy changes that took place in the period: (1) the elimination of teaching certificates or licenses for candidates without BAs and (2) the introduction of compensation incentives or requirements for teachers to attain advanced hours and/or a master's degree. The latter policy change is central to any analysis of the relationship between money and what motivates teachers. A small number of states require teachers to attain a master's as a condition for tenure; in those that do not, the opportunity for salary advancement has served as an important incentive for teachers pursuing advanced degrees.

One should neither under- nor overestimate the significance of this point. It certainly does not diminish the high calling of the profession any more than monetary incentives take away from the calling to cure the sick that motivates doctors. It actually proves very little other than the fact that teachers, like any other employees, respond to monetary incentives. What it does call into question is the oversimplified assumption that teachers are not in it for the money.

Embracing the Paradox of Money and Motivation

In the end, the story of the teacher workforce told by the NEA data is paradoxical. Teachers' views about money, motivation, and their jobs are clear and consistent over time, but they are simultaneously complex, even contradictory. The data clearly show that teachers feel a higher calling to teach and that salary is not among the most important motivators for joining or remaining in the profession. Yet, once they are in the profession, money becomes a significant, if complicated, factor in the way teachers think about their job and their career options for several reasons. First, low salaries can become a problem, driving even dedicated teachers out the door. Second, some teachers who consider leaving are reluctant to do so when they perceive they have too much invested in it, so money may play a role in both the desire to leave and to stay. Finally, teachers are responsive to financial incentives, and their responses are shaped by where they are in their career.

This complex range of attitudes and responses should come as no surprise. The challenge faced by leaders and policy makers is to embrace the complexity, not simplify it or force resolution for the sake of political arguments. The effort to address this challenge will take some courage, though, and require more than oversimplified, doctrinaire responses.

My first experience with such an effort dates back to the late 1990s, when I was a classroom teacher in Denver and a volunteer negotiator for the local NEA affiliate, the Denver Classroom Teachers Association (DCTA). The bargaining team on which I served decided to investigate teacher attitudes toward incentives more closely. Our president, Andrea Giunta, and the local executive director, Bruce Dickinson, got our local into the Teacher Union Reform Network (TURN) and asked the bargaining team to study the report of the National Commission on Teachers and America's Future (NCTAF), *What Matters Most*.[8] Prompted by the NCTAF findings, the team included some questions about possible changes in the salary system on our annual member survey. At the time this was really risky stuff.

First we asked teachers to rate some propositions, including "Teachers should receive extra pay because they work in jobs that are hard to staff like special education, science, and math" and "Teachers should receive extra pay because they work in schools with tough student populations." More than half liked the idea of incentives for working in hard-to-staff subjects, and more than two-thirds supported the idea of incentives for working in hard-to-serve schools. At the time I found this troubling evidence that teachers were willing to break from the solidarity of the single-salary schedule in favor of their own personal interests. For me, the most surprising aspect of these results was that senior teachers were nearly as likely as younger teachers to support the incentives. The results depended more heavily on whether the teachers perceived themselves as eligible for the incentive than on generational differences.

We also asked teachers, "What portion of pay increase, if any, should be based on student performance?" and offered a range of responses: 0 percent, 1–5 percent, 6–10 percent, 11–25 percent, and 26–50 percent. A little more than three-fifths selected 0 percent. Only about 15 percent chose 1–5 percent, and progressively smaller portions chose the others. The response was at first less troubling to me. But Bruce Dickinson, who always had a knack for the kind of democracy that really runs a teachers' union, pointed out that more than 35 percent wanted *some* portion of their pay based on student results. As sound as Dickinson's insight was, these results were even more troubling than the results on the incentives for hard-to-staff subjects and hard-to-serve schools. The attitude seemed to not only embrace individual incentives but also to accept that teachers had some degree of control over student test outcomes. As I saw results come back year after year in DCTA surveys, and as I saw similar results in national surveys, like those conducted by Public Impact, I reached two conclusions.[9] First, there is a core of teachers who believe strongly enough in their own individual efficacy to stake a portion of their pay on it. Second, doctrinaire bargainers like me would need to rethink their positions to be more in tune with this portion of our membership.

In this spirit, it is worth considering results from a different Denver investigation. In 2002 the new superintendent, Jerry Wartgow, and his chief operating officer, Andre Pettigrew, commissioned a poll of teachers that could inform recruiting efforts and policy changes designed to support those efforts. One question cut in a very different direction from DCTA's inquiries about salary systems: "Which of the following would be good parts of a package of incentives to reward teachers for working in a hard-to-serve school?" There was a list of about twelve choices, ranging from supportive parents and paraprofessional time to a $5,000 incentive. Teachers could select as many responses as they wanted, so the answer reflected the breadth of their views rather than a single best choice.

Basing their results on the most popular options selected by more than half of the teachers, the researchers proposed a package of incentives. These included (in order of preference) a strong principal, up-to-date classroom materials, smaller class sizes, relevant professional development, and the $5,000 incentive. The money mattered, but it was far from first on the list. The survey reminds us that teachers think about incentives broadly, not in terms of a single-policy solution. They are interested in the things that enhance their job—good leadership and supports—as well as compensation.

These early Denver-based examples are backed up generally by more sophisticated research, including surveys administered by Public Agenda, Metropolitan Life, and the Bill and Melinda Gates Foundation; the work of economists who consider the relationship between incentives and career choices, such as Mike Podgursky, Eric Hanushek, Steven Rivkin, and Richard Murnane; and the qualitative research being developed by Susan Moore Johnson through her Project on the

Next Generation of Teachers.[10] What is remarkable about the NEA survey findings is how well they predict both the simple lessons from our work in Denver as well as the more carefully developed lessons taught by these researchers.

A New Perspective on Teacher Compensation

So what are teachers in it for? The NEA data tell us: they take up the job in education for the best and most generous reasons. They want to work with kids, serve society, and pursue subjects of study that they love. They also take up the job to make a living doing work that is becoming more and more challenging. It is in this context that leaders and policy makers should embrace the complexity and contradiction of their views. Our teachers, like Ralph Waldo Emerson, find foolish consistency the hobgoblin of little minds. So should those who are engaged in the angry and often very misleading debate on teacher compensation.

At this point, the single-salary schedule, or at least the worst reasoning in its defense, is beginning to appear like one of those foolish consistencies. Those demanding to hold on to it are clinging to a reform that predates World War II. It is not the tool we would use if we were to redesign the profession from scratch. It is not the only fair way to pay people. Depending on the individual interests of teachers, there may even be unfairness baked into it. Prejudice and favoritism will not take over should the single-salary schedule be replaced. Teachers will not, en masse, suddenly become mean-spirited people who refuse to work well with their colleagues or begin cheating on statewide assessments. In short, our worst fears will not be realized.

The story told by the NEA data is not one of a workforce demanding to be paid the way they were fifty years ago. And it is not the story of a workforce that would extort a bonus for a little more effort or commitment. It is the story of a profession that deserves a pay system that realizes, on the one hand, that money matters and, on the other, that teaching is first and foremost a high calling.

In the next ten years there will be an explosion of effort to reinvent both the way teachers are paid and the teaching career in general.

Leaders who take part in that effort will do well to learn from the story told by the data presented in this volume. If they do, they will develop systems that connect the fundamental truth that money is important for teachers—albeit, in complicated ways—to the sense of altruism and generosity that animates their effort on the job. Well-designed pay systems will align both monetary and nonmonetary incentives with the best hopes teachers bring to the job: success in their work with students and effective service in their community and their profession. Because success and effectiveness must be measured, in part, by how much students learn, these future pay systems will have to embrace that too. After all, that's what teachers are in it for. Anything less will not be worthy of the people who do this important work.

A Voice from the Classroom

When I was in high school, I fell in love with learning—actually, the learning process. I knew I wanted to teach. For me, it is the love of geography, history, and government; how we go about learning about those disciplines; and the depth to which young people are willing to go to learn about their world that keep me returning to the classroom every August.

What goes on in my classroom that draws me back there again and again? Take, for example, a given week from mid-spring semester. My AP Human Geography students are working in cooperative groups to analyze the geopolitical situations in Chechnya, Afghanistan, the Israeli-Palestinian conflict, Iraq, and the Balkans. Each case presents multiple challenges. Can the students individually come to understand their own research questions and then help their group synthesize the information so their classmates can understand it? The group researching Chechnya includes one of our senior girl basketball players. It is the week between their winning the regional title and the state competition. They realize they must get their presentation done before leaving. They do. These remarkable students craft a presentation demonstrating their ability to acquire, organize, and analyze information. They speak to the religious split in the Caucasus, the line between the Muslim and Russian Orthodox worlds. They speak to the centripetal power hold Moscow has on Chechnya, explaining how Chechnya is pulled to the powerful core of Russia. They speak to the territory of Chechnya as part of the mountainous Caucasus region and to its important oil resources. They do it! They do the map! They do the geography! PBS NewsHour, here come your new analysts!

From the challenges laid before me as an individual teacher, I understand the ongoing, unfolding history of our profession. The reality is that teaching is like being in the medical profession. You are on call nearly twenty-four hours a day. After the school day come the meetings on individual students, the extracurricular activities, and myriad committee meetings—scheduling, hiring, antibullying, awards, faculty council, and professional development, to name a few. Those are the formal demands on one's time. The informal part of teaching also makes demands and is just as important. Before I walk out the door, I often have students, parents, colleagues, and interns stopping by who want to chat. After walking out the door, I know that I will likely have parent-teacher conferences at the grocery store and that I need to be back in a couple of hours for the ball game or National Honor Society induction. Of course, that's not to mention the need to assess student work and have my lessons updated for class at the beginning bell tomorrow.

Why? Why do I stay with this profession and urge others to enter it? My mind is on my AP students who have come to understand Chechnya, those in my global issues classes who are discussing nuclear weapons in Iran, and my Alaska Studies students who are discussing a Native Lands bill. My mind is on the students who constructed their own learning this week. They are why. They are left with the imperative to create a world that solves the problems created by generations before them. I love learning. I love teaching. And I hope that my students become steadfast in their desire to act on their own learning.

—*Jody Smothers-Marcello*
Sitka High School
Sitka, Alaska

14

Learning to Expect More

JAY MATHEWS

Education Columnist, Washington Post

M ANY YEARS AGO, when I was just beginning to
learn how American high schools worked, I had a
conversation with a history teacher in Pasadena, California. His
school's population was comprised mostly of low-income African
American and Hispanic students. I had known some of them—all
energetic and bright kids—when they played Little League with my
sons. I asked the teacher why this high school, unlike those in neigh-
boring districts, had no Advanced Placement (AP) U.S. History course.
His answer has stuck with me—mostly because I have heard it so many
times since at so many other schools: "Our kids are just not up to it,"
he said with a shrug.

According to the long-term National Assessment of Educational
Progress, we have seen little improvement in reading and math achievement for seventeen-year-olds in the last thirty years.[1] Is it because we
don't get more learning from our teenagers that we don't expect it, or
because we don't expect it that we don't get it? I'm not sure it matters. We
are stuck. A significant portion of Americans have given up on a significant portion of American students. According to a 2001 Phi Delta
Kappa/Gallup poll, 46 percent of respondents thought only some students had "the ability to reach a high level of learning." A 2010 MetLife
survey discovered that many teachers felt that only half of their students would attend any kind of college, even though the fact is that 65
percent of graduating high school seniors enroll in higher education.[2]

Many of us, including a lot of the educators I have interviewed, believe in particular that children from poor families whose parents didn't go to college cannot be expected to go as far as the children of middle-class, college-educated parents. And if we push these children beyond their limits, I've been told, it will do them more harm than good.

If these assumptions were valid, this attitude could be seen as humane. No one wants to hurt a child—particularly teachers, who commit to this profession because they want to help young people, as the NEA numbers attest (figure 2.20). To argue, as many educators I admire do, that the overdose of kindness given to low-income children is often a form of racism and classism, reducing their chances of secure futures, is to risk being called an interfering elitist. What is wrong, well-meaning teachers ask, with the honest menial labor that many of these academically challenged students will do for a living? Not everybody has to go to college.

That fact is indisputable, of course, but do we have the right to decide who will not make it to college? Shouldn't we first see if more challenging and imaginative teaching will give them a different perspective on their potential? Wouldn't it make sense to give more teachers the sophisticated training to handle classrooms in such effective ways that they can change students' lives?

This settling of some children's futures before they graduated from high school was one of the outrages that eventually led the Supreme Court to enforce a more optimistic view of our youth in *Brown v. Board of Education*. Is it possible that the still-troublesome position of the American school teacher—long hours with barely adequate pay, debates over professional status—revealed by the NEA surveys is related to the persistence of such defeatist attitudes in the profession? It is time to employ the research showing how schools can be effective and how teaching can be raised to a new level, to rid ourselves of the pessimism that has influenced American education for a long time.

Challenging Students to Achieve

We say we celebrate teaching, but teaching often seems to take second place to sorting. For instance, many high schools have traditionally not allowed students to take AP courses unless they have a strong B aver-age or a teacher's recommendation. It assumes that all the students who don't meet the qualifying standards are incapable of the extra effort these courses require. And it shows just as little confidence in a teacher's ability to take students who currently might get a 1, the lowest grade on the AP exam, to the point where they get a passing grade of 3—or turn a level-3 student into a level-5 achiever.

A growing number of schools have discarded the requirements and declared that the only qualification for taking an AP course (except for Calculus and foreign languages, where preparation is vital) is a desire to work hard—a move that critics have called reckless and insensitive to the needs of underserved students. But many of those schools have had great success with seemingly ill-prepared teenagers. In 1987 Gar-field High School in East Los Angeles—where math teacher Jaime Escalante made his reputation—produced 26 percent of all Mexican American students in the United States who passed the AP Calculus exams. That outcome showed the power of giving those students more time and greater encouragement to learn. More importantly, it showed how educationally bankrupt hundreds of other schools with large His-panic enrollments were in telling their teenagers that they just weren't ready for AP and would not be allowed to take it.

Teaching beats sorting nearly every time. Many of us recall at least one challenging instructor—mine was American history teacher Al Ladendorff at Hillsdale High School in San Mateo, California—who showed us how much more we could do than we, or our friends and family, imagined. Teachers like that demand classroom attention, assign much homework, give many tests, check every student's progress and ignore the fact that many students, and some of their colleagues, consider them ogres.

The Dangers of Lenience in Grading

Differences in the way grades are assigned form one of the most impor-tant but least discussed factors in explaining schools' success rate with traditionally undervalued students. In the debate over testing, many people think we would be better off if we abandoned No Child Left Behind exam requirements and went back to a system in which student assessments were exclusively administered by teachers. Researchers David Figlio and Maurice Lucas contend that is not a rational or useful way to help more kids learn because we cannot count on all teachers being as challenging as they ought to be.[3]

Figlio and Lucas compared the classroom grades of elementary school students in Alachua County, Florida, to their reading and math scores on two standardized tests: the Iowa Test of Basic Skills (ITBS), which measures children against a national standard, and the Florida Comprehensive Assessment Test (FCAT), which measures them against state learning targets. The Florida testing standards were also used as the basis for the grades teachers put on individual report cards.

The authors found that the grades and test scores were usually "highly correlated," meaning that students with good grades got higher scores than students with bad grades. But there was a deviation: large differences in the portion of children receiving top grades from one teacher to the next. By inflating report card grades, a number of teachers were, in effect, telling their students that they were meeting the state standards when the FCAT tests—where a score of 5 is comparable to an A and a 1 to an F—indicated they were not. Across the sample, 61 percent of B students and 17 percent of A students failed to meet minimum state competency standards. Yet among the students taught by the top half of teachers, as ranked by demanding grading standards, 65 percent of A students attained level 4 or above, with just 5 percent earning level 2 or below. In other words, students in classrooms where more stringent standards were enforced showed significantly better test scores than those in classrooms where A's were handed out like candy samples at a multiscreen theater.

Particularly troublesome is the attitude of parents revealed in the study. When asked to grade their children's teachers, they seemed less happy with those educators who were stringent graders. The researchers found that parents were 50 percent more likely to assign a grade of B or below to a tough teacher than to a relatively laid-back one.

Another study showed that easy grading can also hurt high school-level learning. In an analysis of the early years of the Massachusetts

Comprehensive Assessment System (MCAS), researchers interviewed six hundred students who had failed to pass the new exam, a requirement for high school graduation. The vast majority expressed puzzlement that they could be performing so badly when they had passed their English and math classes.[4] The researchers asked the students what grades they got in those courses. (A number of studies indicate that self-reported grades, although not as good as actual transcripts, are acceptable as a reasonably accurate substitute for report cards.) Almost 90 percent of students who failed the MCAS on their first try reported having a C average or better during the school year.

Lenience in grading is one more sign of school cultures that assume some students just aren't ready for the high standards of instruction that might prepare them for college or for admission to a good trade school or postgraduation job. It explains at least in part the lack of significant achievement gains for high schoolers in the last three decades.

Realizing Raised Expectations—Development, Support, and Four Core Factors

High standards and high expectations in schools are crucial, but they will not be the norm without a teamlike approach to teaching that has every professional in the school pushing in the same direction. Professional development—preferably a nationwide approach—that emphasizes these values and offers concrete strategies for engaging less-advantaged learners may be one way to develop such a team attitude. Some studies reveal that regular support of teachers by talented school leaders and significant amounts of well-coordinated professional development during the school year have a positive effect on school performance. But the NEA survey shows that the amount of time set aside for professional development (an average of six days per year) has not met the standards for schools that have shown big progress (table 2.2). The Knowledge Is Power Program (KIPP) charter schools, for instance, have much longer school days, weeks, and years than public schools, which allows for some form of professional development to take place nearly every day.

In 2005 researchers surveyed principals and teachers from 257 California elementary schools—picked for their similarly high poverty rates—to try to determine why some of the schools reported markedly higher state test averages than others with students from similar backgrounds.[5] Encouraging teacher collaboration and professional development and enforcing high expectations for student behavior (somewhat different than expectations for academic success but possibly the kind of discipline that can spill over into more disciplined learning) correlated positively with school test performance but not as much as four other factors: prioritizing student achievement; implementing a coherent, standards-based instructional program; using assessment data to improve student achievement and instruction; and ensuring the availability of instructional services. Development programs and school administrations can contribute to making these factors central aspects of teaching to higher standards across the board.

KIPP, the most successful public charter school network in raising achievement among low-income students, encompasses all four factors in its mostly middle schools—which, like the California elementary schools, have high poverty rates. Students who have attended all four years of the fifth- through eighth-grade KIPP program have shown tremendous average gains in both math (from the fortieth to the eighty-second percentile) and reading (from the thirty-second to the sixtieth percentile).[6]

That same focus on achievement for low-income students is evident in several schools on *Newsweek*'s annual list of top high schools, a ranking based on participation in AP and International Baccalaureate exams.[7] They include the Preuss Charter School in San Diego; the Hawthorne Math and Science Academy in Hawthorne, California; the South Texas High School for Health Professions in Mercedes, Texas; and the YES Prep Southeast and KIPP Houston high schools in Houston. These schools recruit and train teachers who have high expectations for students and make increasing academic achievement the goal of every day's activities. They take testing seriously and provide resources to raise student levels, including longer school days, coordinated faculty teaching and disciplinary policies, and large numbers of field trips and special projects. As the California study of high-poverty schools shows, this works if the professionals in the school have the training and resources to make it work.

It is clear that more of our kids are up to learning at a much higher level than we think they are. When are we, as Americans, and when are our schools going to shelve outdated, pessimistic attitudes and half-hearted commitments to raising achievement and give our students what they need?

───── ⚬⚬⚬ ───── **A Voice from the Classroom** ───── ⚬⚬⚬ ─────

I have been both a teacher and administrator and fully realize the benefits that accrue to each side. More importantly, I deeply understand how a good relationship benefits the children we serve. Over the years, as I moved into the administrators' rank, I enjoyed ribbing our young teachers about how easy they had it, compared with my own teaching experiences. I had thirty-five active children in my class—all day! I was the art teacher, music teacher, reading teacher, special education teacher, and guidance counselor. I was also called upon to supervise the lunchroom and the recreation periods in the schoolyard. This is not just another boast about how "I walked to school as a child for two miles, uphill both ways." The reality is that in 1968, elementary grades were not served by special area teachers, class sizes were larger, there were only two prep periods per week, and the teachers taught all subjects, much like their earlier counterparts in the one-room schoolhouse.

When I began teaching, there was no talk yet of achievement gaps. The school's student body was predominantly African American and Hispanic, but there were no existing benchmarks by which to compare their performance. Our classes were homogeneously grouped. Six sixth-grade classes were arranged from 6A—kids who today we would classify as gifted and talented—to my 6F group—the discipline cases, the nonreaders, the at-risk kids. My students were needy and hyperactive, and many of them did not speak English. On an instructional level they were, at best, third graders. Today, many of them would be classified as learning disabled, ADD, or ADHD.

Because they were the "bottom" class in the sixth grade, no one in the school expected much from them. My principal gave me a tremendous degree of latitude in structuring the instructional plan to best fit the needs of my students. With no requirement to make Adequate Yearly Progress and close the achievement gap, I was allowed to create an "alternative" classroom focused on my students' personal and social needs first and on their educational needs within the context of what was of interest and relevant to them.

I introduced comic books as a first step toward motivating my class to read and made a performance of Fiddler on the Roof our class project—language arts, math, and history were integrated into the activities of reading and memorizing pages of script, designing a set, and conducting discussions on diversity.

At that time I was working toward my doctorate in educational psychology and research, and I knew about the behavior modification practices that were creeping into the classroom as a technique for dealing with special education students. I created a reinforcement economy whereby desired student behavior was rewarded by a token. A chart indicated what could be "bought." Chewing gum in class was worth five tokens. For ten, a homework assignment could be skipped. A sign of the times: three tokens would buy the privilege of taking the erasers outside to smack out the chalk dust. The biggest prize, however—at a cost of fifteen tokens—was the opportunity to go to my home for lunch. I was single then and lived with my parents a few blocks from the school. My mother would make us sandwiches, and we'd shoot hoops. I implemented this system with the consent and support of my assistant principal, who frequently excused me from lunch duty so that I could spend more time with my "challenged" students.

The behavior modification approach was very effective. The children started taking responsibility for their behavior. They would line up quietly to climb the four flights of stairs to our classroom. The self-discipline also had a positive effect on their achievement. From comic books we graduated to books, and soon they were closing in on reading at grade level. The end-of-year performance of Fiddler on the Roof became a triumphant rite of passage.

What I did in the sixties is still being done by teachers everywhere, but perhaps not quite the same way. Liability constraints make it almost impossible for a child to leave the school during the school day—and certainly not to go to the teacher's home. And the need to make Adequate

Yearly Progress pressures many teachers into teaching to the high-stakes tests administered at the end of each school year. I'd have to fight long and hard to use Fiddler on the Roof as the basis for learning. I was lucky to be able to have those opportunities—and successes—because of the trust and support of my administrators.

—*Daniel A. Domenech*
  American Association of School Administrators
  Arlington, Virginia

15

Brown v. The African American Teacher

The Lingering Effects of Inequality

RENEE MOORE

Humanities Division, Mississippi Delta Community College

THERE'S ALWAYS A STORY behind the numbers. The NEA *Status of the American Public School Teacher* surveys began in 1955, just as the impact of *Brown v. Board of Education* started to reverberate across the South. Although the surveys did not begin to collect information on teachers' race until 1970, in that and subsequent years patterns in the data reveal much about what transpired in the period immediately following the *Brown* decision—some of the most tumultuous years in African American history. What do the data teach us about the impact of desegregation on African American educators, particularly in the Deep South? And what lessons and cautions can we glean from these past experiences as we embark yet again on sweeping school reform aimed primarily at helping minority and poor children?

Missing: African American Teachers

According to NEA survey data, the representation of African American teachers nationally has never been more than 9 percent. However, their numbers have not been evenly distributed across the country. Until the 1990s 53 percent of African Americans lived in the South; of rural African Americans, 91 percent lived there, most in the "Black Belt."[1] As might be expected, the majority of African American *teachers* also lived in the South; the NEA data show that, consistently since 1980, around 15 percent of the southeastern teachers surveyed have been African American.[2]

As I considered the respondents' ages, I noticed that in the 1970 and 1975 surveys, the percentage of black teachers in each age group was, with one or two exceptions, the reverse of the pattern for white teachers (figure 15.1). In 1970 the percentage of white teachers is highest at the beginning and end of the career track; for African Americans the peak is in the middle (thirty to thirty-nine years old). Missing among African American teachers are colleagues age forty and older who would have mentored the younger cohort. By 1975 the peak African American group from five years earlier, now forty to forty-nine years old, is still flanked by lower percentages of teachers at the beginning and end of the career cycle (figure 15.2). In sum, while young white teachers flocked to classrooms in the early and mid-1970s, far fewer young black teachers followed suit; and those who did were likely to find an absence of older African American mentors to guide them. The trends revealed in figures 15.1 and 15.2 mark the start of a disturbing downward trend in new African American teachers that continues to this day.

The peak group of African American teachers in the 1970 survey—those between ages thirty and thirty-nine—would have entered teaching in the early 1960s, as the *Brown* decision was beginning to be implemented in the South. Were they replacements, or were they the last wave of what had been a fairly constant flow of African American teachers that was disrupted by the collateral damage of the resistance to forced desegregation?

Backlash After *Brown*

The drop in new African American teachers (the population after the peak in 1970) might be attributed to the breaking of color barriers in

FIGURE 15-1   Age distribution of African American and white teachers, 1970

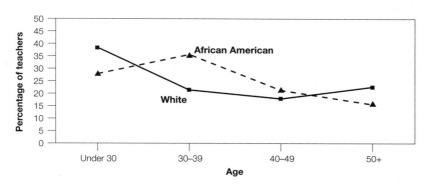

Source: Status of the American Public School Teacher, 1970–1971 (Washington, DC: NEA, 1972).

FIGURE 15-2   Age distribution of African American and white teachers, 1975

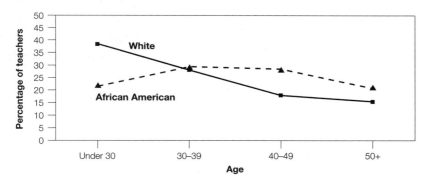

Source: Status of the American Public School Teacher, 1975–1976 (Washington, DC: NEA, 1977).

other professions. However, it might also have been a reaction to what a rising generation of young African Americans saw happening to their schools and the teachers from their communities, as well as what they themselves experienced at the hands of teachers. What happened following *Brown* and desegregation could have soured them on education as a career and sowed disillusionment with school systems, if not with the promise of education itself.

But how do we account for the low numbers before the peak? Teaching was one of the very few professions open to African Americans in the South before the 1960s, and the overwhelming majority of black students were taught in segregated schools by black teachers. Where are those older teachers?

For many years, few people outside the South appreciated its vicious and prolonged resistance to school desegregation. Nearly six years after *Brown v. Board of Education*, only West Virginia and the District of Columbia were completely desegregated and only 6 percent of African American students attended integrated classes.[3] The eight states of the Deep South did not integrate until forced to in the mid-1960s.[4] In some places, such as the Mississippi Delta, it took even longer.

While students may have been slow to see the effects of *Brown*, the aftermath of the decision had a catastrophic impact on the African American teaching force. Thousands of these teachers and administrators, many of them with experience and advanced degrees, were summarily terminated when southern schools were finally desegregated. H. Richard Milner and Tyrone Howard report that "many Black teachers were treated poorly after *Brown* . . . their treatment resulted in a disconnection and imbalances in the Black community, and consequently, Black students seemed to suffer as a result."[5] Veteran African American teachers recall having their complexions examined, being shifted to less-desirable positions, and generally losing professional status after *Brown* was enforced.

All manner of ploys were used to remove or demote these educators, from dismissals and nonrenewal of contracts to establishment of stricter certification requirements for black teachers than for their white counterparts. According to one press report, "In Arkansas . . . virtually no African American educators were hired in desegregated districts from 1958 to 1968. In Texas, 5,000 'substandard' white teachers were employed, while certified African American teachers 'were told to go into other lines of work'"[6] Among the most insidious practices was the reclassification of African American teachers' positions to ones covered by the Title I or Title IV programs of the new federal Elementary and Secondary Education Act (ESEA). Some school districts would deliberately violate the civil rights provisions, triggering the termination of federal funds for those programs, and then tell the teachers that the federal government had eliminated their jobs.[7] Most estimates put the number of African American teachers removed, refused, or demoted during the desegregation process at about thirty-eight thousand.[8] Poor reporting makes it impossible to know the true numbers affected.

African American teachers had little union support against such tactics until much later. The all-black American Teachers' Association (ATA) lacked sufficient political power, and the National Education Association struggled internally over the issue of integration for many years.[9] NEA made no public comments on *Brown* at the time of the decision, even though it had been in formal relations with ATA since 1926.[10] The *Memphis Commercial Appeal* reported a silent protest of the white Mississippi Association of Educators at the 1966 NEA national convention over the merger of NEA with ATA.[11] However, according to a 1970 report in the *New York Times*, as well as the recollections of veterans I interviewed, the NEA later expelled its Mississippi affiliate for refusing to admit African American teachers.[12]

School administrators were also targeted. The years 1954 through 1965 were the most devastating. For example, the number of African American principals in North Carolina alone dropped from 620 to 40.[13] Some of these firings and demotions may have been retaliatory since, in many instances, African American administrators not only had encouraged racial pride but also had been active (although often covertly) in local civil rights work. Another factor may have been unspoken social codes of the era. Black administrators could not be allowed to hold positions of leadership over white faculty or students at the newly integrated institutions. As Russell and Jacqueline Irvine report, "There was a 90 percent reduction in the number of African American principals in the South between the years 1964 and 1973, dropping from over 2,000 to less than 200. Most of them were relegated to 'assistant principals, classroom teachers, or special projects central office personnel.'"[14] More than 50 percent of the African American principals in six states were dismissed as most formerly black schools were closed.[15]

These firings and demotions were carried out under a general heading of "improving the quality of education," with the strong implication being that most African American teachers and administrators were inept or unqualified. Those who were deemed "good teachers" were moved to the predominantly white schools, although many report that, once there, they were placed under the tutelage of white colleagues. The result was the beginning of a much-studied and potentially harmful cultural mismatch between white teachers and black students.[16] But what broader effects did the widespread disregard for and firing of African American teachers have on public education in America, then and now? I contend that the perception of African American students as inherently inferior—or the increasingly popular poverty-deprivation view of these learners—crystallized during this dismal period, when African American teacher voices were limited or silenced entirely.

The removal of teachers who resided in the same communities and shared the same cultural backgrounds as these now-underserved African American students contributed to or reinforced the widespread low expectations with which they were confronted in their desegregated classrooms. Researchers report substantial evidence of a pattern among some white teachers to hold lower academic expectations for their black students than for their white students, a pattern that is often shrouded in a deceptively paternalistic guise.[17]

Just as African American students have been the victims of low expectations in the classroom, African American teachers and administrators have been the victims of low expectations inside the larger education community. Within a profession that has struggled for respect and empowerment, the voices of black educators have been historically muted, particularly in the areas of educational policy and reform.

The Missing Mentors

One of the most touching events of my extraordinary year as Mississippi's Teacher of the Year came after a speaking engagement. I was surrounded by a group of elderly retired African American teachers who were thrilled that I was going to Washington, D.C. and Los Angeles (for the Milken Award ceremony). Like the old mothers at church when I was a child, these teachers gave me a handkerchief in which they had wrapped money for my trip. They held my hands for a long time, repeating how proud they were. It occurred to me that because of the social and political milieu in which they had worked, they would never have been considered for such honors or awards. I referred to them and the African American veteran teachers of the desegregation era whenever I spoke, reminding new teachers of how our predecessors had taught with grace and unwavering faith under conditions we could not imagine.

Teachers like those retirees were my early role models. The first day of my rookie year, a group of African American veterans took me into the teacher's lounge, warmly welcomed me to the school, and then, with motherly sternness, explained how an African American teacher should carry and conduct herself (and why it mattered to my students and the community). They taught me how to become accepted in my new role and not to give up on even the most resistant student. Over the next months and years, they showed me, an African American woman from the North, how to teach these children of the Delta. I did not learn this critical information from my teacher preparation program—in which there were no black instructors, even though most of its graduates would eventually teach in the surrounding, predominantly African American, districts.

Unfortunately, many other new teachers of my generation found themselves thrust into increasingly complex teaching situations, usually in high-needs schools in poor communities, distressingly underprepared to serve their students effectively. One of the consistent problems in American education has been the lagging recruitment of minority teachers. A closely related, often unnoticed, problem is the staggering underrepresentation of African American professors in our nation's teacher preparation programs. This begs a crucial question: Who will prepare a multicultural teaching force for its increasingly multicultural student body? As teacher-educator and researcher Gloria Ladson-Billings observes, "It is not just what we teach students, but also how we teach them that is key to their success in the classroom."[18] This is as true within teacher preparation as it is in any K–12 classroom. More than a generation of aspiring African American teachers has been taught by example (or, rather, lack of examples) that their historical and cultural contributions to education are either insignificant or nonexistent. What we currently describe as an achievement gap may have looked very different had more of those veteran African American educators remained to mentor and prepare succeeding generations of teachers and contribute to the overall growth of the profession.

Moving Beyond the Legacy

Certainly, not all the African American teachers of the past were great, and I am under no nostalgic illusions about the quality of segregated education. Neither am I suggesting that black students can or should be taught exclusively by black teachers. Nevertheless, the impact of the widespread degradation of southern African American educators who were among the most respected members of their communities has left a deep wound. Their mistreatment persists as a symptom of the larger historical pattern of educational disparities toward African American and poor communities that have led to many of the challenges we now face.

Today, students at the predominantly African American schools in the Mississippi Delta are most likely to have the least stable teaching force. This has been a chronic teacher shortage area for more than twenty years: to meet their staffing needs, many schools rely heavily on extended substitutes or temporary instructors from programs such as Teach for America. Meanwhile, hundreds of Mississippi's aspiring African American teachers, most of them products of these underresourced schools, are unable to meet the mandated cut scores on the state's licensing exams. Ironically, the use of exams as a licensure stipulation was originally adopted expressly to prevent black teachers from qualifying for pay raises. As a member of the state licensure commission, I have questioned the continued emphasis on these tests, which the testing company's own norming samples consistently show are skewed against African Americans. The result mirrors that of the old segregationist practices—fewer African American teachers. Balancing such exams with other, more performance-based methods of assessing candidates' pedagogical knowledge and teaching ability would not only improve the overall certification process but also remove an unnecessary barrier to hiring African American teachers.

As the twenty-first century unfolds, developments in technology and pedagogy suggest exciting possibilities and more ethical dilemmas. Will digitally enhanced education be used to help the historically disadvantaged finally catch up—for example, through the creative use of current and future Web-based tools to help compensate for the paucity of African American teachers in teacher education—or will it merely exacerbate existing gaps? Will redesigned teacher preparation programs help draw a more representative pool of teaching candidates to the profession or become yet another obstacle? Will we continue to rely on standardized testing as the gatekeeper to educator certification, or will we develop more comprehensive and rigorous measures of teacher preparation and performance? It is time to make up the ground African American educators lost after *Brown*. History can't be undone, but it need not be repeated if we choose to write new stories.

A Voice from the Classroom

In my fourth year as a public education teacher, I had the "opportunity" to transfer to a small school of 150 kids in the mountainous region of our district. I was ill-prepared for the culture of not only that school but all the people who lived in that valley. The kids showed up every day with no pencils or paper. Several had no change of clothes, were dirty, had holes in their shoes. Often they spoke with a country accent so thick I had to strain to understand.

The principal became a dear friend. She was a native to the valley and had attended this school. As she gave me the background of each family and recounted stories, I began to see the school's value to the whole community. If your family was originally from this valley, chances are you would marry and settle there as well. In addition to the small clapboard churches that dotted the mountainous landscape, this school was the center of all the "goings-on."

One particular afternoon, I piled my lunch tray with homemade meatloaf, green beans, okra, small ears of corn, and cornbread. It was a feast.

I realized that I had taken more than I could handle, and I didn't particularly care for the green beans cooked in fatback. I was about to dump the contents of my tray when one of the high school boys tapped me on the shoulder. He asked why I would waste such a wonderful meal. He pulled me and my half-full tray to the side and pointed to a group of students standing at the door of the kitchen. I watched as each was given a small brown paper bag, which was carefully put into backpacks or coat pockets. The boy explained to me that some local families had fallen on hard times because of a cutback in tobacco payoffs. These families had as many as six or seven children and no means to care for them. The ladies who worked in the cafeteria always fixed extras for these children to take home to help feed the rest. From that day on, I never took what I couldn't eat and always had them give some of my portion to others.

The nine years I spent at that school taught me more about myself and public education than I could have ever learned in a college classroom. Education means something different to us all; sometimes it's simply a matter of learning how to live from day to day.

—*Kelli S. Welborn*
  Joseph Rogers Primary
  Rogersville, Tennessee

16

A Profession?

ANDREW J. ROTHERHAM

Cofounder and partner, Bellwether Education

F OR MORE THAN A half century, the effort to professionalize teaching has been a defining feature of the national conversation about teachers and teaching. In this ongoing debate, making teaching "like law and medicine" has been, and continues to be, a touchstone for many would-be reformers and national organizations. Today, stakeholders in the field of education pursue a variety of national and state accreditation and certification schemes intended to achieve this objective.

Yet there is ample reason to wonder if education is aiming at the right target as it strives to professionalize teaching. Is the focus on law and medicine reductionist, lacking in fundamental applicability to the elementary and secondary education field? Has the focus on creating credentialing and accreditation regimes distracted from the harder work of creating genuinely professional operating norms and cultures in schools?

Neither this essay nor data drawn from the NEA surveys can provide all of the answers to these questions. However, information collected by the NEA should cause us to question just how "professional" teachers' work and workplace conditions really are. Ultimately, we need to consider whether sufficient progress is being made in creating a genuine profession for teachers.

A Brief History

The history of teacher professionalization can be roughly divided into three periods. Initially, district school boards and superintendents issued local licenses to teachers. While certification was a requirement, during this period the profession was characterized by substantial variance and ad hoc arrangements.

The second period of professionalization, occurring at the end of the nineteenth century (at different points in different parts of the country), was marked by a movement toward more uniformity and progressive ideas based on "scientific" notions about efficiency, organization, and regulation. Universities, large urban school districts, and state departments of education began to play a greater role in credentialing teachers.

Not by coincidence, the third phase of teacher professionalization roughly parallels the timeline for the NEA surveys. After World War II, classroom teachers and organizations representing them—the NEA most notable among them—began to gain increasing control and voice. A primary goal of these groups, and new organizations that grew out of their efforts, was to reshape education as a profession akin to law or medicine. This issue continues to dominate the conversation today.

During this period, teacher unionism became a major force, both on the national policy landscape and locally within schools. The American Federation of Teachers began organizing educators along industrial lines to ensure at least baseline working conditions, some uniformity in processes for pay, job responsibilities, and the organization of schools. The NEA subsequently followed suit.

Defining *Professional*

What is noteworthy about this most recent phase of the movement toward professionalization is its emphasis on "professional standards" and the centrality of the idea that true professions are structured like medicine and law. Thus, there has been a growing emphasis on structured coursework, training, and induction regimes for teachers;

uniform standards for teachers and teacher preparation programs; accreditation (for instance, the National Council for the Accreditation of Teacher Education); and formalized paths to entry and advancement. These are the tools the field has seized on to create a profession and where the overwhelming emphasis of the professionalization movement is currently focused. In an effort to follow the examples of law and medicine, the ideal of teacher professionalism has become largely bound up in issues of credentialism and focused on superficial aspects of the legal and medical fields—issues of form rather than content.

In fact, looking at the range of occupations in the U.S. economy that typically require at least a bachelor's degree provides an excellent benchmark for what constitutes a *profession* in the common usage. Law and medicine are not the only professions: consultants, business leaders and managers, journalists, and so forth are also rightly classified as such in the common usage of the term. Today, despite its diversity, professional work can broadly be described by its shared approaches to such issues as:

- *Practitioner agency:* How much control do workers have over various decisions in their daily work? Are they held accountable for end product or process? How is their workday defined?
- *Risk and reward:* How likely is a person to lose a job because of performance or disruptions and changes in the field? Is total compensation commensurate with the risks?
- *Norms and culture:* How are decisions made and conflicts resolved? Do rules and contractual processes drive decision making and operations or are decisions arrived at through collaboration or shared understandings and expectations?

It's not hard to see how these ideas are generally at odds with the industrial organization model that informs much of the teacher unionization movement in the latter part of the twentieth century. For example, in professional workplaces, formal rules are rarely the default mechanism for making decisions or meeting challenges. Instead, norms and culture drive decision making. When disputes arise, for instance, the default is rarely to look at the letter of a contract for resolution. That's not to say there is no acrimony, only that it is usually resolved absent formal mechanisms. Consider issues like grievances, changing work rules, or dealing with performance problems and it is easy to see how this concept of practitioner agency contrasts with today's compliance-driven and contractually based approach to schooling and the organization of schools in most places. Don't take my word for it; peruse teacher contracts or visit databases that catalog contractual provisions, such as the National Council on Teacher Quality's TR[3] Web site.[1] Dispute-resolution procedures are generally laborious and multitiered and organized around an adversarial approach rather than a collaborative one.

It is important to note, however, that professionalism and autonomy are not synonymous. The idea that treating teachers as professionals means leaving them alone to pursue whatever methods they deem most effective can have a deleterious effect on teaching. Doctors, lawyers, stockbrokers, journalists, and other professionals enjoy autonomy, but that agency is bounded within a set of parameters derived from research and experience and is often codified in regulation or law. As long as autonomy is wrongly considered an immutable aspect of professionalism by those advocates who argue that teachers should simply be left alone to teach, schools will default to regulatory strategies to control teachers and efforts to improve teaching and learning will falter.

Similarly, the way most collective bargaining contracts define teachers' work is inconsistent with the standard found in other professions. These contracts specify nearly every detail of the teacher's job, including the length of the workday. In contrast, some local districts are exploring "reform" contracts that allow for substantially greater flexibility. For example, Green Dot Public Schools, a nonprofit network of unionized public schools in Los Angeles and New York, defines a teacher's day by whether or not her work is completed. That approach seems more aligned with the standard governing most professional workplaces. Likewise, while the Green Dot contract is nonspecific about most of the day-to-day organization and operations of schools, most traditional teachers' contracts lay out various processes in painstaking detail.[2]

Although much of the teaching job is still constrained by the industrial model, teacher preparation is becoming more pluralistic, with alternative credentialing and training regimes increasingly common.

In 2005 6 percent of teachers surveyed by the NEA reported that they entered teaching through an alternative route to certification (somewhat lower than other reports of the national average).[3] In some places, nonprofit organizations such as The New Teacher Project have the authority to license teachers. And, in terms of overall numbers, Teach for America—which recruits outstanding college graduates to teach for two years in challenging schools—is now the largest teacher preparation program in the country.

To date, the research evidence from states as diverse as New York and Louisiana shows that the differences within these various routes into teaching are greater than the differences between them. In other words, who the candidates are and their traits matters more than whether they come through a traditional or alternative route into teaching. The only exception to this is emergency credentialed teachers with no training at all, who underperform other teachers as a group.

Given the regulatory infrastructure and costs associated with the "professional" ideal of law and medicine—in particular, long periods of coursework and training—such research raises provocative questions about traditional teacher education. For instance, if teachers coming through routes that carry substantially fewer costs for teaching candidates and taxpayers are performing as well as teachers coming through more costly routes, that raises cost-benefit questions. What this means for the teacher labor market and how these new routes will interact with traditional accreditation and regulatory schemes are open questions. Still, in practice, education is beginning to move toward a much more pluralistic set of ways in which aspiring teachers can enter the profession. Multiple paths are common in many professions—from business to journalism and even in law there exist multiple paths into the field (full-time law school, night schools, elite law schools)—albeit tethered to a single credentialing regime, the bar.

Is the Teaching Profession Professional?

Calls for teaching to be put on par with the traditional professions clearly have rhetorical and political value for efforts to improve the respect, support, and compensation teachers receive. Yet romancing these professions has done little to materially change the circumstances for teachers over the past half century. Teaching today is not much more like law or medicine than it was in the 1950s. In fact, if anything, the field is evolving toward the more pluralistic and informal approaches used by the various professions discussed earlier.

One of the hallmarks of the legal/medical model is its rigorous training and accreditation requirements. Those entering these professions emerge from their education fully equipped to practice. Despite the growing emphasis on credentials in the education literature, teachers are underserved by their formal training. According to the NEA data, only 11 percent of teachers in 2005 identified their training and education as a helpful factor in their work, a decline from 18 percent in 1975 (figure 2.22).

One reason that training falls short is that law and medicine currently have much more established bodies of canonical knowledge than does the field of education. Rather than embrace the challenge of building a similar foundation, distilled through years of experience and a body of research, American education has sought to wish that process away. In other words, in the effort to create the appearance of a professional canon—with the exception of a few specific subjects—American education has arguably manufactured a corpus of theoretical standards instead of organically developing a core of proven or agreed-upon knowledge. Untested in practical application, such imposed ideas have served to undermine or marginalize teachers more than support them and has made their training the object of ridicule rather than respect. The fact that multiple organizations put forward copious standards for teacher professionalism while high school teachers are still left largely on their own to struggle with the problems of adolescent literacy illustrates the problem.

In terms of their daily work routines, professionals need time to prepare for their classes and to interact with one another to build knowledge. On the one hand, the field of education acknowledges the need for preparation, and, on this issue, the NEA data seem to present good news. In 1955 teachers were given an average of four periods of prep time; a half century later, the average had risen to five periods, with little variance in between.[4]

On the other hand, during this same time period our schools became more complicated, the student body they serve more diverse, and, as a result of new federal laws, special-needs students became a fixture in schools rather than a marginalized population. Given the more complicated and growing demands on teachers, the uptick in preparation hours seems negligible. According to the NEA survey data, teachers regularly cite workload and extra responsibilities as significant hindrances to their ability to do their job effectively (figure 2.23). This is perhaps why they reported spending ten hours a week on at-home instructional activities in 2005 (grading, lesson planning), an increase of two hours from 1980, when the NEA first collected these data (figure 2.17).[5] The lack of accommodation for time to learn and prepare in the face of evolving workplace conditions is not encouraging for either the creation of a professional body of knowledge or the ability of teachers to do their best work.

NEA data paint a discouraging picture in other areas as well. For instance, less than a third of teachers report that cooperative and competent colleagues and mentors help them in their work. While this figure is the highest it has been since it was first tracked in 1975, it is hardly what one would expect in a professional workplace. Administrators and specialists were not widely considered as helpful supports either. Fewer than one in five teachers cited them as such in 2005, and in that same year the lack of administrative support was actually singled out as a top hindrance. Finally, just 5 percent found the school environment, organization, and freedom to teach helpful in 2005, a figure that has ranged from 3 percent to 11 percent since 1975 (figures 2.22 and 2.23).[6]

In successful for-profit and nonprofit enterprises, the mentoring and development of talent is considered a core part of the organizational mission. Think about the magnitude of effort investment banks, law firms, consulting businesses, the military, medical residencies, and other enterprises put into developing and supporting talent (and, conversely, their hard-nosed decisions about whom not to develop further). In each of these cases, promising performers are identified and given appropriate growth opportunities.

One thing NEA data show with substantial clarity is that teachers earn less on average than members of many other professions (figure 2.25). They do enjoy benefit packages that are often more generous, but because much of that compensation is deferred, it does not translate to personal cash flow. This may be why the data show that over one-third of teachers reported earning summer income to augment their salary in 2005 (figure 2.27). In other words, despite increasing demands on teachers and a shortage of time because of how schools are organized, teachers still must seek work outside of their core job in order to make ends meet. In addition, because most teachers are paid on the basis of academic degrees and longevity as opposed to measures linked to job performance, this, along with the public perception of low pay, may serve to undermine the public's recognition of teaching as a profession.

Part of the problem with teacher pay—and, more generally, for the field—is a lack of accountability and meaningful standards for evaluation and differentiation. For instance, just 15 percent of teachers reported that student test scores were used as part of their evaluation, a low figure even taking into account all the unassessed subjects that schools offer (figure 2.19). Reports from other sources—most notably *The Widget Effect*, published by The New Teacher Project in 2009—illustrate the perfunctory and ineffective nature of teacher evaluations.[7] We should not idealize evaluations in other fields, as there are always trade-offs and shortcomings. However, results-based accountability of some kind (even if only through consumer choice and preference) is a hallmark of professionalism that remains conspicuously absent from education human capital policies in most places.

Finally, in the very broadest sense, the defining character of education today still owes more to compliance than a truly professional ethos and workplace would dictate. Some of the questions included in the NEA surveys—and many that are not included—speak directly to that issue. In particular, the field still focuses on inputs at the expense of outputs.

Conclusion

While the progress that the education field has made in the last fifty-plus years—for students as well as teachers—should not be discounted, it is reasonable to ask, Have we appreciably improved the professional nature of the work teachers do? The disconnect between the professional rhetoric and aspirations for teaching and the reality today is a fundamental issue, as much cultural as structural, that remains to be addressed.

Without attention to what a true profession would mean within schools, any change in the name of professionalism will likely be one of old ideas in new trappings. The NEA data suggest that, as workplaces, schools remain fundamentally unprofessional places to work in some key ways. Plenty of parties share responsibility for that status quo.

Today, as a practical matter, moving toward real professionalism will likely require several changes. Policy makers must be supportive of a broader range of schooling options and roles for educators. Teacher-run schools and other genuinely progressive approaches to organizing schools are currently quite rare. More scalable solutions include career ladders that allow teachers to take on different roles and leadership responsibilities without leaving the classroom and labor contracts that are based on professional norms and expectations instead of adversarial contractual language.

At the same time, educators must be willing to look for different approaches within the education sector and across other industries. While it has unique aspects, American education is not the first sector to face the challenge of creating a professional work culture for dispersed and often hard-to-measure work at a significant scale.

Finally, the pressure for increased performance that has characterized education improvement efforts for the past two decades must become more central to the culture of schools. Such a change demands the candid and ongoing conversations about collective and individual performance that are vital to any high-performing professional workplace. Anyone who has spent much time in and around schools knows how rare these conversations are and how difficult they are to have within schools as currently organized. It also means a greater tolerance for ambiguity, tension, and non-rules-based decision making. As long as schools are driven by contractual requirements and an adversarial approach in labor-management relations, they will not be professional workplaces.

So, today we remain much better at talking about professionalism than putting it into practice for teachers. Indeed, focusing on some other professions and how they train and organize their practitioners may in fact distract us from the unique challenges the education field faces in its efforts to deliver highly effective instruction to the most diverse group of students in the nation's history. Given the importance of teacher effectiveness to student learning and the challenge of recruiting teachers from a pool of candidates who today have different expectations and employment opportunities than in the past, we do not have another fifty years to get this right.

A Voice from the Classroom

After joining the New York City Teaching Fellows (an alternative certification program), I began a full-time career as a special-needs teacher, taking the place of a colleague. One of the first things a student said to me was, "We ran Ms.——— out, we'll run you out too!" Within the first month I was hit, kicked, spat on, and called every name in the book by my third-grade students, all while learning how to run a classroom for the first time.

These challenges were not entirely unexpected, considering my students' diagnosed disorders and the sudden change in teachers. As I taught this same class for the next three years, though, there were events I did not expect. One that had a particular emotional impact was the disappearance of students. Although my school had an astonishing student retention rate (95 percent) considering its urban environment, my twelve-student special education class was much less stable. While it was not unusual for a student to miss a day for no apparent reason, it was emotionally draining when a desk would stay vacant for days on end.

"A bad case of the flu?" I might initially think. But when attempts to reach parents hit roadblocks like disconnected numbers or outdated contact

information, there was really nothing to do but wait. Sometimes students would come back—maybe with a doctor's note, maybe with mysterious bruises. And then sometimes . . . not at all.

Bit by bit the school would receive the story, usually after a transfer notice was sent by another city school—occasionally from another state. An entire family would move suddenly, children would be sent to live with other family members down South; sometimes we got notices from Children's Services or witness protection.

Suddenly all the time spent working toward a student's future seemed futile. Records would be lost, behavioral goals unattended to, and the services we had fought for forgotten. And how to tell their classmates? I learned with my first disappearance that my students were used to it and did not need an explanation. Yet they felt the loss of classmates to whom they never had a chance to say goodbye. They would refer to desks by previous occupants' names, tell stories, and hand me cards they'd made to send to their friends' new addresses. I couldn't tell them that I didn't know a new address either—I have a box full of these unsent farewell letters.

Concern for these students' welfare overwhelms me on a personal level. Depending on the circumstances, it ranges from worrying if a new school will meet a student's special education needs to having nightmares about his or her physical safety. After a time the feelings wane, but never fully. Years later I'll think of students who disappeared and wonder how they're doing. Sometimes I don't really want to know.

Despite these realities, I continue to teach my special-needs students as if we'll see the year through together. All that I can really do after students have left is to forward all paperwork and notes—if an address is given. If not, I have to trust that these students experienced a sense of community and respect while in our school that can be carried over into their journeys.

—Elizabeth M. DellaBadia
  P.S. 149Q–Christa McAuliffe School
  Jackson Heights, New York

17

The Four Cs

New Norms in an Age of Technology

BARBARA STOFLET

Gatewood Elementary, Minnetonka, Minnesota

IT WAS EARLY FALL in first grade, 1999. We were engaged in solving a real-life math problem that would be relevant to activities later in the day. A.J. approached me with his solution. He asked, "Is this right?" I replied, "I don't know. You have written that 8 + 3 is 11. I know that 8 + 2 = 10, so I wonder if 8 + 3 would be 11?" He came back with, "Yeah. But is it right?" I repeated that I wasn't sure and asked him to prove that he was right. He stood quietly for a minute, then slowly started to return to his desk, shaking his head. As he ambled away, he glanced back at me and muttered, "My kindergarten teacher was WAY smarter than you!" A.J. had been confronted with a different way of teaching math.

Earlier in my career I would have shown A.J. how to solve the problem, given him several similar problems, and graded them for his report card. That day I was questioning instead of answering. I was working on perfecting a newly acquired technique. My district had been awarded one of just a handful of Best Practices grants in our state, the main focus of which was guiding teachers to recognize the wealth of possibilities for student learning if we shifted our instructional practices from being the "sage on the stage" to "the guide on the side." We were, in effect, studying the importance of thoughtful, reflective learning for both teachers and students. The emphasis was on more than just teaching procedures in math. We were expanding our conceptual understanding in order to pass it on to students. Because of this training, I knew that A.J. was at a critical point in his mathematical development. He could be steered toward seeing math as a system of formulae to be memorized, or he could be nudged into developing a firm foundation of the number 10—the base needed to see and use our number system as an infinite bundle of patterns. We have moved from telling students *what* to think to guiding them in *how* to think and approach problem solving.

The Four Cs and the New Technology Divide

As A.J. was learning to reason and justify in math, no one could have predicted the extent to which these critical thinking skills would be needed to cope with a whole new world of information far beyond the mathematics classroom. New technologies—especially communications technologies and the social networking that they enable—are part of today's students' world. And as they flood into the classroom, a technology knowledge gap has grown between students and their teachers. Students have grasped the changes in our world faster than many of their teachers. When students enter classrooms, they often need to "unplug" their world. They're asked to transition into an environment that is very different from the one they just stepped out of.

As a result, A.J.'s educational needs have changed dramatically. Mastery of the traditional three Rs (reading, writing, and arithmetic) is no longer enough. We now have an equal need to critically evaluate the four Cs that have emerged as part of students' experiences with technology: —conversations, content, connections, and collaboration.

- Our students have *conversations* with peers while in their classrooms, but a large percentage of these interactions take place in written form, via phone and computer. Many are carried out without the benefit of body language; instead, generalized language through texting has been invented to fill the void. Now there is an entire communication system using acronyms. The definition of conversation has expanded.

- Today's students learn *content*, but on a new scale. Just a few clicks—and an unprecedented, seemingly infinite amount of information is made available.

- Students today are making fewer *connections* through traditional means—social events, landline phone calls (which might be monitored by adults), writing notes—and are instead linking through technology. They connect information, but, more importantly, they connect with each other. The adage "it's not what you know but who you know" has been inflated exponentially. And communication is time-stamped and recorded with a level of accountability that no other generation has experienced.

- The expansion of conversation, content, and connections makes it more natural (given the ease and speed of communicating) and more necessary (given the amount of data they have to tackle) for today's students to *collaborate*. Today our students are often learning and problem-solving in group settings to creatively address classroom tasks. However, the other three Cs are encouraging even more collaboration, outside the classroom as well as in it. Youth have become adept at working together. They have largely rejected the competitive model followed by previous generations and are supporting each other to become successful.

The central challenge for teachers is to bring critical thinking skills to bear on these issues. Students have taken charge of much of their own learning in the four Cs but are still developing the skills to evaluate them, both critically (evaluating the accuracy and usefulness of content) and ethically or socially (making judgments on how to use content, when to communicate, what collaboration means).

In addition to managing the volume of content, students need to consider the trustworthiness of the information they locate. Very little of it has gone through the strict editing processes once enforced in the world of print. For example, a university law professor recently conducted an experiment to test the reliability of content. He told his morning law class that a chief justice was stepping down—a fabrication. By the end of the day, a national evening news anchor crew was checking the authenticity of the information so that it could be aired. The professor's experiment demonstrated how quickly content, reliable or not, is disseminated.

Collaboration poses another challenge—perhaps the biggest gap in norms. Although students see working together and sharing information as completely natural, they do not always understand the concept of collaboration. They see little wrong with passing answers to tests as a way of supporting each other, which was clearly recognized as cheating, pretechnology. Their collaborative efforts can also be unfocused. This might mean that they are not very good at judging or reluctant to criticize each other's contributions or unable to work together through thorny issues. In one example, a student posted a negative comment about a school issue on Facebook, another student posted a response about its inappropriateness, and then others joined the discussion—but absent guidance on acceptable means of collaboration, the group became contentious. Collaboration can be at the root of many impressive advances, if teachers help students find ways to understand that collaboration is the art of creating a critically evaluated product that blends multiple perspectives while maintaining a balance of contributions. Strong values and constructive social norms need to be the foundation of collaboration for our students.

Preparing Teachers for the Four Cs

We teachers now need to make some corrections in our growth trajectory—and the learning curve is steeper than it has been in the past. If we want to be seen as credible facilitators of learning, we must understand how the four Cs affect learning and behavior and incorporate this knowledge into our practice. Consistent professional development could be a means for equalizing the disparity between students and teachers and equipping teachers with the tools to emphasize critical thinking and literacy skills. We need to consider two key ways of helping teachers tackle the four Cs: rethinking the mode in which professional development is delivered and supporting learning communities.

Aligning District and University Development Programs

The NEA survey data tell us that there has been a steady rise in the proportion of instruction teachers receive from their districts as opposed to colleges or professional associations. While just over half (57 percent) of teachers reported receiving professional development from individual school districts in 1980; that number rose to 81 percent by 2005 (figure 2.14). There are benefits to having professional development tailored to individual districts, but the trend imposes limitations, especially for a teaching force that needs to embrace the technology environment in a hurry. The profession is already very fragmented, divided into districts within states and buildings within districts. In addition, there is a great deal of inequity in the availability of resources. The increasing expectation that each district will meet the professional development needs of teachers at the local level exacerbates the divisions and resource disparities among schools, districts, and states. Funding to bring teachers together to study content and learn from each other would be money well spent; it could foster conversations, content knowledge, connections, and collaboration across the profession.

The nature of this issue also argues against confining professional development on the four Cs to the district level. The challenges posed by technology are universal, or nearly so. Unlike many other issues, which have their own variations district to district, schools are coping with the same problems. Increasingly, students have access to the same technologies and use them in much the same way. Yet the NEA data reveal that, as of 2005, only about one-quarter of teachers reported completing professional development delivered by universities and professional associations, respectively. Spiking an upward trend in this area could unify and equalize professional development, enabling teachers to share and learn across district boundaries.

Another role for the universities would be to introduce programs that yield better alignment between university-level training and professional development in individual districts. Higher education has demonstrated the capacity to conduct impressive research studies. What it lacks is the know-how to apply these results in the real world, making partnerships with K–12 systems mutually beneficial.

Some universities have launched innovative programs with school districts that are designed to ensure that all teachers are challenging students to reason and justify, as A.J. was in first grade. Others have introduced arrangements that put preservice teachers into afterschool programs to address achievement gaps among students. What if universities and school districts partnered to produce a hybrid program aimed at closing the technological achievement gap *between* teachers and students? What if preservice teachers collaborated with classroom teachers on infusing technology into their lessons? The benefits would be manifold. Preservice teachers would gain content and pedagogical knowledge, and teachers in the field would be learning from students who have experienced the technology explosion firsthand.

As teachers develop greater proficiency, further use of technology would allow all districts—urban, suburban, and rural—to be reached. Universities could be the link among districts, spreading methods and practices that have proved effective. In addition, if universities were to work with a number of schools simultaneously, teachers would gain insight from educators in other districts. Another consequence would be that universities would have a direct connection to the rapidly changing needs of preservice teachers as they enter the field.

Learning Communities

We also need to explore options that strengthen professional learning communities. Professional development is one tool for helping teachers manage the four Cs, but it is only part of the equation. Equally important is encouraging teachers to draw on their own experiences and learn from one another about how best to strengthen students' critical thinking skills. Having the time to plan with other teachers, teach what was planned, and then discuss how students responded has enormous potential. Such enriching interactions would also serve to enhance the benefits of any professional development efforts in this area, as learning is enhanced, internalized, and reshaped through dialogue and use. Learning communities may indeed be ideal vehicles or jumping-off points for thinking about how the four Cs work in practice, given the increased role that technology plays in allowing them to flourish.

Unfortunately, practical considerations often impede collaboration. Far too often teachers' calendars and schedules do not allow enough time to give or receive feedback to one another. Nevertheless, according to NEA data, the average number of nonteaching days has increased over the past twenty years, and, over a forty-year span, the number of preparation periods for secondary teachers has also increased from four to five per week (figure 2.18).[1] These trends are indicative of slight movement toward more noninstructional time, which may be utilized to nurture learning communities. In my district, some (minimal, after-school) time has been allocated for teacher collaboration and discussion. Yet it is so minimal that it is confined to collaboration within grade levels, with no opportunity for vertical alignment across grades.

Even greater emphasis should be placed on the use of noninstructional time in support of learning communities. U.S. policy makers should follow the example set by countries such as Korea, Japan, and Germany, where teachers have more time to collaborate and discuss as part of their regular workday.[2] So far, however, our policy makers have not acted on implementing changes despite the obvious benefits—particularly, stronger standings on international exams. The United States is unique in the emphasis it places on instructional hours, compelling teachers to find time before and after school to collaborate with colleagues (figure 2.17).

In the absence of additional time during the workday, the summer months might also be used to support professional communities, allowing teachers to learn the subject matter we present during the school year in more depth and to infuse technology into more lessons. We could very effectively use summer school classes designed to deliver remedial help for our students as a lab school setting for our professional development. We could meet as a class of teachers in the morning, leaving the afternoon available to meet with small groups of students who would benefit from our newly acquired knowledge. We have heard about holding extended-year opportunities for students, but making them available for teachers has the potential to be even more effective. We know that students learn more when we give them timely feedback. The same is true for teachers. It would not be necessary for all teachers to participate in a summer learning program. The professional learning community model could be employed during the school year so that summer participants could share what they learned with teachers who were not able to participate.

––––––––––

We know that the American educational system was built on the three Rs. Those core areas have blended cultures and given us a common language as our society has moved forward. But with the advent of ubiquitous communications technologies, the four Cs—conversation, content, connections, and collaboration—are the skills that, if well guided, will continue to move us forward. They are the present and future for students. Our teachers need to embrace this technologically driven transformation and be part of it. Our students will be moving on with or without us. We can't afford to be left behind.

A Voice from the Classroom

There was never a year in my career without someone assuming the role of the class clown—often kids who wanted to be recognized positively, as do most students, but somehow or other circumstances worked against that. They fall into the role of clown, see that it works, gives them recognition and attention, even if it also earns the occasional afterschool detention. It becomes their self—their core identity in school. But sometimes the opportunity arises to shuck off that role.

There was "Tommy the Clown," as his classmates had been calling him since sixth grade. He was the tallest boy in that year's freshman class, proverbially awkward, and with a voice still undergoing change, which added to his comical bag of tricks. Since September, his little misbehaviors, speaking out of turn, or sudden singing of the Mighty Mouse theme song had earned him quite a few hours after school washing the chalkboard and straightening the rows of desks. Though he seemed to take great pleasure in both tasks, the next day I invariably overheard him dramatically bemoaning his labors to his buddies.

It wasn't unusual for students to read stories and poems aloud in class, and when he took his turn, Thomas would occasionally switch to a rather convincing female falsetto for women characters. During one of our afternoon sessions, the class began reading aloud from *Great Expectations*, and I asked him how Joe the Blacksmith would sound when he spoke. Without hesitation, Thomas opened his book to chapter 2 and began to speak in a slow, deep, and sort-of-fake British accent—with such fluency that it seemed as if he had been practicing this to himself. Then without prompting, he spoke some of Mrs. Joe's lines, with a deeper, scruffier tone. While the effect was hilarious, it seemed to me to be a right-on interpretation of her character, which got me thinking about tomorrow's class.

The next day I began to read a new chapter out loud, and when I came to the part where the army sergeant on the hunt for the escaped convicts speaks, I read in a voice obviously out of character. Several students complained. So I asked if anyone thought they could do better. Tommy the Clown raised his hand. Students cheered him on. And on.

For the next week, Thomas read every bit of dialogue in character for the class. The effect was mesmerizing for all of us. Then a few others began to volunteer to read a character's part. I let Thomas pick who could read which character. He did a great job selecting voices and tones for the characters, which made reading the book an actual pleasure for all. Thomas became sort of a choral director, to the class's enormous delight. And to add to the dramatic effect, I suggested that he include sound effect noises—a door creaking open here, heavy footsteps there—which he undertook with accuracy and gusto. For that month, Thomas had no detentions from me. But he did stop by my room after school a couple times to run new sound effects by me for later in the story.

Thomas, incidentally, majored in music composition and works as a sound engineer. But in his evenings, I'm sure he's reading some novel or other and making noises with his mouth to the great entertainment of whoever is in the room.

—Gary Metras
  Hampshire Regional High School (Retired)
  Westhampton, Massachusetts

18

Laying the Groundwork for Teacher Success

DENNIS VAN ROEKEL

President, National Education Association

A S I REFLECT ON the findings presented in this volume, I am struck by several themes in the data that capture the essence of what I believe teachers need and expect to have in order to be successful in their jobs. Above all, teachers need a fundamental knowledge and understanding of their content area, and they expect a partnership with their colleagues, school administrators, parents, and others to help deliver that content to students. I believe that achieving these conditions will both strengthen the teaching force and go a long way toward improving retention. Thus, we need to look at the quality of pre- and in-service training as well as the support teachers require from colleagues and enlightened administrators to enable them to do their best work. As we nurture our teachers now and in the future, these are the critical areas that must be addressed to ensure that both students and their teachers have the opportunity to achieve their full potential.

Preservice Training for Quality

The NEA survey data reveal that teachers generally perceive support from their colleagues and administrators to be more helpful to their work than their training, education, and knowledge (figure 2.22).

Indeed, in examining long-term trends, it is evident that teachers' appreciation of their education and training is at the lowest level in twenty-five years.[1] These findings suggest several important questions: Why do teachers seem to value their formal training less today than in the past, and why do they value the help received from colleagues on the job more highly than their training experience? Is it because the quality of teacher education programs has become stagnant? If so, where are improvements needed? If not, is there something else missing? There is much to ponder, to be sure.

Some observers continue to hold the quality of teacher training in high regard. For example, comparing teacher preparation programs with those for professionals in other fields (e.g., accounting, architecture, nursing, and law enforcement), Katherine Neville and her colleagues find teacher training to be very comprehensive and quite possibly in the forefront.[2] Certainly, the NEA data and other survey findings confirm that the number of teachers with master's degrees has increased steadily over the past fifty years (figure 2.11). But a recent study of university-based education programs finds teacher education in this country to be principally a mix of weak and mediocre programs, many disconnected from school practice and practitioners.[3]

While teachers' perceptions of their education and training warrant a thorough review of both program quality and relevance, such an examination would be challenging given the various avenues for receiving training and the demand-driven needs that may interfere with program quality and relevance. Although most teachers are trained in public college and university undergraduate programs, a growing number—especially those working in urban schools—have taken nontraditional paths, receiving certification through an alternative training process.[4] In fact, according to the National Center for Education Statistics, nearly one in five (17 percent) of urban teachers have an alternative form of certification, compared with 13 percent of suburban and 9 percent of rural teachers, respectively.[5]

Approximately one-third of all teachers hired are coming through alternative routes—about sixty-two thousand new teachers annually.[6] Such programs vary widely in quality and effectiveness, depending on the intensity of the program. A central component of the successful field-based programs is the capacity of the school to provide meaning-ful information and structured mentoring during the training phase. Yet high-needs schools, in which many of the teacher candidates on alternative tracks are placed, do not generally have the capacity to fol-low through with such intense training responsibilities.

At the state level, affiliates of the NEA have joined in partnership with state affiliates of the American Association of Colleges for Teacher Education (AACTE) to improve the quality of teacher training pro-grams across the country. Through the Partnership for Teacher Quality, both organizations share a strong commitment to teacher preparation and licensure standards and are strengthening state policies on teacher licensure by working closely with governors, state boards of education, state policy analysts, and state legislators. Recent improvements in research, combined with new data systems that track teacher place-ment, retention, and student achievement across states, have helped highlight the need for improvements in teacher preparation programs.

We know that preparation matters greatly for teacher effectiveness, as evidenced by the experiences of the highest-performing countries in the world. Now is the time for our states, with incentives from the fed-eral government, to create world-class teacher preparation programs and impose uniform standards of quality across all training paths to the classroom. It is critical that every candidate receive adequate training and support and meet rigorous standards for skill, knowledge, and abil-ity. If these key components are combined with high-quality content, then stakeholders in universities, school districts, and state licensing agencies can help ensure that preparation and licensure programs are producing the quality teacher candidates our schools need and our stu-dents deserve. Each route for teacher training must be equal in rigor, and every teacher candidate should meet identical standards and mea-sures in order to receive a professional teaching license in any given state.

Professional Development with Relevance

When teachers complete their preparation programs and begin their service in the nation's schools, their need for training and development is ongoing. Yet many teachers experience professional development as superficial, disconnected episodes that don't address their practical needs in the classroom. The NEA data indicate that the time teachers spend on such activities is holding steady at only a handful of days each year (table 2.2).

Examining where teachers obtain their professional development provides some insight into how to best meet their training needs. While school districts have long been the primary providers of in-service training for teachers, their lead over the two other sources of professional development—universities and professional associations—has widened over the past quarter-century (figure 2.14). The proportion of teachers attending training sessions sponsored by universities and associations has remained largely stable, perhaps reflecting limited interest on the part of teachers for sessions that focus on abstract theories and problems. This is consistent with other evidence that professional development programs led by peers and presented in practical settings are more effective than workshops and other formal classes.

The content of professional development is also shifting—moving away from mostly curriculum and instruction concerns toward issues of managing diversity in the classroom (table 2.2). In fact, in the most recent administration of the NEA survey, more teachers reported participating in professional development focused on managing diversity than on standardized testing—and also expressed a greater need for this type of training. This preference may explain in part why so few teachers feel that traditional teacher education is helpful in the classroom. It also points to a possible new direction for teacher training, one in which school districts assume more responsibility for designing programs that are tailored to the increasingly diverse students teachers engage with daily.

Managing diversity in the classroom is especially important for urban educators. To have a real impact on learning, teachers need to understand their students' values, desires, and motivations. Up to a third of teachers in suburban and rural schools have received professional development on managing diversity; in urban schools this number is as many as four out of ten teachers.[7] Diversity exists in many forms, but racial and ethnic diversity, coupled with a higher proportion of low-income students, are often part of urban teachers' experience, requiring competencies well beyond subject matter knowledge.

As school districts gear up to provide professional development that more meaningfully addresses teachers' practical needs, there must also be efforts to expand opportunities for advanced training in subject matter content and pedagogical skills. States and districts need to offer more encouragement and support for teachers to pursue certification through the National Board for Professional Teaching Standards (NBPTS). Since 1989 this process has ensured that teachers have met rigorous requirements through study, expert evaluation, self-assessment, and peer review. The qualifying standards have long served as a guide to school districts, states, colleges, universities, and others with an interest in strengthening the initial and ongoing education of our nation's teachers. Studies clearly document that having NBPTS-certified teachers is significantly related to increased student achievement.[8] Yet only a small fraction of teachers has achieved NBPTS certification.

Beyond recognizing the need for professional development content and standards, schools are also beginning to restructure the way they deliver development opportunities and are redesigning support systems to help teachers succeed. School-based professional communities are the core of these new systems of teacher learning.[9] Schools are moving away from an individualistic view of teacher growth and focusing more on building the collective capacity of school staff. Advocates believe that for teachers, as for students, learning is more effective in interactive contexts. Professional learning communities are a clear departure from other development systems that provide sporadic training events outside the school. To sustain strong teacher relationships, leadership must support such collaborative efforts and inspire them to grow through trust—sufficient trust for teachers to disclose their teaching dilemmas, to ask questions and seek in-depth discussions, to acknowledge differences, and to tolerate conflict.

In all, more financial support and effort should be devoted to improving teacher preparation programs, and states should work with teachers' unions and subject area associations to expand mentoring programs, provide targeted professional development for educators, increase opportunities for NBPTS certification, and expand school leadership initiatives. This kind of collaboration—with teachers at the table in the decision-making process—is crucial for teacher success.

Support to Foster Stability

Good working conditions for teachers, particularly for new entrants, are also critical to their success and that of their students. Beginners can find themselves in sink-or-swim environments, ignored or rejected by their colleagues and principals. Studies show that new teachers who work in a supportive environment and have sustained relationships with colleagues across different experience levels are more likely to remain in their schools than those who lack regular interactions with experienced colleagues.[10]

The NEA survey data reveal that working conditions for teachers have changed over the past twenty-five years, and there have been dramatic shifts in what teachers perceive to be obstacles to their jobs. Workload, testing demands, and student discipline all top the list of hindrances cited most by teachers, while working relations with colleagues and others have become less of a problem (figure 2.23).[11] Fewer teachers today are hindered by unhelpful administrators, negative attitudes of students, and even negative attitudes of parents and other constituents than in the past two decades.[12] In fact, these areas show the greatest improvement overall, and teachers responding to the most recent survey reported that the factors most helpful to them in doing their jobs are competent colleagues and mentors and support from administrators and specialists (figure 2.22).

To help fill the gap in training and meet the need for ongoing professional development, local teachers' unions are partnering with school districts to develop mentoring programs that go well beyond just helping with lesson planning and providing emotional support for those entering the field. Strong mentorships between new and veteran teachers are formally structured to provide the critical support needed at the beginning of a teacher's career but are also helping to maintain the quality of teaching for mentors themselves.

Some programs are now granting master teachers more authority in evaluating the effectiveness of new teachers and making recommendations about their dismissal if they cannot meet standards. Although peer assistance and review programs have been slow to catch on, they have been more successful when implemented through partnerships between school districts and teachers' unions. Under these conditions, teachers feel more protected and are more likely to open up about challenges they face without fear of reprisals. A number of school districts in Ohio, New York, and North Carolina are implementing peer assistance and review programs, and the involvement of local teachers' unions has been crucial to their success. Giving veteran teachers the authority to bolster the quality of those just beginning and to help plan the interventions and professional development for all teachers will afford the profession the level of stability needed to improve public education all around. The key, however, is to design programs that focus on the support of new entrants and to fully fund them. If we are serious about recruiting and retaining new teachers, we have to have greater backing—especially financial—for such programs.

Leadership Designed to Empower

The provision of good teachers and the supports they need to do their job form one of the major civil rights agendas of this decade. Teachers need good leadership to help set goals for their mission and remove obstacles to their success. Strong leadership and teacher empowerment also directly impact student achievement and teacher retention. Studies confirm that teachers who seem "disheartened" are much less likely than their peers to feel supported by their principals and less likely to rate their principals as "excellent" on useful instructional feedback.[13] Disheartened teachers are also more likely to regard insufficient room to grow as a cause for dissatisfaction, suggesting they would be willing to take on more responsibilities. Providing teachers with the leadership and conditions that allow them to practice their craft and to exercise their professional creativity should be an aim of our education system.

Unfortunately, school systems struggle to attract and retain sufficient numbers of high-quality administrators. About half of beginning principals stay on the job for five years or less, not long enough to make staff connections or see reforms through.[14] Turnover rates for school administrators from low-performing, stressed schools seem to be higher, although this may be due in part to reassignments or replacements linked to lagging student performance. Some suggest that the principal's role has outgrown the ability of one person to handle it. Thus, interest is now turning toward restructuring the job to permit principals to devote more time to improving instruction by delegating the managerial tasks to vice or assistant principals.

Nearly all principals have some classroom experience, but many lack sufficient training and experience in coaching teachers. In one major poll, principals reported that their preparation for the job should have included more coaching and leadership skills development, and most believed that typical programs are out of touch with the realities of today's schools.[15] Some respondents, described as *transformers*, had received administrative support from their districts or had, on their own initiative, concentrated on academics and teaching while putting managerial issues aside. However, another group—*coper* principals—seemed overwhelmed and operated in a reactive mode that left little time to devote to instructional matters. The study raises the question of whether some copers could become transformers if they received more appropriate training and could rely on supplemental staff to assume a share of administrative duties. Or, more disturbingly, could failure to provide the resources to compensate for an increasingly complex job reduce some transformers to copers as job stress wears them down?

The NEA has long been a strong advocate of strengthening school leadership. Since 1996 it has engaged in a partnership with seventeen other national organizations—the Learning First Alliance—to provide information, resources, and support for the improvement of student learning. Several years ago, the Alliance conducted a research study to examine the strategies used by five high-poverty school districts that are making great strides in improving student achievement.[16] One key finding was that these districts had redefined leadership roles. They made instructional leadership the primary element of principals' work and provided significant training in leadership techniques. But most notably, the districts expanded the leadership role to include teacher leaders who provided additional instructional support to their colleagues and relieved principals of administrative instructional duties. This leadership role expansion also increased the input of teachers in the design of systemwide teaching practices. Such findings have been used by the Alliance partners to help focus their work in supporting school reform efforts. Moreover, the findings have been used to advocate for sustainable funding at the federal, state, and local levels to help create better systems of instructional supports.

The need for strong, qualified principals in every school cannot be emphasized enough. Policy makers need to promote innovative efforts to prepare and equip administrators to be more effective leaders and coaches. Ultimately, it comes down to hiring and supporting principals who will understand what it means to promote teaching quality through shared responsibilities and distributive leadership, particularly in the unique context of high-needs schools.

Attitudes Concerning Longevity

Finally, I am struck by the optimism revealed in the NEA data about teachers' plans to remain in the profession long-term and what this could mean for reducing attrition rates well into the future—the single biggest challenge to maintaining teacher quality. More teachers are planning on remaining in the profession until retirement than at any other time during the past thirty years (figure 2.24). This is encouraging, since studies show that staffing problems in schools do not result from too few teachers entering the field but, rather, from too many leaving for other jobs.[17]

By retaining high-quality instructional staff, we may also see larger pay-offs in efforts to attract and recruit new teachers to the profession. The survey data show nearly seven out of ten teachers would still have chosen this career if given the opportunity to start over, and this response has become increasingly positive since the early 1990s (figure 2.24). Other nations have learned that if they invest in teaching, they do not have to try to micromanage schools through curriculum and testing mandates. My hope is that this nation will follow their example and continue to expand our investment in the human capital needed to make our schools better than ever before—the very best in the world!

A Voice from the Classroom

I had been teaching almost ten years when Marty Gill came on as principal, just one more of a series of administrators who had come on board over the years. I didn't take much notice of him, since I had been planning my escape from the teaching profession for over a year. Teaching had become too much of the same old thing: same classes, same books, same curriculum, same squabbles over the video machine, the computer lab, the money in the budget. Worse than that, I had become the very thing I never wanted to become—mediocre.

A few days into the semester, I received a message to stop in and see Dr. Gill. Here it comes, I thought, my reputation has preceded me. At least I had the good sense to recognize my own failings before they were pointed out to me. I walked in, sat down, and steeled myself.

"I understand that you are one of our best teachers here," he said. I stared at him stupidly and almost burst out laughing. "I think you may have confused me with someone else," I said at last. "I am sure that I haven't," he replied. "What makes you say that?"

Want an honest appraisal of anything? Talk to the person with one foot out the door—in this case, me. I was bored and frustrated, I told him. I was tired of school politics. I was tired of being blown about with every wind of change without ever having any input in the direction we were going. "I am not a good teacher," I concluded. "I was a good teacher."

Today we throw around terms like "teacher burnout" as if it is some epidemic that teachers catch from the kids, their colleagues, the administration, the parent community. But most of us don't burn out; we smolder alone in our classrooms and we stay that way until the fire goes out completely or someone comes along and relights it. Marty Gill did that for me. He helped me identify what had been lost from my personal teaching equation—creativity. While some teachers crave a comfort zone, I crave change, novelty, innovation—the same things I use to spark my students' interest. *I wanted space to be creative and a voice in the educational community I belonged to.*

Marty listened to me that day without comment. But in the days and weeks that followed, he began to fan the smoking embers. He was a wonderful springboard for new thoughts and ideas, a frequent flyer in my classroom in the minutes between classes. He asked my opinion, he took an interest, he cheered me on. And as time went on, I realized that he was doing the same thing, in different ways, with other members of the faculty. Somehow it felt like we were all coming alive again. By the time a job offer materialized, I was no longer interested. I wasn't going to let that spark that had been rekindled go out; I realized that I loved what I was doing and I wasn't going to walk away from that.

I have been a teacher ever since. Even when I accepted an administrative position, I took an adjunct faculty position at a local college so I could remain a teacher. Over the years I have found that teaching not only fulfills me; it also energizes me to help others waken to their own potential. If I have made a difference in anyone's life in the last twenty years, it is because one principal took the time and interest to make a difference in mine.

—*Lynda Hacker Araoz*
   Mt. Greylock Regional School District
   Williamstown, Massachusetts

19

Teachers and Their Unions

Making Change Work

RANDI WEINGARTEN

President, American Federation of Teachers

O N A CLOUDLESS, early fall morning, just a few days into the new school year, elementary school students had just filed into classrooms at P.S. 234. The hallways were quieting after the bustle of that morning's arrivals—the usual greetings from teachers and children's goodbyes to the parents who delivered them to the door for another school day. Youngsters stowed their backpacks and prepared for their first lesson of the day.

It never started. Just before 9:00 A.M. on September 11, 2001, students at this school just a few blocks north of the World Trade Center heard the first explosion. Within a few minutes, gray smoke blew down the street.

Teachers gathered their students in the gym and cafeteria. As parents began to rush in to take their children home, the crash of a second impact could be heard, and the area became more and more like a war zone as the Twin Towers erupted in flames. By then it was impossible to gain much reliable information, so teachers organized the students for the walk to another school at a safer distance from Ground Zero. The group was still on the sidewalk—walking north, holding each other tightly, teachers ensuring that the students were safe—when the second tower collapsed.

The next morning, although the schools were closed, the teachers, like others throughout the city, made dozens of calls to students' families, checking that all were safe. As it turned out, everyone from P.S. 234—and every other school in the World Trade Center area—was unhurt. By the end of the week, teachers turned to their next concern—resuming school. For the rest of the school year and beyond, they helped their students recover from that day's shocking events and adjust to a changed world.

I tell this story not simply because of the emotional impact of 9/11 and my memories of spending that day helping students and staff in all New York City public schools get home safely.[1] The story illustrates the tender relationship between teachers and their students, a relationship that runs so much deeper than academic lessons. That tenderness and support are the real story behind American public school teachers. The profession has seen much change, and teachers and our unions continue to push for the betterment of teaching. But the goal will always be the same, even under the most adverse circumstances: to enable children to grow and learn.

I often think of the words of psychologist Lee Shulman: "[Classroom teaching] is perhaps the most complex, most challenging, and most demanding, subtle, nuanced, and frightening activity that our species has ever invented."[2] And yet, on any given school day, more than three million public school teachers are working in classrooms around the country performing this most challenging activity: guiding students to an understanding of new facts, new skills, and new ways of thinking (see figure 2.1). What emerges from the fifty years of surveys administered by the NEA is a record of the dedication of our nation's public school teachers helping children succeed through ever-shifting challenges. Teachers' devotion to working with young people and our belief in the value of education to society—the two factors most often cited as reasons for entering the classroom—are among the few constants during a half century of change (figure 2.20). Teachers have remained the everyday heroes in the lives of American children—sometimes literally, as on 9/11.

Partners for Constructive Change

As we move into the second decade of the twenty-first century, teachers and our unions will continue to lead the effort to bring innovative change to improve our public education system. All of our schools must be places that foster academic achievement and provide our children with the knowledge and skills they need to succeed in life. It is essential that we explore promising new approaches. At the same time, we must look to the evidence of what is working now and expand established, proven programs; where we see success, whether in public, private or charter schools, we should learn from it. And we must follow the lead of top-performing countries, replicating their best approaches.

Particular policies and practices may vary from one state or community to another. However, there are certain foundations for student success that form the basis for high achievement in any school or education system. These are the things that teachers will work to develop and implement.

Developing and Supporting the Best Teachers

There must be good teachers supported by good leaders. While teaching is central to better schools, it is a complex craft that requires talented, inspired professionals. But few teachers are great educators on their first day in the classroom. The key to achieving good teaching is to ensure that the infrastructure is in place to support the professional development that will help teachers hone their skills. An effective, continuous, comprehensive, and fair teacher development and evaluation system can help facilitate this process.

Educators and our unions want to partner with school districts to transform teacher evaluation from a perfunctory sorting exercise to a process whose goal is continuous professional improvement. The American Federation of Teachers (AFT) has proposed a framework for such a system, which at this writing is being implemented by more than fifty school districts and their teachers across the nation. This approach enables teachers to receive constant feedback so that we can build on what works and correct what doesn't.

One other element necessary for this approach is the involvement of good leaders. Principals, assistant principals, and other administrators responsible for instructional support can help teachers grow professionally and make sure the resources and backing are available to enable teachers to teach.

Teachers' unions will continue to take the lead in helping new and struggling teachers improve their practice. Peer assistance and review programs implemented by unions in collaboration with administrators have assisted many teachers in improving their skills and have counseled those who could not improve to leave the profession. Effective evaluation systems will render moot the issue of whether tenure protects bad teachers, as some people claim, rather than simply being the due process system that all workers deserve to ensure that they are protected against arbitrary and capricious actions.

Developing the Best Curriculum

The second foundation for student success is a great curriculum and the training and conditions that enable it to be properly implemented. Students need rich, well-rounded curricula in areas ranging from science to the arts, history to mathematics. Instruction should convey not only the content of key subjects but also help students develop higher skills, such as critical thinking, that they will need for college and career. By defining what students should be expected to know at each stage of their education, school systems can develop a well-sequenced curriculum that enables teachers and students to build on what has gone before. For teachers, a good curriculum grounded in common standards also facilitates the sharing of lesson plans and collaboration on instructional methods and best practices. This is the promise of the Common Core Standards, which nearly forty states have adopted and now must implement.

In recent years, curricula have often been distorted by the demands of standardized tests and assessments. Higher academic standards and education legislation such as No Child Left Behind (NCLB) were partly an outgrowth of progressive policies to ensure that all children have an equal opportunity to learn. But NCLB never achieved the right balance between teaching and testing or support and sanctions. One thing that the law demonstrated beyond a doubt is that what gets tested drives what gets taught. School districts throughout the nation increased classroom time for reading and mathematics—the subjects assessed under NCLB. This trend has generally meant that there is less time for science, social studies, history, the arts, and other subjects that constitute a rich curriculum. In the most recent administration of the NEA survey, the demands of teaching to the test were the second-most-cited hindrance to teachers' ability to do their best job (figure 2.23). Teachers will continue to press for education policies that restore balance to what students learn. We will be advocates for a rich curriculum that is aligned with valid assessments—and supported by appropriate instructional materials, books, supplies, and technology.

Building a Culture of Collaboration

Fifty years ago, we teachers worked alone, going into our classroom every morning and closing the door behind us. Today, we understand that this should no longer be the case. Key to reshaping our education system for student success in the twenty-first century is collaboration. Successful schools promote more teaming and collaboration among teachers, a development that should be scaled-up. When teachers look at data and talk to one another about students' development, strengths, and weaknesses, it helps improve the practice of all. Teachers have always helped one another, something that both novices and veterans appreciate, but increasingly it is understood to be a necessary part of building our profession. In recent NEA surveys, the most-cited sources of help have been cooperative and competent colleagues and mentors (figure 2.22).

And collaboration must extend beyond connections among teachers. Schools where students succeed always share this characteristic.

Their success is built on partnerships that engage all stakeholders—teachers, principals, administrators, parents, community leaders. Teachers are eager to move beyond old conflicts and join together to achieve a new vision for American public education. In this vision, our schools are places where teachers and principals work together to help children achieve extraordinary things.

Bringing in the Community

Even with a balanced and rich curriculum taught by great, committed teachers, student success is still influenced by out-of-school factors. While the 9/11 story is a drastic and singular example, students come to school every day with emotional and other concerns prompted by less-traumatic, but still important, events. Teachers must work with the whole student and deal with—and even compete with—the often numerous and serious challenges confronting the youngsters in their classrooms. This is more true than ever as the nation copes with a troubled economy that, at the end of the first decade of the twenty-first century, counted 43.6 million Americans, including more than 15 million children, living in poverty and 14.8 million workers unemployed.[3]

Studies have found that roughly two-thirds of variation in student achievement—or failure to achieve—can be attributed to out-of-school factors. Family socioeconomic status remains the most influential predictor of student achievement; others include hunger, poor health, unstable family circumstances, and community violence.[4] To combat these influences, the AFT is an outspoken advocate of community schools—which expand the services that schools offer to address these issues. Successful community schools become the focal point of their neighborhoods. At a community school students and their families can find health and dental services, early learning programs, housing and nutrition assistance, employment aid, and English language instruction, among many other services. Such in-school programs are clearly important during times of economic crisis.[5] But because they serve the most vulnerable populations, they are a foundation for student success in good and bad times.

In recognizing that community schools are a shared resource and effort, educators also understand that providing our children with the best education possible is a *shared responsibility*. Teachers cannot do it alone—we need the involvement of all stakeholders. We accept and expect accountability, but we also call for everyone with responsibility for our children's education and well-being—teachers, administrators, elected officials, parents, and students—to hold up their end of the bargain. Acceptance by the larger community of this shared responsibility is another foundation for student achievement. In successful schools, accountability is a tool, not the end goal. Our aspiration is to help all children achieve. When accountability—rather than shared responsibility—becomes the focus, practice inevitably shifts to how to do better on tests rather than how to help kids succeed.

The Path Ahead

Ninety percent of our nation's students attend public schools. Nearly fifty million American children are entrusted to our care and depend on us for the education that will prepare them for fulfilling lives.[6] We don't select them, and we don't turn any away. Teachers strive heroically every day to make a difference in our students' lives so that they will not just dream their dreams but achieve them. Children have the right to demand from society the kind of education that will enable them to do so. And the obligation to fulfill that right transcends national, state, local, and community boundaries and lines of authority. Students can't wait for us to agree on the reforms and policies that will fix the problems of our educational system. They can't put their lives on hold; they show up every day even as we continue to debate the future of their schools.

All of us—administrators, teachers, students, parents, and community—have a role to play. The new vision of public education today rejects the blame games that demonize teachers and make them the scapegoats for everything that critics perceive as wrong with America's public schools. Instead, teachers and our unions are focused on building a stronger education system that is defined by excellence, fairness, shared responsibility, and mutual trust. American public education must move beyond the industrial age model that held sway in our classrooms for most of the twentieth century. To this end, teachers also want more of a voice and have fought to be more extensively involved in school operations through participation in curriculum committees and panels addressing budgetary and personnel issues. Teachers have a unique perspective on both current education policy debates and how to implement the myriad policies and demands made on schools and individual educators. We *must* be participants in the discourse on policy and practice, because we are in the classroom every day, we see what our students need, and we do the hard work that helps our children succeed.

Teachers and their unions, if given a real voice, can help shape a new approach that will prepare our children for success in the information age. By embracing the role of change agents that we have always played for our students, teachers will reinvigorate our schools through professionalism and a commitment to the ideal that our children deserve the highest-quality education we can provide. The history of American public education sometimes reads like a catalog of school improvement strategies. Too often, one decade's perceived panacea gives way to the next sure thing, with the root problems left unresolved. It is long past the time to end that cycle.

As I stated on being elected to lead the American Federation of Teachers, the society that we serve, the institutions where we work, and the workforce that we represent are all changing at speeds we never envisioned. But teachers have always been about making change work, and that will continue to be true as we move forward in the twenty-first century.

⸎⸎⸎   A Voice from the Classroom   ⸎⸎⸎

In the early 1990s I was a fifth-grade teacher of English language learners in the Tucson (Arizona) Unified School District bilingual program (Spanish-English). Early on, I noticed that my students really didn't see a connection between their homes and communities and what they learned in school and, therefore, didn't see the value in what they were learning.

I had heard about the Funds of Knowledge for Teaching project, based at the University of Arizona, which worked with teachers of Mexican American students to maximize student learning. Norma Gonzalez, an anthropology professor, and Luis Moll, a professor of education, were training teachers as ethnographers to conduct home interviews of selected students' families. In my experience, home visits were typically to talk to the parents about either behavioral or academic problems. But these home visits would be different. The purpose was to discover the knowledge that these parents possessed that was useful to their families and their communities. For example, a father might have extensive knowledge about construction, raising animals, or repairing machinery or automobiles. A mother might know a lot about preparing certain foods, child care, or herbal remedies to keep her family healthy. We were making a paradigm shift by viewing our students as coming from households rich in social and intellectual resources rather than coming from disadvantaged homes.

Following the interviews, my colleagues and I would attend weekly afterschool meetings to discuss our experiences and develop units of study that would incorporate the knowledge we accumulated as a springboard for the students' learning. I discovered, for example, that one of my students had a coin collection; from this interest, I created learning centers based on different aspects of money—basic economies, how money is printed, the history of the dollar, converting from dollars to pesos, etc. The student whose family I interviewed became an important resource for this unit and took an active role in teaching his peers. He became much more engaged in the learning process and went from being a passive member of the class to an active participant.

Personally, the project changed the way I perceived my students and their families. Observing my students in the context of their homes helped me see the whole child and all the experiences children bring to school. The project also gave families more access to the school by making them feel that they had something to offer to the educational system. Although most of the families with whom I came into contact did not have a working knowledge of the English language, they felt empowered to come to school and participate in programs and conferences. It changed my attitude toward my students and gave me the ability to communicate more effectively and genuinely with their families.

Although I put a lot of extra time and energy into this project, I feel that what I got out of it far outweighed the extra hours that I invested. I participated in something that brought dignity and worth to the cultural practices of my students' families, motivating my students and, in turn, enriching all of our lives.

—Patricia Rendón
Roberts Elementary School (Retired)
Tucson, Arizona

Reflections and Conclusions

20

The American Public School Teacher

Past, Present, and Future

THIS VOLUME WAS CONCEIVED with the aim of developing a better understanding of how the teaching occupation has responded to the challenges of the past half century and how it can most effectively transform itself to meet the demands of the future. We began by presenting a brief overview of the history of American public education from colonial times to the present day, focusing particularly on the years since the mid-1950s, a period characterized by widespread concern about the quality of education and, more specifically, of teachers and teaching. We described how teaching has become ever more complex over this period, a trend owing much to the growing diversity and inclusiveness of our nation's schools and the influence of a powerful reform movement that has created significant obstacles and distractions for educators—in effect, undermining the achievement of many of its own most fundamental objectives. With this historical backdrop as our canvas, we invoked data from NEA teacher surveys administered over the past fifty years, supplemented by information drawn from other sources, to render a broad-stroke statistical portrait of the American public school teacher.

We then invited a distinguished group of scholars, teachers, government and business leaders, policy makers, and other education stakeholders to review the trends revealed in the survey data and offer their individual reflections, interpretations, and insights, focusing particularly on the implications of these trends for the past, present, and future of teaching. Given the wide-ranging backgrounds and experiences that these contributors brought to this task, it is not surprising that they drew different and sometimes conflicting conclusions. Some focused on demographic factors that have shaped the teaching force over the past half century, teasing out important implications for the future of the occupation and its effectiveness in raising student achievement. Others examined trends in teachers' working conditions and offered specific insights and recommendations for their improvement, again with an eye to raising quality and performance. Still others looked at the NEA data and found evidence supporting the need for better teacher education programs, higher and more centralized standards for licensure and certification, or more effective means of evaluating teachers. Finally, several contributors addressed the complex issue of professionalization, seeing the data either as confirmation that the movement to professionalize teaching is on the right path or as support for the view that current professionalization efforts may be misguided. Yet, varied as these commentaries are, there is a common thread that runs through them all. Consistent with the national focus on education quality, each—explicitly or implicitly—acknowledges the critical importance of effective teaching, and all interpret the data through that lens.

In this final section, it is our task to bring together the individual themes and arguments set forth in the commentaries to achieve a better understanding of the evolution of teaching and to help guide its future development. Our encounter with the contributing authors' distinctive interpretations of the data and their accompanying visions for the future of teaching has inevitably led us to develop our own unique perspective. Thus, we build on their collective wisdom, drawing as well on the best research evidence available, to arrive at our own insights, interpretations, and conclusions. We frame our discussion around four broad topical areas that encompass the range of themes and arguments presented in the commentaries: (1) the demographic changes shaping the teacher workforce; (2) the conditions under which teachers practice; (3) teacher training, licensure, certification, and evaluation; and (4) teacher professionalization.

Demographic Trends Shaping the Workforce

We begin with an examination of several important demographic trends that have played a critical role in shaping the teacher workforce and in influencing its quality over the past several decades. These include: the rapid escalation in the number of teachers relative to student enrollments since the mid-1980s; the growing proportions of both younger and older teachers in the nation's schools; the widening demographic disparity between a predominantly white teaching force and an increasingly diverse student body; the ongoing feminization of teaching; and the growing instability of the teacher workforce, as reflected in rising turnover rates.

The Ballooning of the Teacher Workforce

Richard Ingersoll and Lisa Merrill document a long-term pattern of growth in the number of teachers and students in America's schools that dates back to the early twentieth century. For most of this period, the teacher workforce has expanded at a rate only marginally greater than that for student enrollments. But since the mid-1980s, the number of teachers in America's schools has surged, growing at a rate approximately two and a half times that of students. Ingersoll and Merrill attribute this *ballooning* of the teacher workforce to several factors: a concurrent reduction in the average class size of regular primary-level classes; the precipitous growth of special education; a dramatic increase in the number of educators providing elementary enrichment instruction; an upsurge in the number of secondary teachers in core subject areas such as math and science; and the proliferation of programs that were once the responsibility of parents, families, and communities. Several of these underlying causes of the ballooning phenomenon reflect conscious, policy-driven responses to the increasing heterogeneity of America's public schools. For example, the rapid expansion of the special education teaching force over the past two decades is a direct consequence of the implementation of the Individuals with

Disabilities Education Act (IDEA). Because classes serving children with special needs are typically half the size of regular classes, the rate of growth for the special education workforce has been explosive— doubling in just the past two decades, according to Ingersoll and Merrill. As of the 2006–2007 school year, some seven million children, comprising nearly 12 percent of students enrolled in kindergarten through twelfth grade, received educational services as required by IDEA.[1] Class-size reduction (CSR) policies also stem, to some degree, from the growing diversity and inclusiveness of American public education. When asked to name the biggest benefit of CSR policies, a majority of new teachers—more than half at the secondary level and three-fifths at the elementary school level—say that smaller classes enable them to personalize instruction for students with different needs.[2]

The precipitous expansion of the teacher workforce over the past few decades also helps to explain the long-term decline in teacher quality that has been reported in several studies. There is evidence that the average verbal and math aptitude of new female teachers—as measured by their percentile rank on standardized tests—fell steadily between the mid-1960s and 2000 and that this trend was accompanied by a corresponding *increase* in the proportion scoring at the lower end of the test-score distribution, particularly during the 1990s when the ballooning effect was at its peak (figure 2.2). During this same period, the proportion of female educators drawn from the top decile of the test-score distribution dropped by about one-half, presumably because other career opportunities opened up to high-achieving women as labor markets became less segregated by gender.[3] Thus, as the demand for teachers grew—and top candidates increasingly pursued other opportunities—the teacher workforce began to fill its ranks with less-qualified women, at least as measured by their performance on standardized tests. There is, however, evidence that this downward trend in quality may have begun to reverse itself over the past decade, perhaps the result of state-level policies to raise teacher licensure testing requirements.[4] Unfortunately, raising cut scores on teacher tests has had other, less positive consequences, which we take up later in our discussion of licensing policies.

Two Generations of Teachers: The Bimodal Age Distribution

The rapid expansion of the teacher workforce over the past few decades has been accompanied by equally dramatic changes in the distribution of teachers by age and experience. Ingersoll and Merrill point out that the most typical age for teachers has increased from forty-one in 1987–1988 to fifty-five in 2007–2008, and the number of educators fifty years and older now stands at well above one million. But while veteran educators have aged, there has been a simultaneous influx of new, mostly younger teachers into the classroom. Susan Moore Johnson describes the profile of the current teaching force as *bimodal,* with a large cohort of older veterans at one end of the distribution, a substantial number of younger teachers at the other, and a smaller cohort separating the two extremes. As she observes, "Today's districts, schools, and teachers' unions face both the opportunities and challenges of working simultaneously with two distinct generations of teachers." Ingersoll and Merrill call attention to another important challenge related to the shifting age profile of the teaching force: though new teachers are a source of fresh ideas and energy, as more and more veteran educators retire, there will be fewer mentors available to guide and support them, a phenomenon that raises additional concerns about the quality of teaching in the immediate future.

Johnson also directs our attention to the growing number of "career switchers" among the ranks of new teachers. These midcareer entrants, having experienced varied roles and responsibilities in their former workplaces, may bring to teaching an orientation that conflicts with the undifferentiated, cellular structure of traditional schools. This new breed of educators has experienced a career change at least once already, and, as Johnson reminds us, they "could do so again if their school fails to support them in doing the meaningful work they seek." Later, we will consider how these two demographic trends—the emergence of a bimodal age distribution for teachers and the recent influx of career switchers—relate to other areas of change, especially those pertaining to the working conditions in schools.

The Racial Mismatch Between Teachers and Students

Since 1970, when the NEA began collecting survey data on teachers' race, the proportion of African Americans in the teacher workforce has remained largely unchanged, ranging between 7 and 9 percent. Renee Moore's commentary focuses on the two decades following the Supreme Court's landmark decision *Brown v. Board of Education*, which struck down legal segregation. Moore argues that discriminatory policies targeting African American teachers during that period continue to reverberate even today. She reminds us that, in the years following *Brown*, "all manner of ploys were used to remove and demote" African American teachers who had formerly taught in racially segregated schools and cites estimates that some thirty-eight thousand of these teachers were purged from the classroom during this period. Moore examines the impact of this forced exodus on subsequent generations of African American teachers and their students, weaving a poignant narrative that draws on research as well as her personal history as a minority teacher in the Mississippi Delta.

The decimation of the ranks of African American educators during the era of desegregation had lasting effects for minority educators, depriving an entire generation of novice teachers of the mentoring and support that they so desperately needed. Moore writes that, in schools with few veterans to turn to for advice, new teachers of her generation often "found themselves thrust into increasingly complex teaching situations, usually in high-needs schools in poor communities, distressingly underprepared to serve their students effectively." The impact of desegregation on minority *students* has been equally profound, according to Moore. She attributes a chronic shortage of minority teachers in the predominantly African American schools of the Mississippi Delta to the combined impact of the legacy of desegregation and state licensing policies that fail to balance teacher candidates' examination scores with other, performance-based appraisals of teaching ability. To meet their staffing needs, many of these schools rely heavily on extended substitutes and teachers from popular new programs like Teach for America, who tend to be disproportionately white. While Moore explicitly rejects the notion that African American students should be taught exclusively by teachers of their own race, she nonetheless expresses deep concern about research suggesting that white educators tend to have lower academic expectations for minority students.

The demographic mismatch between a largely white teaching force and an increasingly diverse student body is, of course, not limited to the Mississippi Delta but characteristic of schools across the United States. And while evidence does suggest that minority students assigned to teachers of the same race tend to reap an educational advantage—increasing their performance on standardized tests by as much as 2–3 percentile points—this same body of evidence suggests that white children assigned to minority teachers tend to exhibit a comparable *reduction* in achievement. Previous studies offer two broad classes of explanations for why the racial pairing of teachers and students might influence student performance. First, there are explanations based on *passive* teacher effects—that is, effects attributable to the mere presence of a same-race teacher. A minority student may, for example, develop greater self-confidence and higher aspirations when exposed to positive same-race teacher role models. Alternatively, a minority student may tend to avoid too close an association with white teachers in an effort to escape peers' charges of "acting white," and this, in turn, could adversely influence school performance.

A second set of explanations for the achievement advantage associated with the racial pairing of teachers and students rely more on *active* teacher effects resulting from specific teacher attitudes and behaviors that may be associated with race.[5] The tendency for teachers generally, and white teachers in particular, to hold lower achievement expectations for disadvantaged minority students—observed by Jay Mathews and Renee Moore, respectively—would fall into this class, as would the tendency for teachers to devote more instructional time to same-race students. Effects attributable to shared background and cultural bridges that might facilitate learning would also fall into this class of explanations. However, it is important to recognize that even teachers of color are not immune to finding themselves "culturally suspect and challenged" by their racially and/or ethnically matched students.[6] Case studies of novice minority teachers in diverse school environments suggest that "cultural resources need to be developed . . . not assumed."[7]

We actually know very little about the social-psychological dynamic underlying the effect of same-race pairings on student achievement. Yet determining the relative primacy of passive and active effects—and the precise mechanisms through which their influence on student performance is channeled—is a critical antecedent to the development of appropriate policies, recruitment strategies, and training programs. On the one hand, if research were to determine that passive role model effects are dominant in explaining the minority student achievement gains associated with racial pairing, such information could be brought to bear on campaigns aimed at recruiting more minorities to teaching. On the other hand, if active effects were determined to be dominant— and specific, associated teacher behaviors could be identified—that could have tremendous implications for the redesign of teacher training and development programs.[8] Jay Mathews underscores the urgent need for professional development that emphasizes "high standards and high expectations" and "offers concrete strategies for engaging less-advantaged learners." Unfortunately, although models for providing such training exist, research demonstrating their effectiveness in improving student outcomes is all but nonexistent.[9] And yet, according to the most recent NEA survey data, nearly half of all teachers express a need for development in working with diverse classrooms (table 2.2). We cannot change the racial composition of the teacher workforce overnight, but a better understanding of the mechanisms that drive the student performance advantage associated with the active effects of same-race pairings could be instrumental in making *all* teachers more effective in the classroom, regardless of race.

The Increasing Feminization of Teaching

Richard Ingersoll and Lisa Merrill observe that, since the early 1980s, the proportion of females in the teacher workforce has increased steadily—from about two-thirds to approximately three-quarters today. Interestingly, the trend toward increasing feminization of teaching does not result from a corresponding reduction in the rate at which men are choosing teaching as a career; their numbers have also increased substantially, by about 26 percent since the late 1980s. But during this period the number of female educators has increased at more than twice that rate. Ingersoll and Merrill attribute this trend to several factors: (1) more women are taking teaching positions in secondary schools, traditionally a male-dominated domain; (2) the proportion of women entering the workforce overall has increased dramatically, and, though other opportunities are available to them, a significant fraction continue to choose teaching as a career; and (3) with its long summer, winter, and spring breaks, teaching remains a more manageable career than most, especially for mothers of young children who may need to balance the responsibilities of family and career.

Regardless of the causes underlying the increasing feminization of teaching, it is a trend with potentially wide-ranging implications. Ingersoll and Merrill point to the lower compensation and status traditionally associated with female-dominated occupations and express concern about how increasing feminization may affect "the stature and status of teaching," which, in turn, could indirectly influence quality. But the feminization trend might also have more *direct* implications for the quality of teaching, especially as it relates to the educational performance of boys. Boys drop out of school at a higher rate than girls, are more likely to repeat a grade, and receive significantly lower GPAs than their female classmates. And while girls tend to receive slightly lower scores than boys on standardized tests of math and science, boys score *substantially* lower than girls on tests of reading achievement—a gap that is equivalent to about one and a half years of schooling, almost half the size of the corresponding differential between black and white students.[10]

The issues surrounding the effects of matching students and teachers by gender are essentially the same as those pertaining to racial matching. Studies typically report that same-gender pairings are associated with significantly higher student performance on standardized tests, although the effect tends to be subject specific.[11] Boys perform at a significantly higher level in reading when instructed by a male teacher; girls perform better in math and science when assigned to a female teacher. Unfortunately, as with racial matching, positive effects for one gender are associated with negative effects for the other: the matching phenomenon is, it seems, a zero-sum game. Again, following the discussion of racial matching, the underlying dynamic may be either passive or active, and there is little understanding as to which mechanism predominates. If male teachers inspire higher achievement in boys through a strictly passive process—for example, serving as role models or bringing more order to classrooms by their mere presence— the recruitment of more male teachers would likely prove to be the most effective strategy for reducing the gender gap in reading, albeit at the expense of girls' achievement. More than 80 percent of English teachers in grades six, seven, and eight are female. If male-oriented recruitment strategies brought the proportion of male English teachers up to about one-half, it is estimated that the gender gap in reading among eighth graders would be reduced by approximately one-third.[12] However, if research were to determine that the achievement gains associated with same-gender pairing are owing largely to *active* effects—and were able to successfully link these effects to specific teacher behaviors—it should be possible to develop teacher training and professional development programs that would provide teachers of both genders with the tools to raise academic performance for all students across all subjects.

The Growing Instability of the Teacher Workforce

Ingersoll and Merrill report that the teacher workforce became less stable between the early 1990s and the mid-2000s, as reflected in annual turnover rates. They cite evidence that teacher turnover during this period increased by 28 percent—from about 13 percent to roughly 17 percent—and even faster for first-year teachers and minorities. More troubling, however, is their finding that about 45 percent of all teacher turnover occurred in "just one-quarter of public schools and that high-poverty, high-minority, and urban public schools have among the highest rates." More recent data suggest that turnover rates have begun to recede somewhat from their 2004–2005 highs but still remain elevated as compared with those for the previous decade.[13]

The long-term trend of increasing instability of the teaching force could potentially influence the quality of teachers and practice in several ways. First, schools with high turnover may be more likely to have less-experienced teachers who, on average, tend to be less effective.[14] Second, it is more difficult to develop and sustain coherent educational programs and professional learning communities in such schools, which in turn may adversely influence the quality of instruction. Third, the costs in time and effort required to continuously recruit and train replacements divert funds from other educational programs and initiatives that could positively influence the quality of instruction. The cost of replacing public school teachers who either leave teaching altogether or transfer to other schools is estimated to be nearly $5 billion annually.[15]

In a more direct sense, whether turnover positively or negatively influences the quality of teaching depends on the effectiveness of those who leave schools and those who remain behind. A number of studies indicate that teachers with stronger, more marketable qualifications leave teaching at a higher rate than their less qualified colleagues.[16] Further, it is well established that, when educators with stronger credentials move from one school to another, they tend to leave poor, high-minority, low-performing schools for those serving higher-income, higher-achieving, nonminority students.[17] But observable credentials, such as certification or advanced degrees, tend to be only weakly related to teachers' effectiveness in the classroom. More relevant are several investigations comparing the relative educational effectiveness of "movers" and "stayers" based on value-added test-score data.[18] These studies find that teachers leaving schools are typically less effective than those who remain behind, and, among those leaving lower-performing schools,[19] the more effective teachers "tend to transfer to higher-achieving schools, while those less effective move to other lower-performing schools." This sorting process leads inevitably to inequities in the distribution of human capital across schools, which, in turn, exacerbates existing achievement gaps. There is an obvious and critical need for policies and interventions that can effectively reverse this trend.

Until recently, it was unclear whether the elevated rate of teacher mobility out of schools with higher proportions of poor, minority, and low-achieving students was driven more by educators' aversion to teaching students with these characteristics or their desire to avoid the adverse working conditions that are typically found in schools serving such populations. However, according to new evidence based on a methodology that effectively disentangles student demographics from other characteristics of schools, teachers identify *working conditions*— especially, school facilities, administrative support, class size, and salaries—as significantly more important than student characteristics in determining their valuation of schools.[20] This is consistent with the conclusions reached by several contributors to this volume, including Dennis Van Roekel and Dan Brown. Van Roekel argues that good working conditions are critical for the stability of schools, and Brown cites NEA data showing that, when teachers plan to leave the classroom prior to retirement, it is most often due to stress-related factors, such as poor working conditions and low pay, and only rarely for student-related reasons. This has important policy implications, as it suggests that teacher turnover in schools serving high proportions of poor and minority students can be reduced significantly by improving working conditions and, perhaps, by providing incentives for teaching in these schools. But even in schools with better working conditions, student characteristics continue to influence teacher turnover to some degree. And since white educators are more likely to leave schools with high minority enrollments than their minority colleagues, recruiting more teachers of color may be an effective strategy for reducing turnover in these schools.[21]

Changing Working Conditions

Evidence suggesting that the school environment plays a pivotal role in teacher mobility—and therefore, in the equitable distribution of teachers across schools—underscores the importance of school working conditions. As the complexity of teaching has grown over the past several decades, the circumstances and supports that enable educators to do their most effective work have changed as well. Some of the most significant transformations have been in the context of practice: the increasing importance of learning communities, the opportunities for career advancement and role diversification, and the effect of the technology explosion on teaching and administrative responsibilities.

Other long-standing issues—teacher compensation and the role of labor unions—are also being reevaluated in response to the changing work environment.

From Egg Crates to Professional Learning Communities

Historically, teachers have practiced in relative isolation from one another. Many attribute this to the cellular, or "egg crate," organizational structure of schools as well as the deeply rooted norms of privacy and noninterference that have long characterized teachers' professional relationships.[22] Yet over the past two decades, there have been signs that the culture of isolation in schools may be beginning to give way to a greater sense of community and collaboration. There seem to be two reasons behind this emerging trend. First, innovations in the organizational structure of schools—for example, the introduction of thematic courses that cut across disciplines, team-teaching arrangements, and school site councils—have provided more opportunities for interaction and collaboration among teachers. Second, educators themselves have changed their thinking about professional relationships. NEA survey data show that, since the mid-1980s, teachers have increasingly come to identify cooperative, competent colleagues as essential to the performance of their job (figure 2.22). Susan Moore Johnson argues that this cultural change is driven largely by an influx of new teachers who tend to favor interdependence and teamwork over independence and autonomy.

If the transformation of the nation's schools from their egg crate origins to fully developed communities of practice proves successful, it will mean a fundamental shift in how the education workplace is organized and how teachers relate to their colleagues and their jobs. A change of this magnitude would likely have far-reaching consequences—not only for teachers and teaching but for student learning as well. Research suggests that schools that have been successful in nurturing professional learning communities adapt to change more positively, provide fertile ground for the cultivation of teacher leadership, develop practices that engage students in challenging academic work, and embrace an ethos of collective responsibility for student learning.[23] As Randi Weingarten observes, "When teachers look at data and talk to one another about students' development, strengths, and weaknesses, it helps improve the practice of all." But even the strongest advocates caution that, to be effective in raising student achievement, learning communities must be open to new ideas, materials, and assistance from external sources and guard against the temptation to merely validate existing practice.[24]

Although the work environment of many schools is becoming increasingly collaborative, Andrew Rotherham points out that the proportion of educators citing colleagues as key to the performance of their job—less than one-third, according to NEA data (figure 2.22)— is "hardly what one would expect in a professional workplace" and unlikely to sustain professional communities of practice on a larger scale. There seem to be two principal barriers to greater collaboration among teachers and, ultimately, to the development of strong learning communities in schools. First, as Johnson observes, contemporary schools face the challenge of working simultaneously with two distinct generations of teachers, and, when it comes to collaborative work, the two generations' expectations differ substantially. While new teachers acknowledge their interdependence with colleagues and embrace teamwork, veteran teachers—many of whom are approaching retirement—have grown accustomed to working independently and are not eager to adopt a new model of practice. Second, although teachers have seen a modest increase in noninstructional preparation time that could be devoted to collaborative work, Rotherham is right in asserting that this is "negligible" in light of "the more complicated and growing demands on teachers."

Writing from a teacher's perspective, Barbara Stoflet offers an innovative proposal to harness the summer months in support of learning communities, using summer school as a kind of "lab setting." But ultimately, for such a program to be successful, more time for collaboration will be needed during the regular school year as well. NEA survey data show that America's educators spend an average of thirty hours each week in the classroom, as compared with just twenty-one hours per week for teachers in other industrialized countries (figure 2.17). But only two-thirds of these thirty hours are devoted to instruction related to core academic subjects; the remainder is consumed by administrative tasks, fund-raising, assemblies, and the like.[25] Obviously, schools will need to reallocate and prioritize existing time to provide more opportunities for collaborative work if professional learning communities are to take root and flourish in the nation's schools.

Role Diversification in Teaching

Several contributors to this volume share a common vision for greater role diversification and expanded career opportunities for educators, including new leadership roles. Susan Moore Johnson observes that "teachers have the same responsibilities on the first and last days of their career" and further notes that, while most veterans have been content to confine their influence to the classroom, new teachers tend to place substantial value on opportunities to explore diversified roles. Similarly, Dennis Van Roekel cites evidence that teachers with "insufficient room to grow" can become disheartened and suggests that they be afforded the opportunity to "take on more responsibilities." In this same vein, Arne Duncan comments on the growing number of educators who are "dissatisfied with [their] unchanging duties and static career prospects," positing a vision for the future in which talented professionals need not choose between "a love of teaching and career advancement." But Johnson reminds us that diversified roles—especially new leadership roles—can be difficult to implement and often meet "resistance in schools with a strong veteran cohort for whom norms of egalitarianism, autonomy, and seniority still hold sway."

Both Johnson and Van Roekel call attention to the potential for teachers to explore new roles in peer assistance and review (PAR) programs, in which consulting practitioners spend time away from the classroom supporting and assessing new and experienced teachers. These programs provide opportunities for educators to assume differentiated roles as consulting mentors, instructional coaches, and, in some instances, evaluators. Although they have been slow to catch on, PARs have been embraced by teachers in a number of districts, including Toledo, Cincinnati, and Columbus, Ohio, and Rochester, New York. Johnson attributes much of their success to the fact that the position of consulting teacher is "clearly defined, competitively selected, and well supported," while Van Roekel emphasizes the importance of implementing such programs through partnerships between districts and teachers' unions. These two contributors identify and support a broad range of other potential leadership roles for educators in addition to those associated with PARs. For example, Van Roekel promotes various opportunities for teachers to provide support to colleagues, relieve principals of administrative instructional duties, and perform a host of other noninstructional functions, while Johnson sees promise in tiered career structures (although she acknowledges that filling these positions in a way that circumvents charges of favoritism and politics remains a challenge).

Duncan sees other opportunities for the diversification of teaching. He foresees a future in which "teachers are undisputed leaders" in their schools and communities and envisions various roles for educators in school decision making and governance, ranging from serving on school-site councils to filling leadership positions in partnership-based or teacher-run schools. While there are few examples of the latter, public education has a long history of experimentation with school-based management (SBM), and, though some critics dismiss it as a reform that has run its course, efforts to reinvent SBM hold great promise. Traditional models of SBM implemented during the 1990s suffered from a lack of focus on achievement; stakeholder resistance and institutional barriers to implementation; limits on the scope of schools' authority; concentration of authority in the hands of school administrators; and deficiencies in crucial resources, especially information and knowledge. But if site-managed schools had more control over budget, staffing, and instructional programs; if decision-making authority were redistributed at the school level to include the *meaningful* participation of teachers, parents, and other community stakeholders; and if the knowledge base for effective teaching were expanded beyond its current state, the potential of SBM to provide new leadership roles for teachers—*and* improve school performance—could be substantial. One especially promising approach to revitalizing SBM—called *school-based improvement*—incorporates all of these critical elements.[26]

Duncan's vision for the diversification of teaching extends well beyond educators' involvement in school-based decision making. He imagines a future replete with opportunities for teachers to engage in challenging work experiences beyond the classroom—for example, serving as subject matter experts, conducting research, or participating in externships in local industries related to their disciplines—but he also stresses the importance of "scheduled blocks of nonteaching time" to accommodate these expanded roles. Again, as discussed in relation to the development of professional learning communities, the transformation of teaching will require a major reallocation and prioritization of teachers' time.

Technology and Teaching

Among the many changes to teachers' working conditions over the past several decades, few can compare in significance with that of the expanding presence of modern technology in America's public schools. Mainframe computers were not uncommon in school systems as early as the 1960s, but their use was confined largely to administrative support functions. Not until the advent of desktop computing in the 1980s did technology come to play a more significant role in instruction. With the development of the Internet in the 1990s, more and more educators began to see computers as integral to the educational process and advocated for greater access. Fueled by the federal E-Rate program—which provided subsidies for technology infrastructure in public schools—by the late 1990s computers with Internet access became the new standard for technological sufficiency.[27] Between 1996 and 2000 the proportion of classrooms in the nation's public schools with Internet access mushroomed—from 14 to 77 percent.[28] Today nearly all classrooms (97 percent) have one or more computers, and only a small proportion of those machines lack broadband access.[29] But as Michael Dell cautions, "Computers on their own, absent the right training, curriculum, and measurement, won't make a difference . . . it's what people—teachers and administrators—do with technology that has the power to transform lives." In their respective commentaries, Dell and other contributors divide their attention among four key areas in which technology can potentially support public education. These include support for administration, communication, instructional management, and learning.

ADMINISTRATION

Dell sees an important role for technology in providing administrators and teachers with tools that can assist them in identifying trends in attendance, test scores, and other data related to students' progress, facilitating real-time interventions. In addition, he advocates the use of "online dashboards and Internet-based applications" to help guide administrators' decisions concerning "where to invest funding and boost teaching resources." By way of illustration, he points to a Chicago school that successfully increased its on-time graduation rate by 10 percent after implementing just such a system. Meanwhile, Jason Gipson-Nahman offers the perspective of a classroom teacher, commenting on the value of technology in calculating and reporting grades for the 150 students enrolled in his classes as well as for other time-saving functions. He emphasizes that "less time spent on calculating grades . . . means that there is more time for teachers to spend developing lessons and reflecting on their practice." Of course, the administrative support that technology provides to educators is not limited to schools. It also has been critical in transforming central office operations. To cite just one notable example, it is because of the development of sophisticated computerized databases linking information on schools, teachers, and students that new accountability systems based on "value-added" analysis of student test-score data are possible today. For good or for ill, this innovation has been instrumental in changing the face of public education and seems destined to play an important role in teachers' lives well into the foreseeable future.

COMMUNICATION

Technology can also play a key role in fostering better communication among teachers, administrators, parents, and students. Dell focuses our attention on how technology can serve as a catalyst for the development of online communities in which teachers can "share their challenges and collaborate with other educators." From his perspective as a teacher, Gipson-Nahman acknowledges the time-saving virtues of communicating with colleagues, students, and parents by e-mail. But these technological advances in communication are not without potential pitfalls. Another teacher, Barbara Stoflet, comments on the growing inability of students to distinguish between collaboration and cheating when information can be freely accessed and shared online with little oversight. And while increased use of technology for communications has its obvious advantages—such as the ability to share documents instantaneously—it can also lead to inequities. Internet access is now nearly universally available in schools, but across households there is still substantial variability in access according to family income. Today, just one-third of households with incomes of less than $25,000 per year have Internet access, compared with more than 85 percent of those with annual incomes above $100,000.[30] Given this reality, it is not surprising that a recent study of the use of educational technology in schools finds teachers in more affluent schools to be nearly twice as likely as their counterparts in high-poverty schools to use e-mail to share information or address concerns with parents.[31] We have a long way to go before we achieve Arne Duncan's vision of "equitable broadband connectivity." While some of this imbalance in communication may be made up through phone calls or parent-teacher meetings, it remains an area of concern for those seeking to narrow the achievement gaps across socioeconomic groups.

INSTRUCTIONAL MANAGEMENT

In light of the increasing diversity in America's classrooms, today, more than ever, teachers need tools that can help them track student progress, individualize lesson plans, and manage instruction. Dell cites evidence from the most recent NEA survey showing that 45 percent of educators want to better understand how to utilize data in their decision-making processes. He asks us to imagine a classroom in which the teacher has access to "a comprehensive history of students' educational careers—how they performed in previous years, what subjects they excelled in or struggled with, how often they missed school." In his view, the instant availability of such data, combined with applications that can organize it into actionable information, would give teachers "the power to tailor education for every student." In fact, the Michael & Susan Dell Foundation recently worked with the New York City Department of Education to implement just such a system, the Achievement Reporting and Innovation System (ARIS).

Technology can also help teachers manage instruction through the creation of virtual learning communities in which information may be shared inside and outside the classroom. But the success of such programs requires careful planning. Gipson-Nahman recounts his experience at a high school where every student is issued a laptop computer on enrollment. Initially, universal access to technology created a distraction, and he found that teachers spent "inordinate amounts of time trying to keep students on task." His account is consistent with evidence showing that broadening student access to home computers or home Internet service tends to drive down academic performance and widen racial and socioeconomic achievement gaps (researchers speculate that this may be due to the lack of effective monitoring of computer use in the homes of less-advantaged students).[32] Not until Gipson-Nahman's district implemented tools designed to effectively manage students' use of the technology did the universal access program begin to realize its potential. Of course, few schools are able to offer computers to every student; nationally, less than 5 percent of schools have such programs.[33] Before the nation's public schools spend the estimated $9 billion dollars annually that it would take to equip all secondary students with computers for school and home use,[34] it would seem prudent to undertake a rigorous research program to determine the potential of filtering systems—such as the one implemented by Gipson-Nahman's district—to focus the use of technology on learning and mitigate the apparent adverse effects of students' unfettered access to home computing.

LEARNING

It is ironic that, while technology seems to have the potential to transform working conditions in schools by supporting administrative functions, facilitating communication, and improving teachers' ability to manage instruction, its direct role in fostering student learning is less certain. Arne Duncan suggests a range of possibilities for instructional technology, "from customized lesson 'playlists' that respond to an individual student's demonstrated competencies, skills gaps, and learning preferences . . . to tools that help disadvantaged learners or learners with special needs to excel." Yet there have been few rigorous evaluations of the impact of instructional technology on student achievement, and thus far findings have been mixed.[35] Indeed, there is some evidence suggesting that when instructional technology is used for drill and practice rather than as an integral part of a curriculum geared toward the development of higher-level thinking skills, it can actually have a substantial negative impact on learning.[36] This is particularly distressing in light of NCLB's mandate for testing and accountability, which has had the effect of shifting much of the use of instructional technologies from experimental endeavors aimed at improving critical analysis and higher-level skills to routine practice aimed at bolstering students' test-taking ability.[37] Dell's admonishment rings true: technology alone will not make a difference; it's what people do with technology that has the power to transform lives. At this point, however, not only do we have little concrete information concerning the effective uses of specific instructional technologies, but, according to NEA data, half of the nation's teachers express a need for training to improve their ability to integrate technology into classroom instruction (table 2.2). Dedicated staff, like the technology integration specialists at the high school Gipson-Nahman describes, can provide major help to educators seeking to enhance their practice through technological applications; nationwide, however, fewer than one in three schools provide that level of support.[38] Clearly, there is a need for greater technical assistance and professional development in this important area.

Teacher Compensation

Earlier in this chapter, we called attention to evidence of a long-term decline in teacher quality between the mid-1960s and 2000 and speculated that two factors—the dismantling of gender barriers to labor market participation at the beginning of this period and the ballooning of the teacher workforce over the past few decades—may have influenced this trend. A third factor that has almost certainly contributed to the erosion of teacher quality during these years is the steady decline, over roughly the same time span, in teachers' pay relative to that of other college graduates. Class-size reduction (CSR) policies have played a significant role in this downward slide. Faced with an increasingly diverse student population and greater within-class heterogeneity in achievement levels, the need to provide more individualized attention to students of different backgrounds was a major force driving class size reduction. As more funds were allocated for hiring new teachers to reduce class sizes, fewer funds were available to sustain teacher salaries at competitive levels. This apparent trade-off between CSR policies and decisions concerning teacher compensation is not unique to the United States: a 2004 analysis of educational policies in several member countries of the Organisation for Economic Co-operation and Development (OECD) found that those with relatively high statutory teacher salaries (such as Japan, England, and Ireland) also tend to have relatively high student-teacher ratios, while those with relatively low average teacher salaries (such as Sweden, Finland, and Greece) tend to have correspondingly low student-teacher ratios.[39]

But regardless of the forces at play in determining teacher salaries, their relative decline over the past half century is an indisputable fact. A report from the Economic Policy Institute shows that between 1960 and 2000 the "pay gap between female public school teachers and comparably educated women . . . grew by nearly 28 percentage points, from a relative wage *advantage* of 14.7 percent in 1960 to a pay *disadvantage* of 13.2 percent in 2000." Moreover, the report finds that in the years immediately following 2000—a period when *all* college graduates' wages began to stagnate—teachers were hit harder than most, widening the gap even more.[40] As a result, a growing proportion of public school teachers (currently about half, according to NEA data) have found it necessary to earn extra income during the school year by taking school-related and non-school-related jobs, often diverting time and attention away from their principal task—educating America's youth (figure 2.27).

According to a widely accepted model of occupational choice from the field of labor economics, people weigh the expected costs and benefits of alternative career paths and choose that occupation offering the highest net benefit based on their own particular values and circumstances.[41] Consequently, one would expect an increase in teacher salaries to enhance the relative attractiveness of teaching and increase the probability that more highly skilled individuals would choose it as a career. But NEA survey data show that teachers are principally motivated by the *non*monetary rewards of teaching, such as the opportunity to work with young people and contribute to society. Just 3 percent of respondents to the most recent NEA survey cited money as the reason they chose to teach.[42] So what evidence is there that higher salaries would actually attract a higher-quality teaching force? In part, the answer depends on how one measures *quality*. One study using teacher licensure scores as a proxy for quality finds evidence of only a weak relationship between level of teacher pay and teacher quality.[43] But other studies that measure quality in terms of teachers' subject matter expertise, selectivity of undergraduate institution, and cognitive ability have shown stronger effects.[44] For example, one researcher concludes that raising average teacher salaries by about 10 percent would increase teachers' average SAT scores by as much as ten points.[45]

In light of such findings, why have policy makers allowed teacher pay to lag so severely behind that of other occupations, placing the quality of the nation's educational system—and economy—at risk? That was precisely the question that James Hunt Jr. decided to address in his fourth gubernatorial campaign in North Carolina after learning that his state ranked forty-third in the nation in teacher pay. Hunt's description of the efforts he undertook to ensure passage of North Carolina's Excellent Schools Act is testimony to the uphill challenge that politicians, policy makers, educators, and others face in reversing the decline in teacher pay relative to that of other occupations. He recounts the skepticism that he encountered from parents, business leaders, and others along the way, including suggestions that the teachers' union was supporting the legislation for selfish reasons, student test scores were too low, and existing tenure laws made it impossible to get rid of bad teachers. Hunt's objective was to raise North Carolina teachers' pay to the national average, and he attributes his success in that endeavor to "tying those higher salaries to higher standards at every significant step on a teacher's career continuum." Meeting with the public, legislators (Democratic and Republican), business leaders, and representatives of the North Carolina Association of Educators, the North Carolina School Boards Association, and the North Carolina

Association of School Administrators, Hunt fashioned legislation that linked salary increments to the attainment of a master's degree and National Board for Professional Teaching Standards certification, provided paid mentors to guide new teachers, and reworked the state's Fair Employment and Dismissal Act to streamline the process for dismissing incompetent teachers. At every step in the process, Hunt reports that "the key to winning . . . support was the focus on standards."

Eric Hanushek approaches this same question from an entirely different perspective. As an economist, he argues that the "alignment of salaries and productivity of individuals is a natural outgrowth of a competitive economy," resulting in an overall pattern of relative salaries that makes sense to most people. But according to Hanushek, teacher labor markets differ from those for private industries in two important respects. First, salaries are typically determined by collective bargaining between teachers' unions and local school districts (and school districts will not "go out of business" if they negotiate the wrong amount). Second, as public organizations, schools are subject to political forces, and school quality goals depend on government decision making. Thus, teacher salary decisions are partially buffered from the economic forces that underlie salary determination in private, competitive industries. Hanushek argues that the resulting structure of teacher pay—based on the single-salary schedule—tends to "underpay effective teachers while overpaying their ineffective peers," turning policy makers away from any substantial increases in teacher salaries. He considers a number of alternative policy options for raising teacher pay but eliminates all but one because, in his view, they provide no assurances of improved achievement commensurate with expenditures. For example, he considers those policies—like North Carolina's Excellent Schools Act—that "broaden pay from the traditional experience and degree matrix to include details of a teacher's preparation, professional development, and other objective measures" but rejects them because the characteristics typically used to set differentiated salaries "have not been reliably validated against classroom effectiveness."

Hanushek sees the principal obstacle to public support for a substantial teacher pay raise as the insistence of some "that ineffective teachers be paid the same as effective teachers." Thus he offers a "compromise position": removing that "small portion of current teachers" (regardless of their tenure status) who cause "real damage" in exchange for substantially higher pay for the remaining effective teachers. While Hanushek doesn't specify the precise method for judging which teachers should be removed and which should remain, his commentary suggests that value-added test-score performance data would play a significant role in such decisions. Elsewhere, Hanushek estimates that the deselection of the bottom 6 to 10 percent of teachers would boost American students' ranking on international tests from the bottom third of industrialized nations to a position close to the top. He further argues that, since improving student performance would positively impact future U.S. productivity, this reform would pay for itself in relatively few years.[46]

But what are the broader implications of this proposal? First, to realize enduring gains from a teacher deselection policy, the least effective educators would have to be eliminated from the distribution of teachers on an ongoing basis, not at just one point in time. Second, if value-added effectiveness data were to be utilized in the process, each cohort of replacement teachers—including those least effective among them—would have to remain in the classroom for at least three years in order to obtain anything like reliable estimates, and, even then, the inherent flaws of the narrow test-score data on which such estimates are based would limit their validity as measures of teacher quality. Third, focusing on teachers' ability to raise students' standardized test scores, rather than on standards of effective practice, precludes the option of intervening with those educators who prove to be less effective but still above the bottom 6–10 percent. Admittedly, current approaches to raising teacher performance—induction programs, mentoring, professional development, and the like—have not yielded encouraging results, but that makes it all the more important for educators, researchers, and policy makers to concentrate their efforts in those areas rather than abandon them for the revolving-door approach of deselection. Hanushek himself acknowledges that "it would probably be superior . . . to develop systems that upgrade the overall effectiveness of teachers" but has seemingly lost faith in the ability of the education community to develop such systems.[47] Later in this chapter we will offer our suggestions for how this might be accomplished.

Brad Jupp's commentary rounds out this discussion, advocating a position somewhere between those of Hunt and Hanushek. Drawing on NEA survey data, Jupp argues that the reasons teachers "choose teaching as a career, why they stay on the job, and why they leave . . . are complicated, and the subtleties are too often obscured by the overheated debate about the role of financial incentives in teaching." Although he finds evidence that teachers are drawn to the occupation less by money than by "powerful causes and strongly held ideals," he cites other evidence suggesting that the accumulating value of pensions may influence some to remain in the classroom simply because "they have too much invested," while low salaries may drive others "out the door." Furthermore, he interprets the steady growth in the proportion of teachers with master's degrees over the past half century as evidence that educators are receptive to monetary incentives, noting that this trend is likely attributable, at least in part, to the opportunity for salary advancement associated with the attainment of a higher degree. Jupp draws on his prior experience as a negotiator for the Denver Classroom Teachers Association to corroborate his argument, pointing to annual member surveys showing that "more than 35 percent wanted some portion of their pay based on student results, . . . more than half liked the idea of incentives for working in hard-to-staff subjects, and more than two-thirds supported the idea of incentives for working in hard-to-serve schools." Given these findings, Jupp envisions an "explosion of effort" over the next decade to reinvent the way educators are paid and foresees a future in which well-designed pay systems will align monetary and nonmonetary incentives with teachers' success in the classroom (measured in part by how much students learn) and their service to the community and profession. The fundamental issue that remains to be addressed, however, is how school systems will measure student learning and whether such measures will add value to the educational process or subvert that process by diverting attention away from higher-level learning objectives.

The Two Faces of Teachers' Unions

Teachers' unions have long operated under the industrial model of labor-management relations, and, while the adversarial approach to negotiations has given way somewhat in recent years to interest-based bargaining, the scope of negotiations remains focused largely on issues of pay, benefits, working conditions, and job security. Yet Arne Duncan suggests that as teachers become more involved in school-based decision making and begin to assume more diversified roles, "we may be approaching the end of the era of labor-management antagonism and entering a new age of cooperation" in which labor and management share "ownership of the mission and success of public schools, including accepting shared responsibility for improving student learning and closing the achievement gap." He imagines "reinvigorated twenty-first-century unions" that embrace "teaching as a differentiated profession" with a new approach to "the way they represent teachers, the way they conduct business with districts, and the wider opportunities they afford for teachers and administrators to work as partners." The implications of Duncan's vision for the future of unionism are sweeping. Changes might include the reevaluation of the criteria for selecting union staff and school-based representatives, the manner in which budgets are allocated and managed, the way contracts are structured and negotiated (including more flexible options like "living" contracts and school-based compacts), and such traditional elements of compensation as seniority and single-salary schedules, allowing for "a greater recognition of differing levels of skill, experience, and professional goals."

Susan Moore Johnson frames the issues confronting the nation's teachers' unions somewhat differently, focusing more on the generational divide apparent in educators' views of the organizations that represent them. According to Johnson, the two generations of teachers in schools today have "conflicting beliefs, needs, and priorities when it comes to their relationship with unions." Veteran educators "expect their unions to support traditional approaches to pay and autonomy in the classroom," while new teachers "want the unions to provide ongoing training, pursue innovations in pay, create opportunities for differentiated roles, and refuse to defend underperforming teachers from dismissal." Although the NEA data do not deal specifically with these issues, other teacher surveys lend support to Johnson's characterization of the two generations that currently populate both schools and unions. For example, one national study finds that new teachers (those with less than five years' experience) tend to be more receptive than their veteran colleagues (those with more than twenty years' experience) to alternative certification, teacher-run schools, pay-for-performance systems of compensation, and financial incentives for teachers working in low-performing schools or specializing in hard-to-fill subjects.[48] Yet, as Johnson observes, unions must rely on their older members to carry out union work, since new teachers tend to be less engaged.[49]Although, as Johnson suggests, some union presidents may "intensely recruit new members and supplement the traditional bargaining agenda with reform initiatives," veteran members still tend to control the agenda and set organizational priorities. As a result, new members are less likely than their veteran counterparts to feel that their union represents their own values and preferences and less likely to see the union as "absolutely essential."[50]

It is understandable that unions would tend to orient themselves more toward the values and preferences of the veteran cohort of teachers that has provided the most support for their activities and shouldered a disproportionate share of the work. But there is another factor at play that may not be fully appreciated by union leaders, especially those at the helm of state and local affiliates of the NEA. Although both the NEA and American Federation of Teachers (AFT) have been successful in growing their membership over the past few decades, the NEA has actually *lost* substantial market share during this period— slipping from 71 percent of all public school teachers in 1980 to just 62 percent in 2005 (figure 2.3). These seemingly counterintuitive trends— membership gains coupled with market share losses—are largely a function of the ballooning trend discussed earlier. In other words, although NEA's slice of the pie became progressively smaller, the pie itself expanded at such a precipitous rate that the net result was continuous gains in membership—until recently, that is, when membership gains finally plateaued and, for the first time in decades, began to nudge downward. The NEA has, in a very real sense, been buffered from the reality of its declining market share over the past several decades because of the rapid expansion of the teaching force during this same period. Meanwhile, membership among new teachers (those with one to nine years' experience) in either of the two major unions has dropped from 77 percent in 1980 to just 59 percent in 2005, a rate of decline that is *44 percent greater* than that for teachers with ten or more years' experience—and this at a time when veteran teacher retirements are nearing their peak.[51] The implications of these trends should be obvious. If teachers' unions are going to maintain their current membership levels, political clout, and influence over local, state, and national issues, they must broaden their perspective to be more inclusive of the values and preferences of new teachers. This might mean, for example, incorporating more reform initiatives in the traditional collective bargaining agenda, actively promoting the development of professional learning communities in partnership with local districts, and advocating for expanded leadership roles for teachers.

Some might argue that any attempt to redefine the union agenda to better reflect the values and preferences of new teachers would be misguided because, as educators gain more experience, they tend to adopt the more traditional outlook of their veteran peers anyway. Unfortunately, it is impossible to test this hypothesis directly, as there is no source of longitudinal data on teachers that would allow researchers to monitor how their attitudes toward unions change over time. But there is substantial *indirect* evidence that hints at the weakness of the "wait until they come around to more traditional union values" approach. First, the overall rate at which teachers are leaving public education has spiked upward since the early 1990s. This largely reflects a wave of retirements, but attrition among educators with one to nine years of experience has also increased significantly (by 43 percent).[52] Second, new teachers tend to be much less likely than their veteran colleagues to see teaching as a lifelong career (49 versus 74 percent).[53] Third, as Johnson points out, the average age of "career switchers"—who make up almost 40 percent of new teachers—is about thirty-five, compared with an average age of twenty-six for first-career entrants. This means that approximately four in ten new teachers have a "career life-expectancy" that is foreshortened by nearly a decade on their first day in the classroom. In combination, these trends have produced a workforce that is highly skewed in the direction of less-experienced teachers. In fact, as Richard Ingersoll and Lisa Merrill have pointed out, the most typical ("modal") teacher in today's classroom has only *one year* of experience, compared with *fifteen years* of experience just twenty years ago. Whether or not new teachers' attitudes toward unions change over time may thus be a moot point, since fewer and fewer teachers are remaining in the classroom long enough to matter. Finally, although some observers may point to anecdotal evidence suggesting that teachers' views toward unions change over time, they are necessarily referring to *veteran* teachers. Today's new teachers have come of age in a very different society, one in which only about one in eight workers are unionized and where attitudes toward unions have shifted substantially from those of a generation ago.[54]

Training, Licensure, and Evaluation

Formal qualification and licensing requirements have long been prerequisites for entering the field of education. But the increasingly diverse classrooms in which teachers currently practice and growing demands for outcome-based accountability are forcing a wholesale reexamination of teacher preparation, qualification, and evaluation. There is little doubt that all are in need of substantial change—new teacher training must evolve to cover ever more complex content and pedagogic requirements, in-service teachers need ongoing support and development, and, as policy makers focus on student outcomes, evaluation methods must be developed that will deliver fair and accurate measures of success. Yet these issues are as complex as their context. What constitutes reasonable teacher preparation? Should licensing requirements be standardized, and should cut scores be adjusted to compensate for the disproportionate reduction in the number of African American candidates resulting from such policies? What value do induction, mentoring, and professional development programs have for successful teaching? And in all of these areas, is there evidence that any one program or policy is more effective than another?

Traditional Teacher Training and Alternative Pathways into the Classroom

Currently, there is much debate about how best to prepare teachers for the classroom. Not so long ago the path was fairly straightforward. Teaching candidates were required to earn a BA and complete a series of education courses leading to certification. However, many feel that these programs are uneven in quality and have failed to keep pace with the complex demands that new teachers face in the contemporary classroom, leaving them woefully underprepared. This has sparked discussion about how to transform traditional programs, including important questions pertaining to standardization and core teaching knowledge. Meanwhile, a number of preparation and qualification programs have been developed to provide expedited entry to teaching, circumventing more formal pathways. And finally, as resources grow increasingly scarce, the value of advanced degrees has emerged as yet another important focal point of discussion.

TRADITIONAL PRESERVICE TRAINING AND ACCREDITATION

Reacting to NEA survey data suggesting that "teachers' appreciation of their education and training is at the lowest level in twenty-five years," Dennis Van Roekel turns to a widely cited evaluation of university-based teacher education for an explanation. Its conclusion: teacher education in this country consists "principally a mix of weak and mediocre programs, many disconnected from school practice and practitioners."[55] Adding to this dismal assessment of traditional preservice training, a 2010 congressionally mandated study conducted by the National Research Council (NRC) reported that "there is currently little definitive evidence that particular approaches to teacher preparation yield teachers whose students are more successful than others."[56] The NRC's failure to identify substantial evidence in support of one training program over another led it to investigate the current mechanisms for ensuring accountability and quality control in teacher education. After sifting through a mountain of data, reports, and original source materials, the NRC concluded that these mechanisms represent "a patchwork of mandatory and voluntary processes" that are neither "linked in a coherent outcomes-driven accountability system" nor "grounded in solid empirical research about which program elements or accountability mechanisms are most effective, partly because such research is not available."[57]

The NRC's findings notwithstanding, Joseph Aguerrebere sees a lack of "coherence and consistency" in teacher education programs as the root of the problem and calls for a "move toward consensus around training and practice." But the development of consensus around an accepted body of knowledge that will inform training and practice must logically *precede* the formation of consensus around training and practice itself. Unfortunately, as the NRC report stresses, there is currently "a relatively small body of evidence about the effects of particular kinds of instruction and an even smaller body of evidence about the effects of particular approaches to teacher preparation."[58] Aguerrebere clearly favors a national system of accreditation as "the most logical lever for improvement" of the education field's current patchwork of quality-assurance mechanisms. He envisions an independent body that would draw "from the best thinking and research in the field to develop a set of standards and assessments," with the ultimate aim of ensuring some measure of accountability to the public. This is an ambitious goal—one that could ultimately lead to uniform guidelines for teacher training much as the Flexner report led to the standardization of medical education a century ago.[59]

But it is important to recall that in the late nineteenth century, when the American Medical Association initially lobbied for standardization, it was unsuccessful in part because the American public and much of the medical profession had little faith that any particular "brand" of medical education was significantly superior to any other. And yet, by the turn of the century, research exposing the irrationality of treatments such as blistering, bleeding, and purging, combined with mounting evidence of the therapeutic efficacy of modern practices—including public sanitation, vaccination, and antiseptic surgery—had transformed the way medicine was perceived, paving the way for standardization.[60] The impending merger of the nation's two leading teacher training accreditation agencies—the National Council for Accreditation of Teacher Education (NCATE) and the Teacher Education Accreditation Council (TEAC)—presents a unique opportunity for the new entity, the Council for Accreditation of Educator Preparation, to join with other organizations to lead the way in forging a consensus around the small, emerging body of knowledge on effective teaching; in reevaluating and revising that consensus as new research is generated; and, ultimately, in developing appropriate standards and assessments through an evolutionary, organic process.[61] NCATE and TEAC (and other organizations concerned with raising teacher effectiveness) have traditionally drawn on the expertise of a variety of professional associations concerned with education in developing their respective standards, and there is no reason to question the consensus that has emerged. But because that consensus developed largely in the absence of the more rigorous and granular body of research that is now becoming available, the resulting standards are necessarily at a higher level of abstraction than those that guide training in other fields—such as medicine—and are typically based on a more ambiguous body of evidence. Now is the time to draw on that professional consensus for hypotheses about which features of teacher preparation are most promising, subject those hypotheses to rigorous research, and create a new generation of standards not only for teacher training accreditation but for licensure, advanced certification, and teacher evaluation as well.

Alternative Pathways into the Classroom

In addition to the thousand-plus traditional teacher education programs lodged in postsecondary institutions throughout the fifty states, there are another 130 or so alternative pathways designed to prepare individuals for expedited entrance into teaching. These include Teach for America (a program that recruits graduates of some of the nation's leading colleges and universities and provides them with pre- and inservice training), various fellows' programs established by local school districts (often combining expedited entrance into the field with tuition-supported graduate study in education), and numerous other models. About one-third of all new hires currently enter the classroom through such alternative routes.[62]

In keeping with his call for greater consistency and coherence in traditional teacher education programs, Joseph Aguerrebere considers these alternative pathways into the classroom to be problematic. He contends that education stands alone in allowing some candidates to "circumvent traditional preparation through alternate routes" and argues forcefully that this practice makes "education an outlier among professions." However, Andrew Rotherham counters with examples of other professions—including business, journalism, and law—that, according to him, have long accommodated multiple paths for entry. Rotherham fully embraces the "more pluralistic" approach to teacher training that these alternative pathways represent. Arne Duncan's vision for the future of teaching also includes "multiple, equally effective ways to join the profession." And, while Dennis Van Roekel acknowledges that "such programs vary widely in quality and effectiveness," he expresses concern that high-needs schools, where many candidates on alternative tracks are placed, don't have the capacity to support these new entrants with the kind of "meaningful information and structured mentoring" that they require for success. Dan Brown's vivid description of his experience as a New York City Teaching Fellow assigned to a "volatile fourth-grade class" at P.S. 85 in the Bronx is testimony to the fact that Van Roekel's concern is not misplaced. Brown describes how, following days during which he struggled to manage students' "explosive behavior" with virtually no support from school administrators, he would ride the subway home "in a stupor, exhausted and dismayed." In combination with other factors, the total lack of administrative support that Brown encountered "fostered both personal and classroom disorder" that undermined any potential he may have had to succeed, leading ultimately to his departure at the end of the school year.

Given that the NRC found little evidence that would enable it to distinguish one traditional teacher education program from another, it is not surprising that its 2010 report finds an equally "muddled" body of evidence concerning the relative effectiveness of traditional and alternative pathways into teaching. The report describes a situation in which there is "as much variation within pathways as across them" and concludes that "many of the putative distinctions between alternative and traditional pathways are blurred at the program level."[63] In fact, the report points out that, in many states, much of the required course-work of alternative pathways is provided in the same schools of educa-tion that offer "traditional" training and is "similar if not exactly the same" in content.[64] The NRC reviewed a substantial body of research employing a broad range of methodologies (including randomized controlled designs) and commissioned two studies of its own—one in New York City, the other in Florida. It concluded that "inferring that one type of preparation does or does not yield better outcomes for stu-dents is not warranted by the evidence."[65] Of course, it could be argued that the categories of *traditional* and *alternative* are so diverse and vaguely defined that they fail to capture potentially effective program characteristics that cut *across* the two approaches to teacher training. But if effective cross-cutting characteristics exist, they have not been reliably identified in the current body of research. Thus, one of the NRC's key recommendations is for the research community to under-take "new projects and reviews of previous research" with the goal of determining "the relative effectiveness of the components of those pathways and programs."[66]

REDESIGNING THE MA FOR EFFECTIVE TEACHING

NEA survey data show that the proportion of teachers holding mas-ter's degrees has more than doubled over roughly the last fifty years, from 24 percent in 1955 to 52 percent in 2007. About 90 percent of these degrees are awarded by education programs, the vast majority in the field of general education.[67] Generally, local school districts award teachers with a substantial salary "bump"—averaging about 11 percent of base pay—on completion of an advanced degree.[68] In North Caro-lina, for example, the Excellent Schools Act prescribes a 12 percent pay increase for teachers earning a master's degree. Based on salary data collected by the NEA , it is estimated that the total annual expenditure associated with credits earned for any level of education beyond a bach-elor's degree is about $8.6 billion.[69] Given the size of this expenditure, the classroom performance of teachers with advanced degrees has attracted the attention of researchers and policy makers alike. There is a substantial body of research comparing the effectiveness of teachers with and without master's degrees, most of it summarized in two recent reviews.[70] For the most part, this literature offers little evidence that an MA makes a difference in student outcomes. One early investigation reports that the students of teachers holding discipline-specific advanced degrees in mathematics outperform the students of teachers with no advanced degrees or degrees in subjects other than mathematics. However, even this finding must be interpreted cautiously, as the study does not clearly eliminate the possibility that the observed effect may be due entirely, or in part, to the self-selection of teachers with greater aptitude for teaching mathematics into subject-specific advanced degree programs.[71]

In light of these findings, Pam Grossman and Michelle Brown suggest that, before the education community declares "the investment in graduate degrees a failure," it should begin to imagine "what more rigorous graduate programs aimed explicitly at honing professional knowledge and skills might look like." Citing NEA data showing that many teachers earn their master's degrees within the first few years of teaching, they suggest that this practice may be less than optimal— since novice teachers are still "getting their sea legs"—and argue that the MA might be more usefully developed so that it "signals a specialized expertise and skill in an aspect of the practice of teaching" later in a teacher's career. This leads Grossman and Brown to consider how MA programs could be redesigned to link them more closely "to developing clinical expertise." As one possible strategy, they propose fashioning graduate degree programs around preparation for certification by the National Board for Professional Teaching Standards (NBPTS).

But there is little hard evidence that this performance-based credential serves as effective development for those seeking certification. Only two studies have specifically evaluated the impact of the National Board certification process on teachers' development, and, while both produced positive results, each has significant shortcomings. One is limited by its focus on what teachers would do under certain hypothetical situations instead of their actual performance in the classroom.[72] And, although the other examines actual classroom performance, an unusually high rate of attrition among participating subjects renders its validity highly suspect: of about sixty teachers initially expressing interest in participating, only sixteen completed the study, and just nine actually went through the certification process.[73] Other investigations that compare the classroom effectiveness of teachers before, during, and after they earned NBPTS certification have produced equally ambiguous results. Weighing the full body of evidence, the National Research Council concludes that "existing research neither proves nor refutes hypotheses about the effects of the certification process on teachers' practice."[74]

Grossman and Brown consider a broad range of other programs that might serve as models for the redesign of graduate study in education, including Reading Recovery, a one-to-one tutoring intervention for low-achieving first-grade readers; Complex Instruction, an instructional approach designed to provide academic access and success for all students in heterogeneous classrooms; Bread Loaf, a program aimed at improving instruction in literature and writing; and mathematics pedagogy. Ultimately, however, the success of redesigned MA programs will depend on the effectiveness of the programs on which they are based, and that should be clearly determined through rigorous research before allocating scarce resources to these efforts.

Policies Regarding Teacher Licensure

In all fifty states and the District of Columbia teachers must hold a bachelor's degree in order to obtain a license to teach, while other requirements vary from one jurisdiction to another. Typically, teachers are required to complete course work in various domains, participate in an internship or clinical field experience, and pass tests in basic skills, pedagogy, and/or content knowledge.[75] Most states allow exemptions of various kinds from their normal licensure requirements, including those granted for emergency licenses or alternative routes to certification.[76] With regard to this latter practice, Joseph Aguerrebere cautions that "education stands alone as a profession in allowing individuals to practice independently before they are licensed." Thus he expresses concern that alternative routes to certification provide "a backdoor entry" to teaching and strongly advocates the development of mechanisms that would ensure greater consistency and coherence.

Both James Hunt Jr. and Dennis Van Roekel see raising the bar for licensure as a means of ensuring that every public school student in America is taught by a highly qualified teacher. In 1997, as Hunt met with leaders of business and industry to garner support for the Excellent Schools Act, he regularly pointed to North Carolina's high Praxis cut scores as evidence of the elevated standard of teaching in the state. With equal conviction, Van Roekel describes how the Partnership for Teacher Quality has worked closely with governors, state legislators, state boards of education, and policy analysts to strengthen state licensure policies. Others, however, argue that the impact of licensure and teacher testing is more ambiguous. According to these critics, although state tests set a minimum standard, they may also deter some high-quality applicants from choosing teaching as a career.[77]

Early research on licensure requirements reported strong correlations between teachers' test scores and student achievement, but these investigations were based on data aggregated to the district level that tended to inflate estimates.[78] Only recently, with the development of more powerful statistical methods and the availability of data systems that link teachers and students, have researchers begun to unravel the relationship between licensure standards and teacher effectiveness. These more sophisticated analyses find that teachers' performance on licensure exams actually explains very little of the observed variation in student performance gains and that the level of explanatory power varies substantially by subject area.[79] Such findings suggest that, if state licensure tests are to serve as a meaningful screen for high-quality teaching, they will need to be better aligned with research on effective instructional practices and, perhaps, expanded to include performance assessments designed to measure actual teaching skill. Raising cut scores alone will not serve that end.

Another feature of the debate on licensure testing relates to concerns about testing's impact on the diversity of the teaching force and minority achievement. A recent study by Educational Testing Service (ETS) reports that increasingly demanding state testing requirements since the mid-1990s may have lowered passing rates and improved the academic profile of prospective teachers. Between the mid-1990s and the early 2000s, SAT Verbal and Math scores of candidates passing state licensure tests (Praxis II) in twenty states and the District of Columbia increased by 13 points and 17 points, respectively. During this same period, successful test takers' undergraduate GPAs also improved. However, these apparent gains in teacher quality came at a substantial price: states' more restrictive testing requirements seem to be linked to a disproportionate reduction in the number of African American candidates entering the pool of prospective teachers. While passing rates declined substantially for all test takers (from 92 to 80 percent), the steepest drop was for African American candidates (from 74 to just 52 percent).[80]

These findings relate to concerns raised by Renee Moore and lend support to her observation that "hundreds of Mississippi's aspiring African American teachers" are denied entry into the state's teacher workforce because they "are unable to meet the mandated cut scores on the state's licensing exams." Further, when viewed in the context of research showing that same-race pairing of teachers and students boosts student achievement, the ETS findings suggest that policies that raise state testing requirements may conflict not only with the aim of recruiting more African American teachers but also with the goal of improving the academic performance of minority students. Policy makers are, it seems, faced with a potential trade-off between a higher-quality workforce and a more diverse teaching force coupled with higher minority student achievement. Research in North Carolina—based on administrative records covering the universe of teachers and students in the state over an eleven-year period—explores this issue, and the results are revealing. This study concludes that African American teachers "have more consistent success than white teachers in teaching minority students, and this matching effect is greatest in magnitude for [African American] teachers at the lower end of the licensure performance distribution."[81] Even more striking, hypothetical predictive models based on these data suggest that, in racially diverse classrooms, replacing a black teacher who fails to meet the state licensure test cutoff with a white teacher who does meet the cutoff may actually *reduce* student achievement. Obviously, policy decisions designed to raise teacher quality by increasing state testing requirements must be carefully considered in light of the potentially adverse consequences such decisions may have for teacher diversity and minority student achievement. In this regard, Moore suggests that "balancing such exams with other, more performance-based methods of assessing candidates' pedagogical knowledge and teaching ability would not only improve the overall certification process but also remove an unnecessary barrier to hiring African American teachers."

Induction, Mentoring, and Professional Development

The lack of a strong and consistent relationship between teacher performance on state licensure exams and student achievement suggests that even fully licensed teachers may find themselves unprepared for what they'll find when they step into the classroom. New teachers in particular need help learning the culture of their schools and overcoming the difficulties that every classroom population presents. In a workplace where diversity, technology, and standards protocols grow and shift almost daily, ongoing support and development are especially vital. Unfortunately, current evidence suggests that even the most comprehensive induction and mentoring programs have little impact on student outcomes, and evidence of the effectiveness of professional development is similarly lacking.

INDUCTION AND MENTORING

According to NEA survey data, competent colleagues (including mentors) and help from school administrators are among the most valuable supports identified by teachers. Dan Brown clearly had both during his term as a student teacher at DeWitt Clinton High School in the Bronx. Brown's initial exposure to teaching ended with his departure from the Bronx's P.S. 85, after struggling for a year with a heavy workload and a class that "teetered into chaos with unnerving ease." During that year he received little support from either colleagues or administrators—and no mentoring at all. In stark contrast, at Clinton, Brown conferred daily with a seventeen-year veteran teacher who observed his classes and provided "actionable feedback" as well as "structured opportunities for reflecting on past lessons and collaborating on upcoming ones." Furthermore, Brown had the opportunity to learn from the practices of other teachers and received nurturing support and guidance from an administrator who observed his class and provided constructive feedback. Clearly, Brown's trial-by-fire experience at P.S. 85 was exceptional. But so, too, was his experience at Clinton.

Most induction and mentoring experiences today tend to fall somewhere between the two extremes described by Brown. A study of a nationally representative sample of teachers conducted in the 1999–2000 school year provides evidence that induction and mentoring programs vary greatly.[82] Although eight in ten new teachers reported participating in an induction or mentoring program, only about half had opportunities to collaborate with other teachers; just one in ten had a reduced schedule; and, while two-thirds were assigned a mentor, more than a quarter were from another field. The same study found that those teachers who experienced more supports in their induction programs were less likely to move to a different school or leave teaching altogether by the end of their first year. But since teachers were not randomly assigned to programs of varying intensity, it is impossible to determine whether the observed differences in turnover were attributable to the programs themselves, to unmeasured characteristics of the teachers associated with their induction experiences, or to unmeasured characteristics of the schools related to the intensity of the programs offered.

Recently researchers reported the initial findings from the first large-scale randomized controlled study of the impacts of comprehensive teacher induction ever conducted. This ambitious investigation compared highly structured and intensive ("comprehensive") teacher induction programs with the less intensive, traditional programs found in many schools across the country.[83] Each of the two comprehensive programs included in the study incorporated key components associated with programs identified as "successful" in prior research, and these components were, in turn, aligned with widely accepted principles of effective teaching (e.g., one program is modeled on principles established by the Interstate New Teachers Assessment and Support Consortium).[84] Some 418 schools in seventeen school districts were randomly designated as experimental or control schools, and the eligible teachers within each school received either comprehensive induction services (one of the two programs) or no services beyond those normally provided in their district.[85] First-year results, while not conclusive, demonstrate the critical importance of this type of research. Prior studies, confounded by problems of self-selection and other threats to validity, had identified several "critical components" of successful teacher induction/mentoring programs. Yet this carefully designed randomized trial found no evidence that the comprehensive programs incorporating these components had any positive impact whatsoever—on teachers' classroom practices, on their students' achievement, or on their decisions to remain in their schools, their districts, or teaching altogether.

Intensive one-to-one mentoring was the centerpiece of the two comprehensive induction programs evaluated in this study, and, according to Susan Moore Johnson, that may account for the lack of positive findings. Johnson's experience with new teachers suggests that one-to-one mentoring does not provide the kind of support that they seek. Rather, new teachers report valuing the opportunity to work closely with experienced teachers in an "integrated professional culture" in which "all teachers work together as a matter of course, team-teaching in classrooms and clusters or participating on grade-level teams and schoolwide committees." In schools adopting this approach, "induction is incorporated into the work of the school, rather than set apart as an isolated program," and there is movement away from "a professional culture that is dominated by veteran teachers' priorities and practices to one that engages everyone in providing effective instruction for all students." The next step, of course, will be to subject this model—and competing models—to the same kind of rigorous evaluation that was implemented to assess the impacts of comprehensive induction programs emphasizing one-to-one mentoring.

PROFESSIONAL DEVELOPMENT

Even as the education research community seeks to develop and validate effective induction and mentoring programs for new teachers, there remains a parallel—and largely unmet—need for effective

273 The American Public School Teacher

professional development for more experienced practitioners. According to Randi Weingarten, "The key to achieving the good teaching that is central to a better public education system is to ensure that the infrastructure is in place to support the professional development that will help teachers hone their skills." But there is little in the way of a coherent infrastructure for professional improvement in schools today. Rather, there is a "patchwork of opportunities—formal and informal, mandatory and voluntary, serendipitous and planned."[86] Embedding professional development in communities of practice that provide structural supports and a culture conducive to learning is a critical step in the right direction.[87] But the knowledge base for effective teaching is quite limited, and the knowledge base for effective development even more so. For over a decade there has been widespread agreement among educators concerning the key features of "successful" development; yet our understanding of the specific form, intensity, and content of programs that could make a difference for students remains extremely limited.[88]

The most comprehensive review of the literature in this area, conducted in 2007, examined more than thirteen hundred studies that ostensibly assessed the impact of teacher development programs on student outcomes in three content areas.[89] Just nine of the studies (involving a total of 190 teachers) meet current standards of evidence, and all focus exclusively on elementary school teachers and their students. Collectively, these investigations suggest that teacher professional development can moderately influence student outcomes, but because all of the programs investigated were delivered either by their developers or affiliated researchers—rather than through a "train-the-trainer" approach—whether or not any of these interventions could be effectively brought to scale remains an unanswered question. Since the publication of that review, the U.S. Department of Education has commissioned two randomized controlled evaluations of development programs implemented on a larger scale—one dealing with development in early reading instruction, the other focused on middle school mathematics.[90] Neither evaluation has uncovered a significant effect on student achievement.

Beyond the issue of determining the appropriate *content* of training, there is the related question of how such services should be *delivered*.

Dennis Van Roekel observes: "While school districts have long been the primary providers of in-service training for teachers, their lead over the two other sources of professional development—universities and professional associations—has expanded over the past quarter-century." He suggests that this trend may reflect a growing preference of teachers for "programs led by peers and presented in practical settings" rather than "sessions that focus on abstract theories and problems." However, Barbara Stoflet points to the limitations that the current trend imposes, arguing that the profession is already "very fragmented," and "the increasing expectation that each district will meet the professional development needs of teachers at the local level exacerbates the divisions and resource disparities among schools, districts, and states." In this context, she stresses that, since schools across the country are coping with many of the same challenges, more universal programs administered by universities and professional associations could provide greater equity and unity. Advocating greater alignment between university-level training and professional development, she imagines hybrid programs where universities would serve as "the link between districts, spreading methods and practices that have proved effective."

Toward Meaningful Teacher Evaluation

As the education community continues to grapple with issues concerning the appropriate content and delivery of professional development, it has simultaneously begun to reconsider the processes by which teachers are currently evaluated. Ideally, teacher evaluation and professional development should go hand in hand—two interactive components within a single, comprehensive human resource management system. Teacher evaluation should inform professional development decisions, and development should, in turn, influence evaluation through its impact on teachers' behavior and performance. But that is not the reality that exists in most school districts today. In the absence of evaluation systems that accurately identify teachers' specific strengths and weaknesses, professional development has become a sporadic, drive-by affair—or, as Randi Weingarten puts it, a "perfunctory sorting exercise"—rather than a process of continuous professional improvement.

According to a 2009 study of teacher evaluation focusing on some fifteen thousand teachers and thirteen hundred administrators spanning a dozen districts in four states, about three-quarters of educators say that their most recent evaluation failed to identify any potential areas for development.[91] Moreover, none of the evaluation systems examined in the twelve districts provided credible information that would permit administrators to draw meaningful distinctions between the performance of one teacher and another. In systems employing simple binary evaluation ratings ("satisfactory" or "unsatisfactory"), more than 99 percent of teachers were judged to be satisfactory; and in those using a broader range of ratings, 94 percent received one of the top two scores and less than 1 percent were rated unsatisfactory. In light of such findings, it is not surprising that both Randi Weingarten and Andrew Rotherham conclude that most performance assessment systems in use today are badly in need of overhaul.

Reacting to the weakness and superficiality of current evaluation systems, a growing chorus of critics has begun to press for a more outcomes-based approach to assessing teachers' performance, often calling for the expanded use of *value-added modeling* (VAM) of standardized test-score data to generate teacher "effectiveness" ratings.[92] Rotherham laments the fact that, according to NEA survey data, student test scores are used in "just 15 percent" of teachers' evaluations. But in the wake of the recent disclosure of VAM effectiveness ratings for teachers in Los Angeles and amid calls for similar actions in New York City and other locations, it seems prudent to step back for a moment and take stock of the many pitfalls associated with the use of standardized test-score results in teacher evaluations. Previously, we voiced strong criticism of state tests for their narrow assessment of student "achievement" as the accumulation of discrete, disconnected facts. By extension, basing teachers' evaluations on how well their students perform on such tests is to accept an equally narrow measure of effective teaching. Although there is some tendency for teachers who excel on VAM effectiveness measures based on state tests to do well on measures derived from their students' performance on tests of higher-order reasoning, that tendency, in the words of one critic, "is shockingly weak."[93] And while value-added effectiveness scores may provide some information about teachers' proficiency in raising student test scores—albeit of questionable reliability—they provide *no* information about teachers' specific strengths and weaknesses and are therefore incapable of informing critical human resource management decisions. Then there is the purely practical consideration that the vast majority of teachers (about 70 percent) do not teach at grade levels or in subject areas covered by the standardized testing regimes currently administered by states.[94] To expand existing testing programs to cover all teachers would involve significant opportunity costs in both time and resources, necessarily crowding out other important areas of teaching and learning. Finally, VAM effectiveness ratings are confounded by numerous technical limitations—the nonrandom sorting of students and teachers, assessments that are rarely vertically scaled, missing student background information, etc.—that render them unreliable and inappropriate for use as a key performance measure in high-stakes teacher evaluations.[95]

Deficiencies in traditional teacher evaluation systems and concerns about the reliability and validity of VAM effectiveness ratings have led some schools and districts to turn to *standards-based evaluation* as an alternative or supplementary approach to assessing teacher performance. Interest in standards-based evaluation is growing, as evidenced by the commentaries of several contributors to this volume. Arne Duncan advocates teacher evaluations "rooted in clear job descriptions and performance standards" that "include multiple measures tied to student performance and other factors," such as "a teacher's content knowledge or skills in lesson preparation, instructional design, student assessment, or classroom management." Likewise, Randi Weingarten promotes an AFT evaluation framework that integrates a broad range of student outcomes with a standards-based approach to assessing teacher performance.[96] For its part, the NEA recently published a model framework for teacher assessment and evaluation, which, like the AFT framework, stresses the importance of "a clear set of performance standards."[97]

For the past decade, researchers affiliated with the Consortium for Policy Research in Education (CPRE) have studied a number of evaluation systems bearing many similarities to those proposed by Duncan and Weingarten, and their findings are revealing. Across four sites, the CPRE researchers examined the relationship between teachers' scores from various standards-based evaluation systems (all modeled after the Danielson Framework for Teaching) and their students' value-added test-score gains.[98] They found that, over a three-year period, teachers' standards-based scores explained an average of less than 10 percent of the variation in student performance (9 percent for reading and 6 percent for math). Because the evaluation systems examined in the CPRE study focused almost exclusively on generic teaching behaviors rather than content-specific pedagogical skills, these findings are not surprising; nor is the researchers' conclusion that that the effects of such systems on teacher practice were "broad, but relatively shallow."[99]

There is, we believe, a need for a new generation of standards-based evaluation instruments that go beyond generic principles of good teaching practice, reflect the most rigorous research available, and have been validated against substantially broader measures of achievement than those employed in the CPRE studies. An ambitious new study launched in 2009 by the Bill and Melinda Gates Foundation, the Measures of Effective Teaching (MET) project, takes a major step in that direction.[100] The MET project is designed to evaluate various measures of effectiveness, including those based on classroom observations, for some three thousand teachers in six school districts. Participating teachers will be randomly assigned to classrooms, avoiding one major source of selection bias that threatens the validity of much educational research, and classroom practices will be linked to value-added measures of students' performance on state accountability tests as well as supplementary assessments designed to gauge higher-order conceptual understanding. Yet, while the MET project's design is impressive, some have suggested that its strict adherence to several core principles, established a priori, may limit its value and undermine its credibility.[101]

Although leaders of the nation's two largest teachers' unions and many other stakeholders in the field of education have come to share the view that teacher evaluations should be based on multiple measures, including evidence-based standards of practice, there seems to be less clarity concerning which entities or individuals should actually participate in the evaluation process. Both Dennis Van Roekel and Randi Weingarten acknowledge a potential role for peer assistance and review (PAR) panels in the evaluation of teachers' performance, but neither characterizes teacher involvement as *critical* to the effective functioning of standards-based evaluation systems. Indeed, the NEA's recently published framework for assessment and evaluation actually recommends that administrators or supervisors take the lead in summative teacher evaluations.[102] Perhaps such sentiments reflect a long-standing union reluctance to place teachers in positions of judgment vis-à-vis their peers.

There are, however, two very compelling reasons for making teacher involvement—perhaps through an expanded role for PARs—the norm rather than the exception in standards-based evaluation. First, as value-added effectiveness ratings become more readily available, pressure will surely mount to include these measures as one of several components in a complete evaluation. The AFT's framework for evaluation already concedes that "progress on standardized test scores may be considered as part of an overall evaluation system when the measures are valid and reliable."[103] But if school administrators—who would almost certainly be privy to teachers' VAM effectiveness scores—are also charged with conducting standards-based evaluations, it is highly likely that such prior knowledge would bias their subjective ratings. Recent research demonstrates that teacher effectiveness calculated on the basis of several years of value-added test-score data is a substantially stronger predictor of future productivity than subjective performance ratings and that school administrators' perceptions of teachers' ability to raise test scores is highly correlated with overall subjective ratings.[104] Consciously or unconsciously, school administrators would find it in their own best interest to align their subjective ratings of teachers' classroom behaviors with teachers' VAM effectiveness scores. Principals, after all, are under the same accountability pressures as teachers and have no special immunity to the perverse incentives that such pressures create. Placing standards-based evaluations in the hands of peer evaluators (e.g., PARs) would facilitate independent judgments of teachers' practice, uncontaminated by prior knowledge of their effectiveness ratings based on narrowly defined student-achievement gains.

Second, CPRE researchers report evidence that "subject-specific evaluations conducted by evaluators who have expertise (pedagogical content knowledge) in instruction of the subject they are evaluating can improve the validity of teacher evaluation systems."[105] Thus, they found the strongest relationships between standards-based teacher ratings and value-added effectiveness scores in the two sites where teachers played an active role in evaluations.[106] Intuitively, one would expect teachers—particularly those who share the same disciplinary background as colleagues being evaluated—to have substantially greater pedagogical content knowledge than school administrators who typically lack subject-specific training across multiple areas. Moreover, in fully developed systems, PAR evaluation teams can potentially draw on a broad range of expertise from across entire school districts, ensuring that evaluations reflect the most current, subject-specific understandings about effective practice. There is, in brief, good reason to emphasize the role of PARs in evaluation—both as a means for reducing assessment bias and as a mechanism for improving validity in the evaluation process.

The Professionalization of Teaching

The historical portrait of the American public school teacher rendered in these pages suggests an uncertain, and perhaps, difficult road ahead. A half century ago, teaching benefited from a captive labor force of college-educated women with few career alternatives. But as gender barriers to labor market participation crumbled during the latter half of the twentieth century and relative teacher salaries began to decline, many high-aptitude women who might otherwise have pursued a career in teaching were attracted to other occupations, resulting in a gradual erosion of human capital in the field of education.[107] During this same period, teaching grew increasingly complex, attributable in large part to a reform movement that emphasized a narrow approach to teacher accountability at the expense of higher-level student learning and policies that greatly increased the diversity and inclusiveness of the nation's public schools. The combination of these trends has resulted in unprecedented challenges not only for teaching but, more generally, for America's system of public education.

In the coming years, as states begin to make progress toward the development of common standards for student learning and invest in new performance assessments designed to authentically gauge higher-level thinking skills, the complexity of teaching is likely to escalate further. The challenges that teachers currently face will almost certainly pale in comparison with those confronting the next generation of educators. Over the past several decades, one education reform after another has been conceived and implemented in an effort to raise the quality of teaching, in part driven by the need to meet these new imperatives. Predominant among these reforms have been the many policies, initiatives, and institutional arrangements designed to advance the professionalization of teaching. But is professionalization the best means for advancing the quality of education? And, if so, how can the education community best prioritize its efforts to attain that end? We conclude this chapter with a brief discussion of the thoughts of several of this volume's contributing authors on the movement to professionalize teaching, as well as our own ideas about the most promising way forward.

The Medical Model

In the mid-1980s, influential reports on the future of teaching by the Holmes Group and Carnegie Corporation set the education field on its current course toward professionalization.[108] From the start, medicine served as the preferred standard for professional work, as reflected in early advocates' adoption of terminology such as *clinical experience*, *intern*, and *practitioner* and the education community's enthusiastic embrace of innovations such as the professional development school, modeled after the teaching hospital. Today, the allure of medicine's successful transformation to professional status remains as strong as ever. Arne Duncan, Joseph Aguerrebere, and other contributors to this book espouse visions for the future of teaching that are, in large part, shaped by this paradigm. Thus, Duncan imagines a profession in which training is "built around a combination of academic and hands-on experience—mirroring the rigor and relevance of . . . the medical profession" and advocates "year-or-longer residencies that [would] include intensive observation, mentoring, and coaching by master teachers."

But after a quarter of a century, teaching has made little progress toward the achievement of full professional status. Shifting societal demands, growing discontent over the perceived failures of the nation's public schools, and an economic crisis second only to the Great Depression have contributed to the lack of progress, forcing teaching into a defensive posture and redirecting attention toward more fundamental concerns, including recent efforts to preserve tens of thousands of teaching jobs threatened by a failing economy. Meanwhile, the medical profession, subject to many of the same social, economic, and cultural forces that have influenced teaching, has undergone substantial changes of its own. Given these dynamic circumstances—in which the environment is in constant flux and the goal itself is a moving target—it is reasonable to ask if the movement toward professionalization is on the right path or whether a midcourse correction might be needed.

Andrew Rotherham describes the education community's long-standing affinity for the medical model as "reductionist," arguing that it lacks fundamental applicability to the field of education and consequently distracts from the harder work of "creating genuinely professional operating norms and cultures" in schools. In Rotherham's assessment, the professionalization movement has lost sight of its ultimate objective, emphasizing only the most "superficial aspects of the traditional professional model." Thus, he argues: "Rather than embrace the challenge of building a [foundation of knowledge similar to that in medicine], distilled through years of experience and a body of research, American education has sought to wish that process away. In other words, in the effort to create the appearance of professional canon, [the field of] education has arguably manufactured a corpus of theoretical standards instead of organically developing a core of proven or agreed-upon knowledge."

While taking a somewhat more optimistic view than Rotherham, Pam Grossman and Michelle Brown nonetheless express significant concerns of their own about the current direction of the movement to professionalize teaching. They point to the impressive growth in the proportion of teachers earning master's degrees over the past fifty years as an indication that the new emphasis placed on professionalization has had an effect. However, citing the lack of consistent evidence linking advanced degrees to higher student achievement, they also remind us of the Holmes report's admonishment regarding the pitfalls of credentialism, whereby a profession's entry requirements are not backed up by improved outcomes. Grossman and Brown also express concern over the reluctance of some educators to be held accountable for student outcomes, arguing that such a position is inconsistent with the goal of professionalization. They assert that for an occupation to attain professional status, it must not only demonstrate "accountability for client outcomes" but also other key attributes, including autonomy and—importantly—a recognized knowledge base.

Rotherham draws an indelible line between teaching and medicine, emphasizing the many differences that distinguish the two fields. Yet, in some respects, these occupations share common "professional" attributes, having been shaped by many of the same social, economic, and cultural forces. Just as teaching has experienced a rise in accountability demands in the form of the No Child Left Behind Act and its mandated state testing requirements, the medical profession has encountered similar demands from providers, insurers, employers, regulators, and consumers. Indeed, medicine's adoption of industrial process control methods—such as continuous quality improvement, benchmarking, and total quality management—has been in direct response to these new demands, resulting in greater measurement of treatments and outcomes.[109] And, just as doctors once enjoyed substantial autonomy in the practice of medicine—with little interference from those outside the profession—teachers also exercised much control over their professional lives in "loosely coupled" systems where classroom practices were largely buffered from centralized policy centers.[110] Now both have lost several degrees of freedom in the exercise of professional discretion and judgment. Teachers have come under increased scrutiny and control as a result of a standards movement that closely prescribes the scope and content of instruction, while doctors—practicing within a changing milieu featuring spiraling health-care costs, an increasingly well-informed public, and the widespread proliferation of managed care—routinely submit to processes for reviewing the medical necessity of services, controls on inpatient admissions, and strict limits on the time they can spend with patients.

But despite these commonalities, teaching and medicine differ greatly in terms of the third, and perhaps most critical, attribute of professions identified by Grossman and Brown. Whereas medicine has developed a recognized knowledge base reflecting a history of rigorous research, teaching has made only limited progress in this area. The many gaps in knowledge identified throughout this chapter underscore this point. For nearly every topic examined, reported findings are inconclusive, inadequate, or mixed. In the absence of a body of knowledge comparable to that in medicine, the field of education has failed to achieve consensus regarding even the most fundamental issues, including what constitutes effective practice. Relying on a combination of "expert judgment," "best practices," and "conventional wisdom"—which, in turn, are informed by an inconclusive body of evidence—educators struggle to develop meaningful training, induction, mentoring, and professional development programs and engage in endless debates concerning the appropriateness of current licensure, certification, and evaluation procedures.

Of course, it is possible to impose consensus from above through policies aimed at greater centralization, and some policy makers advocate that approach. But only when teachers and others with a stake in public education achieve common understandings based on rigorous research will they succeed in replacing uncertainty and contentiousness with the unity of purpose necessary to achieve the twin objectives of professionalization identified in the Holmes report: improved status and conditions for teachers and better outcomes for students. The current emphasis on what Rotherham calls "the superficial aspects of the traditional professional model" is not so much *misplaced* as it is logically *out of sequence*. The education field must first make significant progress toward developing an undisputed, widely recognized knowledge base. After that, establishing a new generation of licensure procedures, certification processes, training models, induction/mentoring programs, professional development, and evaluation frameworks—all fully aligned with student achievement objectives—will come more easily.

The professionalization of teaching is, of course, not the only area in which progress depends on the creation of an evidence-based body of knowledge. For example, although schools have made great strides in improving access to instructional technologies, the potential impact of these new tools ultimately rests on the effectiveness of the instructional strategies on which they are based. Until research is successful in identifying proven models of effective practice, instructional technologies will continue to fall short of their promise to revolutionize teaching. And as schools restructure to accommodate and nurture professional learning communities, we must ask, as Judith Warren Little did two decades ago, "Does teachers' time together advance the understanding and imagination they bring to their work or do teachers merely confirm one another in present practice?"[111] As she correctly observes, to be effective in boosting student performance, collaboration among educators must be open to new ideas, materials, and knowledge from external sources.[112]

Although the field of education has not yet developed a foundation of knowledge comparable to that in medicine, it is by no means starting at zero. Years of research have yielded many useful insights, practices, and understandings. Yet as the preceding pages so clearly document, much of this research remains inconclusive. The limited use of sophisticated research designs, inadequate outcome measures that fail to assess higher-level thinking skills, and, until recently, the lack of advanced multilevel statistical modeling techniques have combined to severely restrict the field's ability to move beyond its current state of ambiguity. Andrew Rotherham suggests that the education community has lacked the will to organically develop a core of proven knowledge, choosing to "wish that process away" and focus instead on the superficial aspects of professionalization—what the Holmes report called *credentialism*. It seems more accurate to conclude that, more often than not, education researchers have simply lacked the requisite tools to develop a sound and widely recognized body of knowledge.

Building a Recognized Knowledge Base

Today, teaching has reached a defining moment in its long journey toward professional status. Unlike any other time in the past half century, the field is poised to build a foundation of knowledge rivaling that in medicine, the profession that it has long emulated in so many ways. But to accomplish that end, teachers—and others who share their commitment to the advancement of public education—must acknowledge the limits of their present level of understanding and reject the tendency to canonize prevailing wisdom. At the same time, the accumulated insights of decades of research and practical experience—though limited and inconclusive—can serve as the basis for generating hypotheses and shaping the research agenda going forward.

Already, knowledge in the field of education is growing at an accelerating pace. Whereas much research conducted in the past several decades has been limited to case studies and simple cross-sectional designs that left many questions unanswered, an increasing number of investigations today employ quasi-experimental and randomized controlled designs that make it possible to draw valid causal connections. But important obstacles remain. Many of the most recent studies rely heavily on administrative data collected by schools, districts, and states. Constrained by limited budgets, researchers have found the prospect of conducting investigations with such a "natural harvest" of data attractive.[113] This approach has proven to have its limitations, however. Some studies report instances where administrative databases fail to properly match students with teachers, lack test-score data for consecutive years, or include tests that have not been scaled to represent a progression of content knowledge. Others warn that findings should be interpreted with caution, pointing to missing data, nonrandom assignment of students and teachers to classrooms, inaccuracies introduced by summer learning, and insufficient student background data. Finally, most recent studies have little choice but to measure educational outcomes exclusively in terms of students' performance on state standardized tests. Such a narrow indicator of educational "achievement" leads to questionable findings and ultimately distorts the broader mission of public education.

Some recent investigations supplement administrative data with information derived from teacher surveys, administrator interviews, and other sources. All too often, however, this strategy falls short of overcoming the fundamental weaknesses and limitations of existing data. The most ambitious—and promising—study of this type is the aforementioned Measures of Effective Teaching (MET) project.[114] Funded by the Bill and Melinda Gates Foundation, this ongoing investigation is unprecedented in its scope. It seeks to link the practices and behaviors of classroom teachers to the achievement gains of their students in an effort to determine which practices are most effective. But instead of relying solely on students' performance on state tests designed for accountability purposes to measure achievement outcomes, the MET project will employ supplemental assessments designed to evaluate higher-order thinking skills. The study also plans to use digital video technology to record about twenty-four thousand individual lessons delivered by some three thousand teachers and will employ and train hundreds of educators to score the lessons. Finally, to ensure that results are not compromised by the composition of the classes to which participating teachers are assigned, in the second year of the study teachers will be assigned to classes by lottery. With these innovations, the MET project addresses many of the shortcomings of prior studies and seems destined to set a new standard for the design of field-based education research.

Yet even such a well-conceived study cannot overcome all of the limitations inherent in research conducted in traditional public school settings. For example, parents of students assigned to teachers perceived to be less effective may insist that their children be reassigned or simply engage the services of a private tutor. And while the project's utilization of supplemental assessments of higher-level thinking represents an important advance over most other studies, other potential outcomes remain unassessed, simply because to do so would encroach too much on already limited instructional time.

As one potential strategy for addressing these remaining limitations, we propose an expanded role for the nation's professional development schools (PDSs).These schools already have been pivotal in the ongoing movement to professionalize teaching and are widely acknowledged both as training centers for the preparation of future educators and as laboratories for experimentation and development.[115] We envision these schools—in partnership with colleges and graduate schools of education—assuming a major new leadership position in a nationwide effort to forge a knowledge base for the field of education comparable to that in medicine. Thus, we propose extending the school year in PDSs by a week or more to accommodate the administration of a battery of assessments designed to measure a wide range of educational outcomes, including critical analysis and higher-level thinking skills in *every* school subject, without sacrificing instructional time. Our vision includes PDSs working collaboratively to develop common assessments and coordinated approaches to scoring, analyzing, and reporting results—all with the aim of facilitating joint research efforts. Such collaborative work would likely include the development of a universal strategy for training cadres of former educators to score performance assessments with a high degree of consistency and inter-rater reliability; a unified approach to the collection and management of data; and a common methodology for conducting value-added analyses of assessment results and background data. Finally, we propose that PDSs develop compacts with students and parents as a condition of enrollment, acknowledging their agreement to commit to a longer school year, accept random classroom assignment, complete a detailed background questionnaire, and a host of other conditions designed to ensure the validity of research conducted within these institutions.

With such an infrastructure in place, professional development schools would become unparalleled centers of knowledge creation. Joint research projects examining new instructional strategies, innovative technological applications, novel approaches to school structure and organization, revamped professional development programs, and other initiatives could easily be coordinated across partnerships of participating schools and their affiliated colleges and graduate schools of education. Just as teaching hospitals regularly join together in coordinated studies designed to validate new pharmaceutical products and medical procedures, PDSs could play an analogous role in the field of education. Of course, such an ambitious venture would require significant and sustained funding, but the potential benefits would be enormous.

In the absence of a recognized education knowledge base—one validated against outcome measures designed to assess a broad range of student skills and capabilities in controlled school environments—the effort to professionalize teaching seems bleak. It is now commonly recognized that teachers represent the most important variable within schools in determining student outcomes. Yet we have very little understanding of which teacher attributes are associated with effectiveness in the classroom or which instructional practices best promote student learning. Given that uncertainty, it is not surprising that policy makers have attempted to increase the quality of teaching by simply eliminating those educators who fail to raise student test scores.

As teaching becomes increasingly complex, educators can no longer rely on those practices and strategies that served the occupation well in simpler times. Teachers, researchers, policy makers, and others with a stake in public education must take up the challenge to elevate this critical occupation to full professional status. The stakes are high, not because professionalization will enhance the standing of teachers—although that itself is a well-deserved outcome—but because professionalization, through the establishment of a strong body of knowledge, will result in better outcomes for students, a more productive economy, and a more secure future for our nation's democratic institutions and ideals.

Notes

Chapter 1

1. W. J. Bushaw and S. Lopez, "A Time for Change: The 42nd Annual Phi Delta Kappa/Gallup Poll of the Public's Attitudes Toward the Public Schools," *Phi Delta Kappan* 92, no. 1 (September 2010): 9–26. With the exception of the reference to Gallup poll data and the performance of U.S. students on international assessments, this paragraph draws on and partially paraphrases the arguments presented in G. Sykes, "Serving our Children: Building an Occupation of Teaching" (NEA Working Paper, 2009).

2. K. Rousmaniere, "In Search of a Profession: A History of American Teachers," in *Portrait of a Profession*, ed. D. M. Moss, W. J. Glenn, and R. L. Schwab (New York: Rowman & Littlefield Education, 2005).

3. Ibid.

4. D. L. Angus, *Professionalism and the Public Good: A Brief History of Teacher Certification* (Washington, DC: Thomas B. Fordham Foundation, 2001).

5. A. C. Ornstein and D. U. Levine, *Foundations of Education*, 10th ed. (Boston: Houghton Mifflin, 2007).

6. A few public high schools had existed from the early part of the nineteenth century, beginning with the nation's oldest, the English High School, located in Jamaica Plain, MA, and founded in 1821.

7. *Stuart v. School District No. 1 of Village of Kalamazoo*, 30 Michigan 69 (1874).

8. Ornstein and Levine, *Foundations of Education*.

9. Angus, *Professionalism and the Public Good*.

10. L. D. Webb, *The History of American Education: A Great American Experiment* (Upper Saddle River, NJ: Pearson/Merrill/Prentice Hall, 2006), 176; cited in Ornstein and Levine, *Foundations of Education*.

11. T. D. Snyder, *120 Years of American Education: A Statistical Portrait* (NCES 93-442), National Center for Education Statistics (Washington, DC: U.S. Department of Education, 1993).

12. Angus, *Professionalism and the Public Good*.

13. Benjamin W. Frazier, *Summary of Teacher Certification Requirements*, U.S. Office of Education Circular No. 223 (Washington, DC: Government Printing Office, 1946), cited in Angus, *Professionalism and the Public Good*.

14. Angus, *Professionalism and the Public Good*.

15. National Commission on Teacher Education and Professional Standards, *Journey to Now, 1946–1961: The First Fifteen Years of the Professional Standards Movement in Teaching as Reflected in Keynote Addresses* (Washington, DC: NEA, 1961), 29, cited in Angus, *Professionalism and the Public Good*.

16. A. E. Bestor, *Educational Wastelands: The Retreat from Learning in Our Public Schools* (Urbana: University of Illinois Press, 1953), and R. Flesch, *Why Johnny Can't Read—and What You Can Do About It* (New York: Harper, 1955), cited in Angus, *Professionalism and the Public Good*.

17. P. Schrag, "Schoolhouse Crock: Fifty Years of Blaming America's Educational System for Our Stupidity," *Harper's Magazine*, September 2007, 36–44.

18. J. Coleman, *Equality of Educational Opportunity* (Washington, DC: Government Printing Office, 1966).

19. National Commission on Excellence in Education, *A Nation at Risk: The Imperative for Educational Reform* (Washington, DC: Department of Education, 1983).

20. *Tomorrow's Teachers* (East Lansing, MI: Holmes Group, 1985); *A Nation Prepared: Teachers for the 21st Century* (New York: Carnegie Forum for Education and the Economy, 1986).

21. Http://childstats.gov; *The Worst of Times: Children in Extreme Poverty in the South and Nation, SEF Research and Policy Report* (Atlanta: Southern Education Foundation, 2010).

22. Anthony Milanowski, "What Professions Compare with Teaching?" *Principal Leadership: High School Edition* 9, no. 7 (2009): 9.

23. *Swann v. Charlotte-Mecklenburg Board of Education*, 402 U.S. 1 (1971).

24. The Immigration and Nationality Act of 1965 established family reunification as the principle basis for immigration to the United States.

25. Http://childstats.gov.

26. Sykes, "Serving our Children: Building an Occupation of Teaching."

27. Http://childstats.gov.

28. In *Pennsylvania Association for Retarded Children (PARC) v. Pennsylvania* (PPA, 1971) and *Mills v. Board of Education* (DC, 1972), the courts ruled that children with disabilities had the right to a free, appropriate education in the least restrictive environment. By 1975 more than thirty states had affirmed this right through legislation.

29. The law was initially called the Education for All Handicapped Children Act (EAHCA) of 1975, Pub. L. No. 94-14220, U.S. C. 1400 *et seq.*; the 1990 Amendments to EAHCA changed the name to the Individuals with Disabilities Education Act (IDEA), and, although the name was changed again in the 2004 reauthorization, we use the more commonly recognized IDEA title to identify the law throughout this volume.

30. *What Do Teachers Think? NEA Research Bulletin* 40, no. 4 (1962).

31. *Promises to Keep: Creating High Standards for American Students; Report on the Review of Education Standards from the Goals 3 and 4 Technical Planning Group to the National Education Goals Panel* (Washington, DC: National Education Goals Panel, 1993), cited in L. Shepard, J. Hannaway, and E. Baker, *Standards, Assessments and Accountability* (Washington, DC: National Academy of Education, 2010).

32. Shepard, Hannaway, and Baker, *Standards, Assessments and Accountability*.

33. W. J. Popham, *Unlearned Lessons: Six Stumbling Blocks to our Schools' Success* (Cambridge, MA: Harvard Education Press, 2009).

34. M. S. Tucker, *Standards Movement in American Education*, http://education.stateuniversity.com/pages/2445/Standards-Movement-in-American-Education.html.

35. Shepard, Hannaway, and Baker, *Standards, Assessments and Accountability*; P. E. Barton *National Education Standards: Getting Beneath the Surface* (Princeton, NJ: Educational Testing Service, 2009).

36. S. Thompson, "The Authentic Standards Movement and Its Evil Twin," *Phi Delta Kappan* 82, no. 5 (January 2001): 358–362.

37. Popham, *Unlearned Lessons.*

38. M. Polikoff, A. C. Porter, and J. Smithson, "The Role of State Student Achievement Tests in Standards-Based Reform" (working paper, University of Pennsylvania Graduate School of Education, Philadelphia, 2009), cited in Shepard, Hannaway, and Baker, *Standards, Assessments and Accountability.*

39. K .M. Doherty, "Poll: Teachers Support Standards—with Hesitation," *Education Week on the Web* 20, no. 17 (2001), http://counts.edweek.org/sreports/qc01/articles/qc01story.cfm?siug=17intod-s1.h20, cited in S. M. Johnson, *The Workplace Matters: Teacher Quality, Retention, and Effectiveness* (Washington, DC: NEA, 2006).

40. L. A. Banicky and A. J. Noble, "Detours on the Road to Reform: When Standards Take a Back Seat to Testing" (publication T01.022.2), Delaware Education Research and Development Center, University of Delaware, Newark, July 2001, http://www.rdc.udel.ed/reports/t010222.pdf, cited in Johnson, *The Workplace Matters.*

Chapter 2

1. W. J. Bushaw and S. J. Lopez, "A Time for Change: The 42nd Annual Phi Delta Kappa/Gallup Poll of the Public's Attitudes Toward the Public Schools," *Phi Delta Kappan* 92, no. 1 (2010): 9–26; W. Howell, P. E. Peterson, and M. West, "The 2010 Education Next—PEPG Survey," *Education Next,* August 25, 2010, http://educationnext.org/the-2010-education-next-pepg-survey/.

2. A. Ripley, "A Call to Action for Public Schools," *Time,* September 20, 2010.

3. *The 2009 MetLife Survey of the American Teacher: Collaborating for Student Success* (New York: MetLife, 2010), http://www.metlife.com/assets/cao/contributions/foundation/american-teacher/MetLife_Teacher_Survey_2009.pdf; *Primary Sources: America's Teachers on America's Schools* (New York: Scholastic and the Bill and Melinda Gates Foundation, 2010), http://www.scholastic.com/primarysources/pdfs/Scholastic_Gates_0310.pdf; J. Johnson, A. Yarrow, J. Rochkind, and A. Ott, "Teaching for a Living: How Teachers See the Profession Today," October 19, 2009, http://www.publicagenda.org/pages/teaching-for-a-living; J. Coopersmith, *Characteristics of Public, Private, and Bureau of Indian Education Elementary and Secondary School Teachers in the United States: Results From the 2007–08 Schools and Staffing Survey* (NCES 2009-324), National Center for Education Statistics, Institute of Education Sciences (Washington, DC: U.S. Department of Education, 2009); *Status of the American Public School Teacher 2005–2006* (Washington, DC: NEA, 2010).

4. The *Status of the American Public School Teacher* survey is administered during the academic year, which spans two calendar years. For simplicity, when referencing the year of administration for the survey, we use the year corresponding to the fall term of the academic year. Thus, the "2005 survey" refers to the survey conducted during the 2005–2006 academic year. This convention is followed for all surveys that span two years, including the U.S. Department of Education's *Schools and Staffing Survey.*

5. "The Status of the American Public School Teacher," *Research Bulletin of the National Education Association* 35, no. 1 (1957): 4–63.

6. *Status of the American Public School Teacher 2005–2006.*

7. Using data from the National Center for Education Statistics, all school districts are first sorted into nine strata on the basis of student enrollment. In the first sampling stage, districts are sampled from within each stratum with a probability of selection proportionate to the size of the stratum (i.e., larger districts have a higher probability of selection than smaller districts). In the second sampling stage, teachers are randomly

selected from rosters of teachers provided to the NEA by the sampled school districts. The probability of selection for teachers is equal across the strata, yielding a self-weighted sample. For the first administration of the survey in 1955, the first sampling stage was defined using the population of the area served by a school district rather than student enrollment in the district. With this exception, all other sampling procedures used between 1955 and 2005 are the same.

8. E. de Leeuw and W. de Heer, "Trends in Household Survey Nonresponse: A Longitudinal and International Comparison," in *Survey Nonresponse*, ed. R. M. Groves, D. A. Dillman, J. L. Eltinge, and R. J. A. Little (New York: Wiley, 2002), 41–54.

9. MetLife maintains that the annual survey of teachers it has conducted since 1984 is nationally representative. However, the absence of detailed technical information concerning the administration of the survey (e.g., sampling frame, response rates) makes it difficult to determine the accuracy of this claim.

10. While the majority of analyses referenced by commentators are presented in this chapter as tables or figures, a select few are not. Selected analyses were excluded as data displays if they reflected a more nuanced or narrow aspect of the teaching occupation unique to a specific commentator. While the more nuanced analyses may be an important part of the commentator's argument, we determined that, given space limitations, they could stand on their own without a separate display. Additionally, some analyses of survey data for which a data display would have limited value (e.g., a single percentage in a single year) were excluded. Endnotes for each commentary indicate those analyses that are not presented in this chapter.

11. In the 1955 *Status of the American Public School Teacher* report, elementary schools include schools with grades K–6 as well as schools with self-contained instruction for grades 7 and 8. Secondary schools include all other grades or combinations of grades.

12. S. P. Choy, E. A. Medrich, and R. Henke, *Schools and Staffing in the United States: A Statistical Profile, 1987–88*, National Center for Education Statistics, Institute of Education Sciences (Washington, DC: U.S. Department of Education, 1992); Coopersmith, *Characteristics of Public, Private, and Bureau of Indian Education Elementary and Secondary School Teachers*.

13. Teachers self-identified as "elementary" or "secondary" school teachers in the 1960 *Status* survey without reference to specific grade levels. The only additional information given about elementary teachers is that they taught a single class as opposed to multiple classes. The absence of grade-level information for teachers identified as elementary or secondary teachers makes it impossible to link the survey results to average class sizes for teachers in later years. Consequently, we show results only for 1987 and 2007 and provide the 1960 averages as a point of reference.

14. *Education at a Glance 2009: OECD Indicators* (Paris: OECD, 2009).

Chapter 3

1. National Research Council of the National Academy of Sciences, *Preparing Teachers: Building Evidence for Sound Policy* (Washington, DC: National Academies Press, 2010).

2. Data not shown. SASS estimates are based on data analyses of the 2007–2008 administration. For further information on the SASS program, see J. Coopersmith, *Characteristics of Public, Private, and Bureau of Indian Education Elementary and Secondary School Teachers in the United States: Results From the 2007–08 Schools and Staffing*

Survey (NCES 2009-324), National Center for Education Statistics, Institute of Education Sciences (Washington, DC: U.S. Department of Education, 2009), http://nces.ed .gov/surveys/SASS/.

3. J. Bransford and L. Darling-Hammond, eds., *Preparing Teachers for a Changing World: What Teachers Should Learn and Be Able to Do* (New York: National Academy of Education, 2005), is probably the most comprehensive and well-researched compendium of knowledge in the field.

4. D. H. Gilmour, *Teacher Quality in a Changing Policy Landscape: Improvements in the Teacher Pool* (Princeton, NJ: Educational Testing Service, 2007), http://www.ets.org/ Media/Education_Topics/pdf/TQ_full_report.pdf.

5. Data not shown.

6. A. Baber, *Teacher Certification and Licensure/Testing Requirements* (Denver, CO: Education Commission of the States, 2008), http://mb2.ecs.org/reports/reportTQ.aspx? id-1137.

7. *What Matters Most: Teaching for America's Future* (New York: National Commission on Teaching and America's Future, 1996); and *The Holmes Partnership Trilogy: Tomorrow's Teachers, Tomorrow's Schools, Tomorrow's Schools of Education* (New York: Peter Lang, 2007).

8. M. C. Reynolds, ed., *Knowledge Base for the Beginning Teacher* (Washington, DC: American Association of Colleges for Teacher Education, 1989).

Chapter 4

1. Data not shown.

2. In 2005, teachers reported spending a total of fifty-two hours per week on all instructional and noninstructional duties both during and after school hours. Data about instructional hours are shown in figure 2.17; data about noninstructional hours are not shown.

3. Data not shown.

4. Data not shown.

5. In 2005, 61 percent of teachers reported that they earned half or more of their total household income (data not shown).

Chapter 5

1. In 2005, 90 percent of teachers reported they had access to a computer with Internet connectivity and e-mail at school (data not shown).

Chapter 6

1. N. C. Aizenman, "U.S. to Grow Grayer, More Diverse: Minorities Will Be Majority by 2042 Census Bureau Says," *Washington Post*, August 14, 2008.

2. S. Farkas, J. Johnson, and A. Duffett, *Stand by Me: What Teachers Really Think About Unions, Merit Pay and Other Professional Matters* (New York: Public Agenda, 2003), 35.

3. R. M. Ingersoll, "Short on Power, Long on Responsibility," *Educational Leadership* 65, no. 1 (September 2007): 23–24.

4. B. Berry, *The Teachers of 2030: Creating a Student-Centered Profession for the 21st Century*, Oct. 2009, May 2010, http://catalog.proemags.com/publication/1e41a2a8#/1e41a2a8/1.

5. Ibid.

6. C. T. Kerchner, J. E. Koppich, and J. G. Weeres, *United Mind Workers: Unions and Teaching in the Knowledge Society* (San Francisco: Jossey-Bass, 1997).

Chapter 7

1. In 2005, 90 percent of teachers reported they had access to a computer with Internet connectivity and e-mail at school (data not shown).

2. L. D. Rosen and M. M. Weil, "Computer Availability, Computer Experience and Technophobia among Public School Teachers," *Computers in Human Behavior* 11, no. 1 (1995): 9–31.

Chapter 8

1. *Tomorrow's Teachers* (East Lansing, MI: Holmes Group, 1985); *A Nation Prepared: Teachers for the 21st Century* (New York: Carnegie Forum for Education and the Economy, 1986).

2. D. Goldhaber and D. Brewer, "When Should We Reward Degrees for Teachers?" *Phi Delta Kappan* 80, no. 2 (1998): 134, 136–138; M. Roza and R. Miller, "Separation of Degrees: State-by-State Analysis of Teacher Compensation for Master's Degrees," http://www.crpe.org/cs/crpe/download/csr_files/rr_crpe_masters_jul09.pdf.

3. S. G. Rivkin, E. A. Hanushek, and J. F. Kain, "Teachers, Schools, and Academic Achievement," *Econometrica* 73, no. 2 (2005): 417–458.

4. D. Goldhaber and D. Brewer, "Evaluating the Effect of Teacher Degree Level on Educational Performance," in *Developments in School Finance 1996*, ed. W. Fowler (Washingon, DC: National Center for Education Statistics, 1997), 197–210; and D. Goldhaber and D. Brewer, "Why Don't Teachers and Schools Seem to Matter? Assessing the Impact of Unobservables on Educational Productivity," *Journal of Human Resources* 32, no. 3 (1997): 505–523.

5. Roza and Miller, "Separation of Degrees."

6. *Tomorrow's Teachers*, 42.

7. *A Nation Prepared.*

8. D. Goldhaber and E. Anthony, "Can Teacher Quality Be Effectively Assessed? National Board Certification as a Signal of Effective Teaching," *Review of Economics and Statistics* 89, no. 1 (2007): 134–150; see http://www.mitpressjournals.org/doi/abs/10.1162/rest.89.1.134.

9. For examples see http://www.cde.ca.gov/pd/ps/te/nbptshighered.asp.

10. See, for example, B. Sunstsein, *Composing a Culture: Inside a Summer Writing Program with High School Teachers* (Portsmouth, NH: Heinemann, 1994).

11. American Physical Therapy Association, "Working Operational Definitions of Elements of Vision 2020, *Vision 2020* (2007), http://www.apta.org/AM/Template.cfm?Section=Vision_2020I&Template=/TaggedPage/TaggedPageDisplay.cfm&TPLID=285&ContentID=32061.

12. A. Threlkeld and K. Paschal, "Entry-Level Physical Therapist Education in the United States of America," *Physical Therapy Reviews* 12, no. 2 (2007): 156–162.

13. S. Fitzgerald, "Physical Therapy Goals for 2020 Well on Way to Fruition," *Medical News* (October 2007), http://www.medicalnewsinc.com/physical-therapy-goals-for-2020-well-on-way-to-fruition-cms-85.

Chapter 9

1. Data not shown.

2. I found differences of this magnitude for disadvantaged students in Gary, Indiana; see E. A. Hanushek, "The Trade-Off Between Child Quantity and Quality," *Journal of Political Economy* 100, no. 1 (1992): 84–117. For an overview of the results of similar studies, see E. A. Hanushek and S. G. Rivkin, "Teacher Quality," in *Handbook of the Economics of Education*, ed. E. A. Hanushek and F. Welch (Amsterdam: North Holland, 2006), 1051–1078.

3. Hanushek and Rivkin, "Teacher Quality."

4. E. A. Hanushek and R. R. Pace, "Who Chooses to Teach (and Why)?" *Economics of Education Review* 14, no. 2 (1995): 101–117; S. P. Corcoran, W. N. Evans, and R. S. Schwab, "Changing Labor Market Opportunities for Women and the Quality of Teachers 1957–1992," Working Paper 9180 (Cambridge, MA: National Bureau of Economic Research, 2002); M. P. Bacolod, "Do Alternative Opportunities Matter? The Role of Female Labor Markets in the Decline of Teacher Quality," *Review of Economics and Statistics* 89, no. 4 (2007): 737–751.

5. E. A. Hanushek, "The Failure of Input-Based Schooling Policies," *Economic Journal* 113, no. 485 (2003): F64–F98.

6. In 2005, 6 percent of teachers reported they earned additional income because of performance or incentive pay (figure 2.27). Also, 13 and 7 percent of teachers, respectively, indicated that they had the *opportunity* to earn additional income for teaching a subject area with a staff shortage or teaching in a "challenging to staff" school in the district (data not shown).

7. E. A. Hanushek, "Teacher Deselection," in *Creating a New Teaching Profession*, ed. D. Goldhaber and J. Hannaway (Washington, DC: Urban Institute Press, 2009), 165–180.

8. M. Barber and M. Mourshed, *How the World's Best-Performing School Systems Come Out on Top*, McKinsey and Company, 2007, http://www.mckinsey.com/clientservice/Social_Sector/our_practices/Education/Knowledge_Highlights/Best_performing_school.aspx.

Chapter 10

1. A number of these studies focused specifically on North Carolina. See D. Goldhaber, L. Cramer, and H.-J. Choi, "A Descriptive Analysis of the Distribution of NBPTS Certified Teachers in North Carolina," *Economics of Education Review* 26, no. 2 (2007): 160–172; L. Bond, T. Smith, W. K. Baker, and J. Hattie, *The Certification System of the National Board for Professional Teaching Standards: A Construct and Consequential Validity Study* (Greensboro: Center for Educational Research and Evaluation, University of North Carolina, 2000).

Chapter 11

1. This commentary draws on an earlier article, R. Ingersoll and L. Merrill, "Who's Teaching Our Children?" *Educational Leadership* 67, no. 8 (2010): 14–20. Support for our research came from a grant to the National Commission on Teaching and America's Future from the Bill and Melinda Gates Foundation and from a grant (no. 0455744) from the Teacher Professional Continuum Program of the National Science Foundation. H.

May and D. Perda provided valuable assistance with the SASS data analyses. For further information on the SASS surveys, see National Center for Education Statistics, *Schools and Staffing Survey and Teacher Follow-Up Survey* (Washington, DC: U.S. Department of Education, 2005), http://nces.ed.gov/surveys/SASS/.

2. T.D. Snyder, A.G. Tan, and C.M. Hoffman, *Digest of Education Statistics, 2005* (NCES 2006-030), National Center for Education Statistics (Washington, DC: U.S. Department of Education, 2006).

3. Trends prior to 1960 are not shown in figure 2.2.

4. In this analysis primary schools are defined as having grades K–4.This differs from how school level is defined in figure 2.16.

5. According to analyses of NEA data not shown here, the number of hours that teachers dedicated to instruction-related activities outside of class increased from nine to ten hours between 1985 and 2005.

6. R. M. Ingersoll and D. Perda, "Is the Supply of Mathematics and Science Teachers Sufficient?" *American Educational Research Journal* 47, no. 3 (2010): 563–594.

7. Data from the 1970s are not shown in figure 2.6.

8. R. Ingersoll and D. Perda, *How High Is Teacher Turnover and Is It a Problem?* (research paper, Consortium for Policy Research in Education, University of Pennsylvania, 2010).

9. Ingersoll and Perda, "Is the Supply of Mathematics and Science Teachers Sufficient?"

10. See, for example, D. B. Tyack, *The One Best System: A History of American Urban Education* (Cambridge, MA: Harvard University Press, 1974); and D. C. Lortie, *Schoolteacher: A Sociological Study* (Chicago: University of Chicago Press, 1975).

Chapter 12

1. Figure 2.2 shows the precipitous growth in the teacher workforce since the early 1980s. See the commentary by Ingersoll and Merrill (chap. 11) in this volume for a discussion of various factors associated with this growth.

2. Data not shown.

3. M. Fultz, "The Displacement of Black Educators Post-*Brown*: An Overview and Analysis," *History of Education Quarterly* 44, no. 1 (2004): 11–45.

4. T. S. Dee, "Teachers, Race, and Student Achievement in a Randomized Experiment," Working Paper 8432 (Cambridge, MA: National Economic Bureau of Research, 2001).

5. W. H. Marinell, "Will Mid-Career Entrants Help Avert a Teacher Shortage, Reduce Racial and Gender Imbalances, and Fill Vacancies in Hard-to-Staff Subjects and Schools?" (paper, American Educational Research Association, San Diego, April 2009).

6. H. G. Peske, E. Liu, S. M. Johnson, D. Kauffman, and S. M. Kardos, "The Next Generation of Teachers: Changing Conceptions of a Career in Teaching," *Phi Delta Kappan* 83, no. 4 (2001): 304–311.

7. Data not shown. The percentage of teachers with one to nine years of experience who reported that they plan to teach until retirement increased from 53 percent to 61 percent between 2000 and 2005.

8. A . Keigher, *Teacher Attrition and Mobility: Results from the 2008–09 Teacher Follow-Up Survey* (NCES 2010-353), National Center for Education Statistics (Washington, DC: U.S. Department of Education, 2010),

9. S. M. Johnson and the Project on the Next Generation of Teachers, *Finders and Keepers: Helping New Teachers Survive and Thrive in Our Schools* (San Francisco: Jossey-Bass, 2004).

10. S. Glazerman, E. Isenberg, S. Dolfin, M. Bleeker, A. Johnson, M. Grider, and M. Jacobus, *Impacts of Comprehensive Teacher Induction: Final Results from a Randomized Controlled Study*, 2010, http://ies.ed.gov/ncee/pubs/20104027/.

11. Johnson et al., *Finders and Keepers*.

12. Data not shown.

13. J. York-Barr and K. Duke, "What Do We Know About Teacher Leadership? Findings from Two Decades of Scholarship," *Review of Educational Research* 74, no. 3 (2004): 255–316; M. J. Donaldson, S. M. Johnson, C. Kirkpatrick, W. Marinell, J. Steele, and S. Szczesiul, "Angling for Access, Bartering for Change: How Second-Stage Teachers Experience Differentiated Roles in Schools," *Teachers College Record* 110, no. 5 (2008): 1088–1114.

14. S. M. Johnson, J. P. Papay, S. E. Fiarman, M. S. Munger, and E. K. Qazilbash, "Teachers Leading Teachers: Realizing the Potential of Peer Assistance and Review" (Washington, DC: Center for American Progress, 2010).

15. S. M. Johnson, *Teachers at Work: Achieving Success in Our Schools* (New York: Basic Books, 1990).

16. Data not shown.

17. J. G. Coggshall, A. Ott, E. Behrstock, and M. Lasagna, "Supporting Teacher Talent: The View from Generation Y," *Public Agenda*, 2009, http://www.publicagenda.org/pages/supporting-teacher-talent-view-from-Generation-Y.

18. Data not shown.

19. Interviews were conducted with thirty local union presidents in six states. See S. M. Johnson, M. L. Donaldson, M. S. Munger, J. P. Papay, and E. K. Qazilbash, *Leading the Local: Teachers Union Presidents Speak on Change, Challenges* (Washington, DC: Education Sector, 2007).

Chapter 13

1. Financial reasons are not among the top five reasons shown in figure 2.20.

2. Financial reasons are not among the top five reasons shown in figure 2.21.

3. Financial hindrances are not among the top five hindrances shown in figure 2.23.

4. The percentages shown in figures 2.20 and 2.21 differ from those presented in the text because the figures show the *average* of the top reasons reported between 1970 and 2005 and 1980 and 2005, respectively. The text references data for 2005 in particular, which are not shown.

5. Data not shown.

6. Data on the percentage of teachers holding less than a bachelor's degree are not shown.

7. T. D. Snyder, *Mini-Digest of Education Statistics, 2008* (NCES 2009-021), National Center for Education Statistics, Institute of Education Sciences (Washington, DC: U.S. Department of Education, 2009).

8. *What Matters Most: Teaching for America's Future* (New York: National Commission for Teaching and America's Future, 1996).

9. See, for instance, S. Farkas, J. Johnson, and A. Duffett, with L. Moye and J. Vine, *Stand by Me: What Teachers Really Think About Unions, Merit Pay and Other Professional Matters* (New York: Public Agenda, 2003).

10. See S. Farkas, J. Johnson, and T. Follet, with A. Duffett and P. Foley, *A Sense of Calling: Who Teaches and Why* (New York: Public Agenda, 2000); A. Duffett, S. Farkas, A. J. Rotherham, and E. Silva, *Waiting to Be Won Over: Teachers Speak on the Profession, Unions and Reform* (Washington, DC: Education Sector, 2008); *The 2009 MetLife Survey of the American Teacher: Collaborating for Student Success* (New York: MetLife, 2010), http://www.metlife.com/assets/cao/contributions/foundation/american-teacher/MetLife _Teacher_Survey_2009.pdf; and *Primary Sources: America's Teachers on America's Schools* (New York: Scholastic and the Bill and Melinda Gates Foundation, 2010), http://www .scholastic.com/primarysources/pdfs/Scholastic_Gates_0310.pdf.

Chapter 14

1. B. D. Rampey, G. S. Dion, and P. L. Donahue, *NAEP 2008 Trends in Academic Progress* (NCES 2009–479), National Center for Education Statistics (Washington, DC: U.S. Department of Education, 2009).

2. *The 2009 MetLife Survey of the American Teacher: Collaborating for Student Success,* Part 2: *Do Teachers Expect Enough of Students?* (New York: MetLife, 2010).

3. D. N. Figlio and M. E. Lucas, "The Gentleman's A," *Education Next* 4, no. 2 (2004): 60–67.

4. This study was supported by the Massachusetts Insight Education and Research Institute, the Nellie Mae Education Foundation, and the University of Massachusetts Donahue Institute.

5. T. Williams, M. Kirst, and E. Haertel, *Similar Students, Different Results: Why Do Some Schools Do Better? A Large-Scale Survey of California Elementary Schools Serving Low-Income Students* (Mountain View, CA: EdSource, 2005).

6. J. Mathews, *Work Hard. Be Nice: How Two Inspired Teachers Created the Most Promising Schools in America* (Chapel Hill, NC: Algonquin Books, 2009), 283.

7. Http://www.newsweek.com/feature/americas-best-high-schools.html.

Chapter 15

1. P. S. Kusimo, *Rural African Americans and Education: The Legacy of the Brown Decision* (Washington, DC: ERIC Clearninghouse on Rural Education and Small Schools, 1999).

2. Data not shown.

3. "Education: Progress Report I," *Time,* http://www.time.com/time/archive.

4. Kusimo, *Rural African Americans and Education.*

5. H. R. Milner and T. C. Howard, "Black Teacher, Black Students, Black Communities, and *Brown*: Perspectives and Insights from Experts," *Journal of Negro Education* 73 (Summer 2004): 1–16.

6. G. Toppo, "Thousands of Black Teachers Lost Jobs," April 28, 2004, *USAToday,* http://www.usatoday.com/news/nation/2004-04-28-brown-side2_x.htm.

7. J. Haney, "The Effects of the *Brown* Decision on Black Educators," *Journal of Negro Education* 47, no. 1 (1978): 88–95.

8. Kusimo, *Rural African Americans and Education;* B. J. Holmes, "New Strategies Are Needed to Produce Minority Teachers," in *Recruiting and Retaining Minority Teachers,* ed. A Dorman, Policy Brief No. 8. (Oak Brook, IL: North Central Regional Educational

Laboratory, 1990); S. King, "The Limited Presence of African American Teachers," *Review of Educational Research* 63, no. 2 (1993): 115–149.

9. Toppo, "Thousands of Black Teachers Lost Jobs."

10. Available at NEA Timeline, ATA History, https://sites.nea.org/aboutnea/atatimeline.html. Note that NATCS later changed its name to ATA.

11. R. Dewing, "Desegregation of State NEA Affiliates in the South," *Journal of Negro Education* 38, no. 4 (1969): 395–403.

12. See Jon Nordheimer, "Mississippi Unit Dropped by NEA: Refusal to Join with Blacks Cited by Teachers Group," *New York Times*, April 14, 1970, 37.

13. C. F. Karpinski, "Faculty Diversity: *Brown* and the Demise of the Black Principal" (paper, American Educational Research Association, San Diego, CA, 2004).

14. R. W. Irvine and J. J. Irvine, "The Impact of the Desegregation Process on the Education of Black Students: Key Variables," *Journal of Negro Education* 52, no. 4 (1983): 410–422.

15. Karpinski, "Faculty Diversity."

16. See, for example, T. S. Dee, "The Race Connection: Are Teachers More Effective with Students Who Share Their Ethnicity?" *Education Next* 4, no. 2 (2004): 52–59; L. D. Delpit, "Skills and Other Dilemmas of a Progressive Black Educator," *American Educator* 20, no. 3 (1996): 9–11, 48; M. Dickar, "Hearing the Silenced Dialogue: An Examination of the Impact of Teacher Race on Their Experiences," *Race, Ethnicity and Education* 11, no. 2 (2008): 115–132; D. Downey and S. Pribesh, "When Race Matters: Teachers' Evaluations of Students' Classroom Behavior," *Sociology of Education* 77, no. 4 (2004): 267; N. E. Hyland, "Being a Good Teacher of Black Students? White Teachers and Unintentional Racism," *Curriculum Inquiry* 35, no. 4 (2005): 429–459; J. Irvine, "Culturally Relevant Pedagogy," *Education Digest* 75, no. 8 (2010): 57–61; G. Ladson-Billings, "It's Not the Culture of Poverty, It's the Poverty of Culture: The Problem with Teacher Education," *Anthropology and Education Quarterly* 37, no. 2 (2006): 104–109; A. Mitchell, "African American Teachers: Unique Roles and Universal Lessons," *Education and Urban Society* 31, no. 1 (1998): 104–122.

17. R. W. Irvine and J. J. Irvine, "The Impact of the Desegregation Process on the Education of Black Students: Key Variables," *Journal of Negro Education* 52, no. 4 (1983): 410–422.

18. G. Ladson-Billings, *Beyond the Big House: African American Educators on Teacher Education* (New York: Teacher College Press, 2005), 89.

Chapter 16

1. Http://www.nctq.org/tr3/home.jsp.

2. For a comparison tool, see A. J. Rotherham, "Understanding Teachers Contracts," *Education Sector*, 2010, http://www.educationsector.org/publications/understanding-teachers-contracts.

3. Data not shown.

4. Data not shown.

5. Data for 1980 are not shown in figure 2.17.

6. Data on "school environment, organization, and freedom to teach" are not shown as a "help" in figure 2.22 because this response was not one of the top five responses reported.

7. See http://widgeteffect.org/.

Chapter 17

1. Data on the number of preparation periods for secondary teachers are not shown in figure 2.18.

2. *Education at a Glance 2009: OECD Indicators* (Paris: OECD, 2009).

Chapter 18

1. In 2005, 11 percent of teachers identified their training, education, and subject matter knowledge as a help to doing their job. See *Status of the American Public School Teacher, 2005–2006* (Washington, DC: NEA, 2010), table 64 in online appendix, http://www.nea.org/assets/docs/2005-06StatusAppendixB.pdf.

2. K. Neville, R. Sherman, and C. Cohen, *Preparing and Training Professionals: Comparing Education to Six Other Fields* (New York: Finance Project, 2005).

3. A. Levine, *Educating School Teachers* (Washington, DC: Education Schools Project, 2006), http://www.edschools.org/pdf/Educating_Teachers_Exec_Summ.pdf.

4. C. E. Feistrizer, "Teaching While Learning: Alternate Routes Fill the Gap," *EDge* 5, no. 2 (2009), http://www.pdkmembers.org/members_online/publications/edge/edgev5n2.pdf.

5. National Center for Education Statistics, *Schools and Staffing Survey* (Washington, DC: U.S. Department of Education, 2009), http://nces.ed.gov/surveys/SASS/.

6. Ibid.

7. Data not shown.

8. D. Goldhaber, "National Board Teachers Are More Effective, but Are They in the Classrooms Where They're Needed Most?" *Education Finance and Policy* 1, no. 3 (2006): 372–382.

9. J. W. Little, *Professional Community and Professional Development in the Learning-Centered School,* Working Paper (Washington, DC: NEA, 2006).

10. S. M. Johnson, "Supporting and Retaining the Next Generation of Teachers," *Research Briefs from the Visiting Scholars Series: Teacher Quality and Achievement Gaps* (Washington, DC: NEA, 2007).

11. In 2005, 1 percent of teachers identified "lack of teacher cooperation/unprofessional teachers" as a hindrance to doing their job (data not shown).

12. In 2005, 6 percent of teachers identified "negative attitudes of public/parents/state legislator" as a hindrance to doing their job. See *Status of the American Public School Teacher,* table 63 in online appendix, http://www.nea.org/assets/docs/2005-06Status AppendixB.pdf.

13. A. L. Yarrow, "State of Mind," *Education Week* 29, no. 8 (2009): 21–23.

14. D. Viadero, "Turnover in Principalship Focus on Research," *Education Week* 29, no. 9 (2009): 1.

15. J. Johnson, "The Principal's Priority 1," *Education Leadership* 66, no. 1 (2008): 72–76, http://www.ascd.org/publications/educational_leadership/sept08/vol66/num01/The_Principal's_Priority_1.aspx.

16. W. Togneri, *Beyond Islands of Excellence: What Districts Can Do to Improve Instruction and Achievement in All Schools—A Leadership Brief* (Washington, DC: Learning First Alliance, 2003), http://www.learningfirst.org/sites/default/files/assets/biefullreport.pdf.

17. *No Dream Denied: A Pledge to America's Children,* National Commission on Teaching and America's Future, 2003, http://www.nctaf.org/documents/no-dream-denied_summary_report.pdf.

Chapter 19

1. The description of events involving P.S. 234 on September 11, 2001, and in the days following the attack on the World Trade Center is a composite of accounts from recordings of teachers and others from P.S. 234 at the National September 11 Memorial and Museum, http://www.national911memorial.org/site/PageServer?pagename=New_Museum_Collection_Attacks; T. Fields-Meyer, "Shelter from the Storm," *Time*, March 18, 2002; "The Heroes," *Newsweek*, September 27, 2001, www.newsweek.com/2001/09/26/the-heroes.html; "Our Heroes," *New York Teacher*, September 26, 2001, http://nysut.org/newyorkteacher/2001-2002/010926safety.html. For an account of a similar experience, see "School Dazed—Teachers and Students at P.S. 150 Learn How to Bounce Back," *U.S. News and World Report*, http://www.usnews.com/usnews/9_11/articles/911school.html.

2. L. S. Shulman, *The Wisdom of Practice: Essays on Teaching, Learning, and Learning to Teach* (San Francisco: Jossey-Bass, 2004), 504.

3. C. DeNavas-Walt, B. D. Proctor, and J. C. Smith, "Income, Poverty, and Health Insurance Coverage in the United States: 2009," U.S. Census Bureau Current Population Reports (Washington, DC: Government Printing Office, 2010), 14, 16, 18, http://www.census.gov/prod/2010pubs/p60-238.pdf; Bureau of Labor Statistics, U.S. Labor Department, "The Employment Situation—September 2010," October 8, 2010, http://stats.bls.gov/news.release/pdf/empsit.pdf.

4. R. Rothstein, "How to Fix Our Schools," Economic Policy Institute Issue Brief 286, October 14, 2010, citing J. S. Coleman, *Equality of Educational Opportunity* (Washington, DC: Government Printing Office, 1966).

5. See also L. Benson, I. Harkavy, M. Johanek, and J. Puckett, "The Enduring Appeal of Community Schools," *American Educator* 33, no. 2 (2009): 22–47; and S. M. Fine, "Community Schools: Reform's Lesser-Known Frontier," *Education Week*, February 1, 2010, http://www.edweek.org/ew/articles/2010/02/03/20fine.h29.html.

6. T. D. Snyder and S. A. Dillow, *Digest of Education Statistics, 2009* (NCES 2010-013), National Center for Education Statistics, Institute of Education Sciences (Washington, DC: Department of Education, 2010), table 3, http://nces.ed.gov/programs/digest/d09/index.asp.

Chapter 20

1. These data are for the 2006–2007 school year; see http://nces.ed.gov/fastfacts/display.asp?id=59 (February 2010).

2. See *Lessons Learned: New Teachers Talk about Their Jobs, Challenges, and Long-Range Plans*, no. 1 (Washington, DC: National Comprehensive Center for Teacher Quality and Public Agenda, 2007), fig. 5C.

3. S. P. Corcoran, "Human Capital Policy and the Quality of the Teacher Workforce," in *Creating a New Teaching Profession*, ed. D. Goldhaber and J. Hannaway (Washington, DC: Urban Institute Press, 2009).

4. D. H. Gitomer, *Teacher Quality in a Changing Policy Landscape: Improvements in the Teacher Pool* (Princeton, NJ: Princeton University Press, 2007).

5. The estimate of the educational advantage associated with the racial pairing of teachers and students and the discussion of active and passive effects is drawn from two sources: T. S. Dee, "Teachers, Race, and Student Achievement in Randomized Experiment," *Review of Economics and Statistics* 86, no. 1 (2004): 195–210; and T. S. Dee, "A

Teacher Like Me: Does Race, Ethnicity, or Gender Matter?" *American Economics Review* 95, no. 2 (2005): 158–165.

6. B. Achinstein and J. Aquirre, "Cultural Match or Culturally Suspect: How New Teachers of Color Negotiate Sociocultural Challenges in the Classroom," *Teachers College Record* 110, no. 8 (2008): 1505–1540.

7. Ibid. In turn, Achinstein and Aguirre cite Hernandez-Sheets as the originator of this idea. See R. Hernandez-Sheets, "Trends in the Scholarship on Teachers of Color for Diverse Populations: Implications from Multicultural Education" (paper, American Educational Research Association, New Orleans, April 2000).

8. Dee, "Teachers, Race, and Student Achievement in a Randomized Experiment."

9. For a review of the literature in this area, see E. Hollins and M. T. Guzman, "Research on Preparing Teacher for Diverse Populations," in *Studying Teacher Education: The Report of the AERA Panel on Research and Teacher Education*, ed. M. Cochran-Smith and K. Zeichner (Mahwah, NJ: Erlbaum, 2005).

10. Evidence of lower GPAs among boys can be found at http://nationsreportcard.gov in a figure entitled "Trend in Grade Point Average, by Gender," based on data from U.S. Department of Education, Institute of Education Sciences, National Center for Education Statistics, High School Transcript Study (HSTS), various years, 1990–2005. Other evidence of differential educational outcomes for boys and girls can be found in T. S. Dee, "Teachers and the Gender Gaps in Student Achievement," *Journal of Human Resources* 42, no. 3 (2007): 528–554. The gender gaps in reading, math, and science reported by Dee are for seventeen-year-old boys and girls, based on their performance on the 1999 National Assessment of Educational Progress.

11. V. Lavy, "Do Gender Stereotypes Reduce Girls' or Boys' Human Capital Outcomes? Evidence from a Natural Experiment," *Journal of Public Economics* 92, no. 10–11 (2008): 2083-2105, finds same-gender matching effects that account for between 0.05 and 0.18 standard deviations in student performance, depending on subject area. Dee, in "Teachers and the Gender Gaps in Student Achievement" and "A Teacher Like Me," estimates that same-gender pairing accounts for about 0.05 standard deviations in achievement on standardized tests in math, science, and literature. R. G. Ehrenberg, D. D. Goldhaber, and D. J. Brewer, *Do Teachers' Race, Gender, and Ethnicity Matter? Evidence from NELS88*, NBER Working Paper W4669 (Cambridge, MA: National Bureau of Economic Research, Cambridge, 1995), finds that same-gender matching influences teachers' subjective evaluations, but not students' test scores. Dee reports in "Teachers and the Gender Gap" a propensity for low-achieving boys to be assigned to male teachers and suggests that Ehrenberg, Goldhaber, and Brewer's failure to find a testing effect may be due to nonrandom assignment of students to teachers.

12. In "Teachers and the Gender Gap," Dee bases this calculation, which assumes that the effects of male teachers are additive across grades, on data from the U.S. Department of Education's 1999–2000 *Schools and Staffing Survey* (SASS).

13. A. Keigher and F. Cross, *Teacher Attrition and Mobility: Results from the 2008–2009 Teacher Follow-Up Survey* (Washington, DC: National Center for Education Statistics, 2010).

14. J. E. Rockoff, "The Impact of Individual Teachers on Student Achievement: Evidence from Panel Data," *American Economic Review Proceedings* 94, no. 2 (2004): 247–252; S. G. Rivkin, E. A. Hanushek, and J. F. Kain, "Teachers, Schools, and Academic Achievement," *Econometrica* 73, no. 2 (2005): 417–458; T. J. Kane, J. E. Rockoff, and D. O. Staiger,

What Does Certification Tell Us About Teacher Effectiveness? Evidence from New York City, Working Paper 12155 (Cambridge, MA: National Bureau of Economic Research, 2006).

15. *Teacher Attrition: A Costly Loss to the Nation and to the States* (Washington, DC: Alliance for Excellent Education, 2005).

16. R. Murnane, J. Singer, and J. Willet, "The Career Paths of Teachers: Implications for Teacher Supply and Methodological Lessons for Research," *Educational Researcher* 17, no. 6 (1988): 22–30; T. Stinebrickner, "A Dynamic Model of Teacher Labor Supply," *Journal of Labor Economics* 19, no. 1 (2001): 196–230.

17. See, for example, D. J. Boyd, H. Lankford, S. Loeb, and James H. Wyckoff, "Explaining the Short Careers of High-Achieving Teachers in Schools with Low-Performing Students," *American Economic Review Proceeding* 95, no. 2 (2005): 166–171.

18. E. A. Hanushek, J. F. Kain, D. M. O'Brien, and S. G. Rivkin, *The Market for Teacher Quality*, Working Paper 11154 (Cambridge, MA: National Bureau of Economic Research, 2005); D. Goldhaber, B. Gross, and D. Player, *Are Public Schools Really Losing Their Best? Assessing the Career Transitions of Teachers and Their Implications for the Quality of the Teacher Workforce*, Working Paper 12 (Washington, DC: National Center for Analysis of Longitudinal Data in Education Research [CALDER], 2007).

19. D. Boyd, P. Grossman, H. Lankford, S. Loeb, and J. Wyckoff, *Who Leaves? Teacher Attrition and Student Achievement*, Working Paper 23 (Washington, DC: CALDER, 2008), 2.

20. E. L. Horng, "Teacher Tradeoffs: Disentangling Teachers' Preferences for Working Conditions and Student Demographics," *American Educational Research Journal* 46, no. 3 (September 2009): 690–717.

21. K. J. DeAngelis and J. B. Presley, *Leaving Schools or Leaving the Profession: Setting Illinois' Record Straight on Teacher Attrition*, IERC 2007-1 (Edwardsville: Illinois Education Research Council, 2007); E. A. Hanushek, J. F. Kain, and S. G. Rivkin, "Why Public Schools Lose Teachers," *Journal of Human Resources* 39, no. 2 (2004): 326–354.

22. D. C. Lortie, *Schoolteacher: A Sociological Study* (Chicago: University of Chicago Press, 1975); J. W. Little, "The Persistence of Privacy: Autonomy and Initiative in Teachers' Professional Relations," *Teachers College Record* 91, no. 4, (1990): 509–536.

23. J. W. Little, "Norms of Collegiality and Experimentation: Workplace Conditions of School Success," *American Educational Research Journal* 19, no. 3 (1982): 325–340; P. Grossman, S. Wineburg, and S. Woolworth, "Toward a Theory of Teacher Community," *Teacher College Record* 103, no. 6 (2001): 942–1012; M. McLaughlin and J. Tolbert, *Professional Communities and the Work of High School Teaching* (Chicago: University of Chicago Press, 2001); V. Lee and J. Smith, "Collective Responsibility for Learning and Its Effects on Gains in Achievement and Engagement for Early Secondary School Students," *American Journal of Education* 104, no. 2 (1996): 103–147.

24. J. W Little, *Professional Community and Professional Development in the Learning-Centered School* (Washington, DC: NEA, 2008).

25. F. Hess, "The Human Capital Challenge: Toward a 21st Century Teaching Profession," in Goldhaber and Hannaway, *Creating a New Teaching Profession*, 115–136.

26. D. Drury, *Reinventing School-Based Management* (Alexandria, VA: National School Boards Association, 1999).

27. A. Goolsbee and J. Guryan, "The Impact of Internet Subsidies in Public Schools." *Review of Economics and Statistics* 88, no. 2 (2006): 336–347.

28. J. Wells and L. Lewis, *Internet Access in U.S. Public Schools and Classrooms: 1994–2005* (NCES 2007-020), National Center for Education Statistics (Washington, DC: U.S. Department of Education, 2006).

29. L. Gray, N. Thomas, L. Lewis, and P. Tice, *Teachers' Use of Educational Technology in U.S. Public School: 2009* (NCES 2010-040), National Center for Education Statistics (Washington, DC: U.S. Department of Education, 2010).

30. National Telecommunications and Information Administration, *Digital Nation: 21st Century America's Progress Toward Universal Broadband Internet Access* (Washington, DC: U.S. Department of Commerce, 2010).

31. Gray et al., *Teachers' Use of Educational Technology in U.S. Public Schools.*

32. J. Vigdor and H. Ladd, *Scaling the Digital Divide: Home Computer Technology and Student Achievement,* Working Paper 48 (Washington, DC: Urban Institute/Center for Analysis of Longitudinal Data in Education Research, 2010).

33. L. Gray, N. Thomas, L. Lewis, and P. Tice, *Educational Technology in U.S. Public Schools: Fall 2008* (NCES 2010-034), National Center for Education Statistics (Washington, DC: U.S. Department of Education, 2010).

34. Vigdor and Ladd, *Scaling the Digital Divide.*

35. W. E. Blanton, G. B. Moorman, B. A. Hayes, and M. L. Warner. "Effects of Participation in the Fifth Dimension on Far Transfer," *Journal of Educational Computing Research* 16, no. 4 (1997): 371–396; C. E. Rouse and A. B. Krueger "Putting Computerized Instruction to the Test: A Randomized Evaluation of a 'Scientifically Based' Reading Program," *Economics of Education Review* 23, no. 4 (2004): 323–338; Goolsbee and Guryan, "The Impact of Internet Subsidies in Public School"; X. Li, M. S. Atkins, and B. Stanton. "Effects of Home and School Computer Use on School Readiness and Cognitive Development Among Head Start Children: A Randomized Controlled Pilot Trial," *Merrill-Palmer Quarterly: Journal of Developmental Psychology* 52, no. 2 (2006): 239–263.

36. H. Wenglinsky, *Does It Compute? The Relationship Between Educational Technology and Student Achievement in Mathematics* (Princeton, NJ: Educational Testing Service, 1998).

37. A. Trotter, "Getting Up to Speed." *Education Week* 26, no. 30 (2007): 30–33.

38. Gray, Thomas, Lewis, and Tice, *Educational Technology in U.S. Public Schools.*

39. See *Teachers Matter: Attracting, Developing and Retaining Effective Teachers* (Paris: OECD, 2005), fig. 3.13; student-teacher ratios are correlated with, but not equivalent to, class size.

40. S. Allegretto, S. Corcoran, and L. Mishel, *The Teaching Penalty: Teacher Pay Losing Ground* (Washington, DC: Economic Policy Institute, 2008), 2.

41. For a more complete description of the occupational choice model for labor economics, see Corcoran, "Human Capital Policy and the Quality of the Teacher Workforce."

42. Data not shown.

43. E. A. Hanushek, J. F. Kain, and S. G. Rivkin, *Do Higher Salaries Buy Better Teachers?* Working Paper 7082 (Cambridge, MA: National Bureau of Economic Research, 1999).

44. C. F. Manski, "Academic Quality, Earnings, and the Decision to Become a Teacher: Evidence from the National Longitudinal Study of the High School Class of 1972," in *Public Sector Payrolls,* ed. D. A. Wise (Chicago: University of Chicago Press, 1987), 291–316; D. N. Figlio, "Can Public Schools Buy Better Quality Teachers?" *Industrial and Labor Relations Review* 55, no. 4 (2002): 686–699.

45. Manski, "Academic Quality, Earnings, and the Decision to Become a Teacher."

46. E. A. Hanushek, "Teacher Deselection," in Goldhaber and Hannaway, *Creating a New Teaching Profession*, 165–180.

47. Ibid., 174.

48. S. Farkas, J. Johnson, and A. Duffett, *Stand by Me: What Teachers Really Think About Unions, Merit Pay and Other Professional Matters* (New York: Public Agenda, 2003).

49. Ibid; 20 percent of new teachers versus 46 percent of their veteran colleagues report being actively engaged in union activities.

50. Ibid; at the national level, 14 percent of new members versus 24 percent of veteran members feel that their union represents their own values and preferences; 30 percent of new members see the union as "absolutely essential," compared with 57 percent of veterans

51. These data are derived from a separate analysis of the NEA survey data not presented in chapter 2.

52. According to our calculations, based on SASS data for 1991–1992 and 2008–2009, the annual rate of attrition for teachers with one to nine years' experience has increased from 6.0 to 8.6 percent (a 43 percent increase) over this time span, while the attrition rate for teachers with ten or more years' experience has increased from 4.5 to 7.5 percent (a 67 percent increase). U.S. Department of Education, National Center for Education Statistics, *Schools and Staffing Survey,* data files for 1991–1992 and 2007–2008.

53. Farkas, Johnson, and Duffett, *Stand by Me.*

54. In 2010, 11.9 percent of the U.S. labor force was unionized, according to the Bureau of Labor Statistics; see *News Release: Union Members—2010,* USDL-11-0063, January 21, 2011), http://www.bls.gov/news.release/pdf/union2.pdf.

55. This statement by Dennis Van Roekel summarizes the conclusion reached in A. Levine, *Educating School Teachers* (Washington, DC: Education Schools Project, 2006).

56. National Research Council (NRC), *Preparing Teachers: Building Evidence for Sound Policy* (Washington, DC: National Academies Press, 2010), 174. The NRC report was conducted by the Committee on the Study of Teacher Preparation Programs in the United States, made up of eighteen scholars from a broad cross-section of colleges and universities and several project staff persons.

57. Ibid., 3.

58. Ibid.

59. A. Flexner, *Medical Education in the United States and Canada* (New York: Carnegie Foundation for the Advancement of Teaching, 1910). For a brief history and description of the Flexner Report, see A. H. Black, "The Flexner Report and the Standardization of American Medical Education," *Journal of the American Medical Association* 291 (2004): 2139–2140.

60. Black, "The Flexner Report."

61. Allied organizations might include, for example, the Partnership for Teacher Quality (a partnership of NEA state affiliates and the American Association of Colleges for Teacher Education), the National Board for Professional Teaching Standards, and the Interstate New Teacher Assessment and Support Consortium.

62. NRC, *Preparing Teachers.*

63. Ibid., 35.

64. Ibid.

65. Ibid., 41–42.

66. Ibid., 54–55.

67. Although most degrees are awarded by education programs, the content of these degrees varies. Analyses of the 2007–2008 *Schools and Staffing Survey* reveal that among all teachers with master's degrees, about 65 percent are awarded in a general education field (e.g., elementary education, administration) with the remainder spread across subject-specific disciplines.

68. D. Goldhaber and D. Brewer, "Why Should We Reward Degrees for Teachers?" *Phi Delta Kappan* 80, no. 2 (1998): 134, 136–138.

69. M. Roza and R. Miller, *Separation of Degrees: State-by-State Analysis of Teacher Compensation for Masters Degrees* (Seattle: Center on Reinventing Public Education, 2009).

70. E. A. Hanushek, "The Failure of Input-Based Resource Policies," *Economic Journal* 113, no. 485 (2003): F64–F68; D. Harris and T. Sass, *Teacher Training, Teacher Quality, and Student Achievement,* Working Paper 3 (Washington, DC: National Center for Analysis of Longitudinal Data in Education Research, 2008).

71. The study in question is D. Goldhaber and D. Brewer, "Evaluating the Effect of Teacher Degree Level on Educational Performance," in *Developments in School Finance 1996,* ed. W. Fowler (Washington, DC: National Center for Education Statistics, 1997), 197–210. The authors report that "a teacher with a B.A. in mathematics, or an M.A. in mathematics, has a statistically significant *positive* impact on students' achievement relative to teachers with no advanced degrees or degrees in non-mathematics subjects . . . We also see that teachers with B.A. degrees in science have a positive impact relative to those who teach science but have either no degree or a B.A. in another subject . . . It is possible that the positive findings for teachers' degrees in mathematics and science do not reflect the training that they have in those subjects but simply that mathematics and science degrees serve as proxies for teacher ability. To test this hypothesis we re-estimated all models, including whether a teacher has a mathematics or science degree in the English and history regressions. If mathematics and science degrees serve as proxies for teacher quality, we would expect the coefficients on these variables to be significant and positive in all of the subject areas, including English and history. This is not the case. Neither the mathematics nor the science degree level variables are statistically significant in the English and history regression. This result clearly suggests that, in mathematics and science, it is the teacher subject-specific knowledge that is the important factor in determining 10th-grade achievement." Ibid., 206. We have two concerns about the authors' interpretation of this "test": (1) teachers with degrees in mathematics or science may have higher ability or aptitude than those with degrees in other areas, but that ability may be specific to math or science and not transferable to other subject areas; and (2) teachers with degrees in mathematics or science have demonstrated an interest in these subject areas and, therefore, when assigned to teach an out-of-area subject, such as English or history, may not bring the same motivational level to the task. Combined, we feel that these alternative explanations of the test results make it less clear than the authors suggest that it is teachers subject-specific knowledge that is the important factor in determining achievement.

72. D. Lustick and G. Sykes, "National Board Certification as Professional Development: What Are Teachers Learning?" *Education Policy Analysis Archives* 14, no. 5 (2006): 1–43.

73. L. Darling-Hammond, J. M. Atkin, M. Sato, and R. C. Wei, "Influences of National Board Certification on Teachers' Classroom Assessment Practices" (unpublished paper, Stanford University, March 2007).

74. NRC, *Assessing Accomplished Teaching: Advanced-Level Certification Programs* (Washington, DC: National Academies Press, 2008), 8.

75. NRC, *Preparing Teachers*.

76. Ibid., 47–48.

77. J. Angrist and J. Guryan, "Teacher Testing, Teacher Education, and Teacher Characteristics," *American Economic Review* 94, no. 2 (2004): 241–246.

78. R. Strauss and E. Sawyer, "Some New Evidence on Teacher and Student Competencies," *Economics of Education Review* 5, no. 1 (1986): 41–48; R. Ferguson, "Paying for Public Education: New Evidence on How and Why Money Matters," *Harvard Journal of Legislation* 28, no. 2 (1991): 465–498; R. Ferguson and H. Ladd, "How and Why Money Matters: An Analysis of Alabama Schools," in *Holding Schools Accountable: Performance-Based Reform in Education*, ed. H. Ladd (Washington, DC: Brookings Institution, 1996), 265–298.

79. C. Clotfelter, H. Ladd, and J. Vigdor, "Teacher-Student Matching and the Assessment of Teacher Effectiveness," *Journal of Human Resources* 41, no. 4 (2006): 778–820; C. Clotfelter, H. Ladd, and J. Vigdor, *How and Why Do Teacher Credentials Matter for Student Achievement?* Working Paper 12828 (Cambridge, MA: National Bureau of Economic Research, 2007); D. Goldhaber, "Everyone's Doing It, but What Does Teacher Testing Tell Us About Teacher Effectiveness?" *Journal of Human Resources* 42, no. 4 (2007): 765–794; D. Goldhaber and M. Hansen, "Race, Gender and Teacher Testing: How Informative a Tool Is Teacher Licensure Testing?" *American Educational Research Journal* 47, no. 1 (2010): 218–251.

80. Gitomer, *Teacher Quality in a Changing Policy Landscape*.

81. Goldhaber and Hansen, "Race, Gender, and Teacher Testing," 244.

82. R. M. Ingersoll and T. M. Smith, "Do Teacher Induction and Mentoring Matter?" *NASSP Bulletin* 88, no. 638 (2004): 28–40.

83. S. Glazerman, S. Dolfin, M. Bleecher, A. Johnson, E. Isenberg, J. Lugo-Gil, M. Grider, E. Britton, and M. Ali, *Impacts of Comprehensive Teacher Induction: Results from the First Year of a Randomized Controlled Study* (Washington, DC: U.S. Department of Education, Institute of Education Sciences, 2008).

84. The key components of "successful" induction programs identified in prior research include: (1) carefully trained mentors; (2) a curriculum of intensive support for beginning teachers; (3) a focus on classroom instruction; (4) constructive feedback through ongoing formative assessment; and (5) outreach to school and district administrators to ensure their support for the program.

85. *Eligible teachers* are defined as beginning K–6 teachers who were new to teaching and were not already receiving induction support from a teacher certification or preparation program. There were 1,009 eligible teachers in the 418 participating schools.

86. S. M. Wilson and J. Berne, "Teacher Learning and the Acquisition of Professional Knowledge: An Examination of Research on Contemporary Professional Development," *Review of Research in Education* 24 (January 1999): 173–209.

87. Little, *Professional Community and Professional Development in the Learning-Centered School*.

88. A. J. Wayne, K. S. Yoon, P. Zhu, S. Cronen, and M. S. Garet, "Experimenting with Teacher Professional Development: Motives and Methods," *Educational Researcher* 37, no. 8 (2008): 469–479.

89. K. Yoon, T. Duncan, S. Lee, B. Scarloss, and K. Shapley, *Reviewing the Evidence on How Teacher Professional Development Affects Student Achievement* (Washington, DC: U.S. Department of Education, Institute of Education Sciences, 2007).

90. M. Garet, S. Cronen, M. Eaton, A. Kurki, M. Ludwig, W. Jones, K. Uekawa, A. Falk, H. Bloom, R. Doolittle, P. Zhu, L. Sztejnberg, and M. Silverberg, *The Impact of*

Two Professional Development Interventions on Early Reading Instruction and Achievement (Washington, DC: U.S. Department of Education, Institute of Education Sciences, 2008); M. Garet, A. Wayne, F. Stancavage, J. Taylor, K. Walters, M. Song, S. Brown, S. Hurlburt, P. Zhu, S. Sepanik, F. Doolittle, and E. Warner, *Middle School Mathematics Professional Development Impact Study* (Washington, DC: U.S. Department of Education, Institute of Education Sciences, 2010).

91. D. Weisberg, S. Sexton, J. Mulhern, and D. Keeling, *The Widget Effect* (New York: The New Teacher Project, 2009), http://widgeteffect.org.

92. For a review and critique of VAM, see E. Baker, P. Barton, L. Darling-Hammond, E. Haertel, H. Ladd, R. Linn, D. Ravitch, R. Rothstein, R. Shavelson, and L. Shepard, *Problems with the Use of Student Test Scores to Evaluate Teachers* (Washington, DC: Economic Policy Institute, 2010).

93. J. Rothstein. Review of *Learning about Teaching* (Boulder, CO: National Education Policy Center, 2011), http://nepc.colorado.edu/thinktank/review-learning-about-teaching.

94. *Teacher Assessment and Evaluation: The National Education Association's Framework to Transforming Education Systems to Support Effective Teaching and Improve Student Learning* (Washington, DC: NEA, 2010).

95. For a more complete description of the technical limitations of VAM effectiveness ratings, see Baker et al., *Problems with the Use of Student Test Scores to Evaluate Teachers.*

96. *A Continuous Improvement Model for Teacher Development and Evaluation* (Washington, DC: American Federation of Teachers, 2010).

97. *Teacher Assessment and Evaluation,* 5.

98. H. Heneman III, A. Milanowski, S. Kimball, and A. Odden, "Standards-Based Teacher Evaluation as a Foundation for Knowledge- and Skill-Based Pay," *CPRE Policy Briefs,* no. RB-45 (2006).

99. Ibid., 7.

100. Bill and Melinda Gates Foundation, *Working with Teachers to Develop Fair and Reliable Measures of Effective Teaching,* 2010, http://gatesfoundation.org/highschools/Documents'met-framing-paper.pdf.

101. J. Rothstein, Review of *Learning about Teaching.* Specifically, the project's stated premises—that, wherever feasible, teacher evaluations should include student achievement gains and that any additional components of evaluations should be related to achievement gains—seem to prematurely rule out several potential conclusions.

102. *Teacher Assessment and Evaluation.*

103. *A Continuous Improvement Model for Teacher Development and Evaluation,* 6.

104. D. N. Harris and T. R. Sass, *What Makes for a Good Teacher and Who Can Tell?* Working Paper 30 (Washington, DC: Center for Analysis of Longitudinal Data in Education Research, 2009).

105. H. A. Gallagher, "Vaughn Elementary's Innovative Teacher Evaluation System: Are Teacher Evaluation Scores Related to Growth in Student Achievement?" *Peabody Journal of Education* 79, no. 4 (2004): 104.

106. Heneman et al., "Standards-Based Teacher Evaluation as a Foundation for Knowledge- and Skills-Based Pay."

107. As reflected in their percentile rank on standardized achievement tests; see "The Ballooning of the Teacher Workforce" section in this chapter.

108. *Tomorrow's Teachers* (East Lansing, MI: Holmes Group, 1985); *A Nation Prepared: Teachers for the 21st Century* (New York: Carnegie Forum for Education and the Economy, 1986).

109. R. Mullner and M. Jewell, "The Medical Outcomes Mandate," *Journal of Medical Systems* 23, no. 3 (1999): 171–173.

110. K. E. Weick, "Educational Organizations as Loosely Coupled Systems," *Administrative Science Quarterly* 21 (1976): 1–9.

111. Little, "The Persistence of Privacy."

112. Little, *Professional Community and Professional Development in the Learning-Centered School.*

113. A. Odden, "Lessons Learned About Standards-Based Teacher Evaluation Systems," *Peabody Journal of Education* 79, no. 4 (2004): 126–137.

114. Gates Foundation, *Working with Teachers.*

115. A. Levine, *Educating School Teachers* (Washington, DC: Educational Schools Project, 2006).

About the Authors

DARREL DRURY oversees the National Education Association's Surveys and Data Analysis Group, Higher Education Research Center, and Center for the Study of Education Support Professionals. He formerly served as a faculty member and research scientist at Yale University, where he conducted a broad range of studies focusing on the effective organization and management of public education systems. More recently he held positions as director of Policy and Evaluation Research at Metrica, Inc.; director of Policy Research at the National School Boards Association; and vice president for Research and Evaluation at New American Schools. Drury has published extensively, much of his work aimed at providing research-based guidance to policy makers seeking to improve America's public schools. He is the author or coauthor of several major works, including *School-Based Management: The Changing Locus of Control in American Public Education* (1994), *Learning to Hope* (1995), *Reinventing School-Based Management* (1999), *Exploring New Directions* (2000), *Charting a New Course: Fact and Fiction About Charter Schools* (2000), *Building Capacity: Professional Development for New and Experienced Teachers* (2002), and *Evaluating Success* (2002). In addition, he is the author of numerous journal articles, book chapters, and policy briefs. Drury, a former Fulbright Scholar, received his BA with honors from Vanderbilt University and earned his MA and PhD in sociology from Brown University. He also attended Københavns Universitet (Copenhagen, Denmark) and La Ciudad Universitaria (Madrid, Spain) and completed postdoctoral training in psychosocial epidemiology and advanced epidemiological methods at Yale Medical School.

JUSTIN BAER is a senior research analyst at the National Education Association (NEA). His work focuses on helping the NEA's affiliates understand the conceptual and technical underpinnings of new models of teacher compensation and identifying and disentangling the range of factors associated with chronically underperforming schools. Prior to joining the NEA, Baer directed and collaborated on a variety of large-scale surveys, assessments, and program evaluations at the American Institutes for Research, including the Progress in International Reading Literacy Study, the National Survey of America's College Students, and the National Assessment of Adult Literacy. He earned his doctorate in sociology from the University of Washington.

About the Contributors

JOSEPH A. AGUERREBERE is president and CEO of the National Board for Professional Teaching Standards (NBPTS), an independent, nonprofit organization that establishes rigorous standards to advance the quality of teaching and provides a national voluntary teacher certification. Aguerrebere earned his BA in political science and master's and doctorate degrees in educational administration from the University of Southern California. Prior to heading NBPTS, he served as a public school teacher and administrator, professor of educational administration at California State University, Dominguez Hills, and a deputy director at the Ford Foundation.

DAN BROWN is an English teacher at the SEED Public Charter School of Washington, D.C., and the author of *The Great Expectations School: A Rookie Year in the New Blackboard Jungle* (2007). He holds a bachelor's degree from New York University and a master's degree in education from Teachers College, Columbia University. He became a teacher in 2003 through the New York City Teaching Fellows. He blogs regularly for the Teacher Leaders Network and the *Huffington Post*.

MICHELLE BROWN is a doctoral student in the Stanford University School of Education Curriculum Studies and Teacher Education programs. She is an instructor in the Stanford Teacher Education Program and was a research assistant on the Protocol for Language Arts Teaching Observation project. Her research interests include adolescent literacy and intervention curricula and policy. Before pursuing graduate study, she taught high school English and reading in New Orleans. She holds a BA in literature and Hispanic language and literature from New College of Florida.

MICHAEL DELL is the founder, chairman, and chief executive officer of Dell Incorporated. In 1992 he became the youngest CEO ever to earn a ranking on the *Fortune* 500. In 1998 Dell and his wife formed the Michael & Susan Dell Foundation to manage the philanthropic efforts of the Dell family. He serves on the foundation board of the World Economic Forum and on the executive committee of the International Business Council and is a member of the U.S. Business Council. Dell also serves on the Technology CEO Council and the governing board of the Indian School of Business in Hyderabad, India.

ARNE DUNCAN was appointed U.S. secretary of education in 2009. Previously he served as chief executive officer of the Chicago Public Schools and before that ran the nonprofit education foundation Ariel Education Initiative. He was part of the team that later started the Ariel Community Academy, one of the top elementary schools in Chicago. Duncan graduated magna cum laude from Harvard University in 1987, majoring in sociology. He holds honorary degrees from the Illinois Institute of Technology, Lake Forest College, and National-Louis University.

JASON GIPSON-NAHMAN teaches at the Next Step Public Charter School in Washington, D.C., and previously taught general, honors, and AP Physics at T. C. Williams High School in Alexandria, Virginia. He is a fellow with the Knowles Science Teaching Foundation. Gipson-Nahman received his EdM in teaching and curriculum from the Harvard Graduate School of Education and a BS in mechanical engineering and a BA in Spanish from the University of Texas at Austin.

PAM GROSSMAN is the Nomellini Olivier Professor of Education at Stanford University. She is a research collaborator with the National Center for Analysis of Longitudinal Data in Education Research and has served on the American Educational Research Association's council and executive board. Her research interests include teacher education, teacher knowledge, and the teaching of English in secondary schools. Grossman received her PhD in curriculum and teacher education from Stanford University and her BA in English from Yale University.

ERIC A. HANUSHEK is the Paul and Jean Hanna Senior Fellow at the Hoover Institution of Stanford University. He is a member of the National Academy of Education and the International Academy of Education, a fellow of the Society of Labor Economists and the American Education Research Association. In 2004 he was awarded the Fordham Prize for Distinguished Scholarship. Hanushek is a Distinguished Graduate of the U.S. Air Force Academy and completed his PhD in economics at the Massachusetts Institute of Technology.

JAMES B. HUNT JR. was four-term governor of North Carolina and is a nationally recognized leader in education. His early childhood Smart Start program won the Kennedy School's Innovations in American Government Award. Hunt was a founder and chairman of the National Board for Professional Teaching Standards, the founding chair of the National Commission on Teaching and America's Future, and a recipient of the NEA Friend of Education Award. In 2006 he was recognized as one of the ten most influential people in American education.

RICHARD M. INGERSOLL is a professor of education and sociology at the University of Pennsylvania. After teaching in both public and private schools for a number of years, he earned a PhD in sociology from the University of Pennsylvania. From 1995 to 2000 he served as a faculty member in the sociology department at the University of Georgia. Ingersoll's research is concerned with the character of elementary and secondary schools as workplaces, teachers as employees, and teaching as a job.

SUSAN MOORE JOHNSON is the Jerome T. Murphy Professor in Education at the Harvard Graduate School of Education, where she served as academic dean from 1993 to 1999. She studies and teaches about teacher policy, organizational change, and administrative practice. A former high school teacher and administrator, Johnson directs the Project on the Next Generation of Teachers, which focuses on how best to recruit, support, and retain a strong public teaching force. She has written four books and numerous articles about teachers and their work.

BRAD JUPP is a senior program adviser in the Office of the Secretary at the U.S. Department of Education on loan from the Denver Public Schools (DPS). For the past twenty-four years he served as a teacher, union leader, and senior administrator in DPS, most recently as senior academic policy adviser to former superintendent Michael Bennet. Jupp taught middle school language arts in DPS and was lead teacher of the DPS Alternative Middle School. He was also an activist in the Denver Classroom Teachers Association (DCTA); from 1990 to 2002 he served as the chief negotiator for the DCTA's bargaining team.

JUDITH WARREN LITTLE is dean and Carol Liu Professor of Education Policy in the Graduate School of Education, University of California, Berkeley. Her research interests center on the organizational and policy contexts of teaching and teacher education. She has published numerous papers and two books in the areas of teachers' work, school reform, and teacher policy. Little is an elected member of the National Academy of Education and a fellow of the American Educational Research Association. She received her BA, a teaching credential in English, and her PhD in sociology from the University of Colorado.

JAY MATHEWS is the *Washington Post*'s education columnist and the author of several best-selling books on education. His annual Challenge Index rating of U.S. high schools is available online at washingtonpost.com. Mathews is a recipient of the Education Writers Association National Education Reporting Award, the Benjamin Fine Award for Outstanding Education Reporting, and the Eugene Meyer Award. In 2009 he won the Upton Sinclair Award for being "a beacon of light in the realm of education." He attended Occidental and Harvard colleges.

LISA MERRILL is a third-year doctoral student in the Education Policy Program at the University of Pennsylvania's Graduate School of Education. Prior to enrolling in graduate school, Merrill taught eighth-grade math for three years in Brooklyn, and her experience in the classroom directs much of her research agenda. Currently she is working on a film project documenting teachers' experiences in schools with the hope that it will promote the inclusion of teacher voices in the national conversation on schooling.

RENEE MOORE, a National Board Certified Teacher, teaches English at Mississippi Delta Community College. Previously, she served as a classroom teacher in the Mississippi public schools and was named the 2001 Mississippi Teacher of the Year. Moore is a member of Mississippi's Commission on Teacher and Administrator Education, Certification, and Licensure and serves on the board of directors of the National Board for Professional Teaching Standards. Part of the Teacher Leaders Network and a published author, she also maintains a blog, TeachMoore.

ANDREW J. ROTHERHAM is an education analyst and cofounder and partner at Bellwether Education, a national education reform nonprofit. He has served at the White House and on the Virginia Board of Education and is a member of the board of the University of Virginia's Curry School of Education and the Visiting Committee to Oversee the Harvard Graduate School of Education. Rotherham is coeditor of *A Qualified Teacher in Every Classroom*, author of *Achieving Teacher and Principal Excellence*, and a columnist for *Time*. His blog is Eduwonk.com.

BARBARA STOFLET is a sixth-grade teacher at Gatewood Elementary in Minnetonka, Minnesota. She is currently enrolled in a doctoral educational leadership program at Minnesota State University, Mankato. Stoflet was named Minnesota Teacher of the Year in 2001 and 2002 and was the recipient of the Presidential Award for Excellence in Math and Science Teaching in 2008.

DENNIS VAN ROEKEL, a twenty-three-year teaching veteran and longtime activist and advocate for children and public education, is president of the National Education Association (NEA). He previously served as the NEA's vice president and secretary-treasurer and has held key positions in all levels of the association, including Arizona Education Association president and Paradise Valley Education Association president. Van Roekel earned a BA from the University of Iowa and a master's degree in math education from Northern Arizona University.

RANDI WEINGARTEN is president of the American Federation of Teachers, where she has launched major efforts to place education reform and innovation high on the nation's agenda. Before that she served on the Federation's executive council and for twelve years was president of the United Federation of Teachers, representing educators in New York City's public schools. Weingarten holds degrees from Cornell University's School of Industrial and Labor Relations and the Cardozo School of Law. She previously taught history at Clara Barton High School in Brooklyn.

Index